D1426527

THE LIFE AND DEATH OF DIETRICH BONHOEFFER

By the same author

CANADA RIDE
JOURNEY INTO A PICTURE
THE MAN ON THE ISLAND
MOTHER OF THE MAGNIFICENT

For Children

PEOPLE WITH SIX LEGS

THE
LIFE AND DEATH OF
DIETRICH
BONHOEFFER

by

MARY BOSANQUET

HODDER AND STOUGHTON

Copyright © 1968 by Mary Bosanquet

First printed 1968

SBN 340 04446 2

All rights reserved. No part of this publication may be reproduced or
transmitted in any form or by any means, electronic or mechanical including photocopy, recording or any information storage and retrieval system,
without permission in writing from the publisher.

PRINTED IN GREAT BRITAIN FOR HODDER
AND STOUGHTON LIMITED, ST. PAUL'S HOUSE,
WARWICK LANE, LONDON, E.C.4 BY C. TINLING
AND CO. LIMITED, LIVERPOOL, LONDON AND
PRESCOT

FOREWORD

It was in 1948 that I made the acquaintance of the author of this book. By that time she had already written her book *Canada Ride* which still enjoys a wide circulation in Germany.

When four years ago I received a letter in which Mary Bosanquet modestly informed me of her intention to write a life of my brother, I could not quite suppress my alarm, and wrote to her frankly expressing my concern, but I can say today with real pleasure that Mary Bosanquet's book has proved my anxieties to be groundless.

Her exceptional sensitivity, together with her painstaking and perceptive study of my brother's writings, have enabled her to present in this book an excellent picture of Dietrich Bonhoeffer's life. She has recognised Dietrich for the man he was. She has sought out many who knew Dietrich and received their impression of him. I myself have spent many hours in talking to her about Dietrich and was impressed by the delicate perspicuity with which she was able to elucidate obscure passages in his thought, and by the warm interest with which she addressed herself to the theological questions which were burning in Dietrich's soul. I can fully agree with her interpretation and believe that it will facilitate the approach to his writings and make a very considerable contribution to the understanding of his life and character. For there are no inventions in Mary Bosanquet's book. By means of her fluid presentation the writer carries us through the various stages in my brother Dietrich's life. She gives some account of his ancestry and illuminates at each stage the cultural and political background of the nineteenth and twentieth centuries in Germany. She gives a picture of his childhood and youth and conveys the atmosphere of our home, which had such a strong creative influence on his development, and she portrays our large circle of brothers and sisters and the Berlin of those days in which Dietrich grew up and studied. The author follows with care his personal and theological development, describes the genesis of his writings and discusses them. She describes vividly his participation in the Church struggle and in the political resistance to Hitler, and finally his imprisonment in Tegel military prison, selecting significant passages from the letters of that period.

To have discovered in this book a distorted picture of the twin brother to whom I was bound with such powerful ties of affection would have been a bitter grief to me. But this has nowhere been the case. Mary Bosanquet has been able to show how the Grace of God rested upon his life in all its manifold endeavours, and in all the joys and sorrows of the road which led Dietrich home to Him.

Sabine Leibholz–Bonhoeffer

PREFACE

THIS book owes much to the many relations and friends of Dietrich Bonhoeffer who have helped me with their reminiscences, and especially to his sister, Mrs. Sabine Leibholz, who has spent many hours of her time in striving to recreate the past and to give me a living picture of the brother to whom she was so closely bound by ties of affection and natural affinity.

But the man to whom I owe more than could possibly be expressed in these few words is Dr. Eberhard Bethge, whose own exhaustive theological and psychological study of his friend's life has appeared in German and is now being translated into English. The unstinting generosity with which, over the past five years, he has made available to me not only his time, but also the unique material and extensive information which for almost twenty years he has been assembling and setting in order, reflects not only his own magnanimity, but certainly also the spirit of the man whose pupil he became, and whose intimate friend he remained, all through the most intensely-lived period in both of their lives.

ACKNOWLEDGEMENTS

To the S.C.M. Press for permission to quote from the following books:
Creation and Temptation, First Combined Edition, 1966
Ethics, 1955
Life Together, 1954
The Cost of Discipleship, First Cheap Edition, 1964
Letters and Papers from Prison, Revised Translation, 1967

To Wm. Collins Sons and Co. Ltd. for permission to quote from:
Sanctorum Communio, 1963

To Wolf Dieter Zimmermann and the Kaiser Verlag, Munich for permission to quote from:
Begegnungen mit Dietrich Bonhoeffer, 1965

To Eberhard Bethge and the Kaiser Verlag, Munich for permission to quote from:
Dietrich Bonhoeffer, Theologe, Christ, Zeitgenosse, 1967

AUTHOR'S NOTE

In order to spare the reader the irritation often attendant upon the "*op. cit.*" footnote, the titles of works quoted will be repeated. After the first reference, abbreviations will be used in footnotes in the following instances, as shown below:

Unpublished memoir written for his family by Karl Bonhoeffer: KB's Memoir.

Eberhard Bethge, *Dietrich Bonhoeffer, Theologe, Christ, Zeitgenosse*, 1st edition: E.B., *D.B.*
Begegnungen mit Dietrich Bonhoeffer, herausgegeben von Wolf Dieter Zimmermann, 2nd edition: *Begegnungen*
Dietrich Bonhoeffer, *The Cost of Discipleship*, 1964 edition: *C. of D.*
Dietrich Bonhoeffer, *Gesammelte Schriften, herausgegeben von* Eberhard Bethge (4 volumes), 1st edition: *G.S.* I–IV
Dietrich Bonhoeffer, *Creation and Temptation*, combined edition: *C. and T.*
Dietrich Bonhoeffer, *Letters and Papers from Prison*, 1967 edition: *L. and P.*

The following German words or initials will be used in the text in preference to the English paraphrase:

Bruderrat : Council of Brothers
Bruderhaus : House of Brothers
V.K.L.: *Vorläufige Kirchenleitung* – Provisional Church Government
Abwehr : Counter-Espionage Department
R.S.H.A.: *Reichssicherheitshauptamt* – Principal Security Department of the Reich

CONTENTS

The quotations which precede the four parts of this book are the four verses of the prose poem "Stations on the Road to Freedom," written by Dietrich Bonhoeffer a few months before his death, translated by Frank Clarke.

ILLUSTRATIONS

Key to Acknowledgements

[1] Eberhard Bethge
[2] Sabine Leibholz-Bonhoeffer
[3] Maria von Wedemeyer-Weller
[4] Rotraut Vorbergatelier

Part I

DISCIPLINE

If you set out to seek freedom, then learn
                above all things
to govern your soul and your senses, for fear
                that your passions
and longings may lead you away from the path you
                should follow.
Chaste be your mind and your body, and both
                in subjection,
obediently, steadfastly seeking the aim set before them;
only through discipline may a man learn to be free.

                                  Dietrich Bonhoeffer

CHAPTER I

It must have been evening before Bonhoeffer reached Flossenbürg. The "trial" went on throughout the night. The prisoners were interrogated once more and confronted with one another. All were condemned.

The last picture that we have of Bonhoeffer comes from the prison doctor, who wrote many years later:

"On the morning of the day, some time between five and six o'clock, the prisoners, among them Admiral Canaris, General Oster and Sack, the Judge Advocate General, were led out of their cells and the verdicts read to them. Through the half-open door of a room in one of the huts I saw Pastor Bonhoeffer, still in his prison clothes, kneeling in fervent prayer to the Lord his God. The devotion and evident conviction of being heard that I saw in the prayer of this intensely captivating man, moved me to the depths."[1]

So the morning came. Now the prisoners were ordered to strip. They were led down a little flight of steps under the trees to the secluded place of execution. There was a pause. For the men about to die, time hung a moment suspended. Naked under the scaffold in the sweet spring woods, Bonhoeffer knelt for the last time to pray. Five minutes later, his life was ended.

That was on April 9th 1945. Three weeks later, Hitler committed suicide. Before a month had passed, the Third Reich had fallen and the victims of the regime were free. On such a delicate thread of time Bonhoeffer's life had hung.

For many weeks after this, Germany was in a state of chaos which made normal communication impossible. No one knew what had become of Dietrich. It was towards the end of June that his elder brother, Karl Friedrich, wrote from Leipzig to his children who were in the Harz Mountains:

". . . and now? The last time I was in Berlin was at the end of March . . . there was no news at all of Uncle Dietrich, who had been deported from Berlin in February by the S.S. . . . that was more than two months ago . . . Uncle Dietrich had a long conversation with some-

[1] *Begegnungen mit Dietrich Bonhoeffer, herausgegeben von* Wolf Dieter Zimmermann, p. 192.

body in Passau on April 5th. From there he was to go to the concentration camp of Flossenbürg near Weiden.

"Why has he not returned . . . ?"[1]

While the family waited in anguished uncertainty, the report of his death was first received in Geneva, whence it was telegraphed to Bishop Bell in Chichester. Still his family in Berlin heard nothing.

But on July 27th his aged parents, as was their custom, turned on their radio to listen to the broadcast from London. A memorial service was in progress. The triumphant measures of Vaughan Williams' "For all the Saints" rolled out loud and solemn from many hundred voices. Then a single German was speaking in English. "We are gathered here in the presence of God," said the disembodied voice, "to make thankful remembrance of the life and work of his servant Dietrich Bonhoeffer, who gave his life in faith and obedience to His holy word . . ."[2]

So the news came.

To his friends and colleagues and devoted students who were to hear it in the course of the next months, it seemed like a total end. None could have guessed then that in the twenty years which followed his death his name would travel through the whole Christian world of Europe and America, penetrate the intellectual defences of Eastern Europe, and even make its way to Japan. Yet so it was to be. This intense enigmatic figure, a hero to some of his Christian friends, a renegade to others, passionately opposed to violence yet ready to be involved in it when he believed that the cause of truth could not otherwise be served, who could combine daring originality of thought with unwavering fidelity to his faith, this man who seemed lost to the world in that tragic spring of 1945, was to fire the theological imagination of a whole succeeding generation.

He was born in 1906 in Breslau, into a world that was soon to end.

Only thirty-five years before, William I, King of Prussia, had been proclaimed Emperor of all Germany in the Palace of Versailles, and the country had been united at last under a single ruler. Only twelve years later, William's grandson was to abdicate, and Germany was to lie prostrate after a crushing military defeat; and with that the stage would be set for a still greater tragedy, in which the child born that day in the large Breslau house was to find his life and lose it and find it again one-hundred-fold.

[1] Quoted by Eberhard Bethge in Dietrich Bonhoeffer, *Theologe, Christ, Zeitgenosse*, p. 1043.

[2] *Bonhoeffer Gedenkheft*, editor Eberhard Bethge, pp. 5–6.

Dietrich Bonhoeffer's ancestors had fitted with an unobtrusive distinction into the jigsaw puzzle of German history. The family can be traced back to 1403 in the annals of Nymwegen. In 1513 Caspar von Bonhoeffer moved to Schwäbisch Hall, a free city of the Empire in the State of Würtemberg, where for nearly three hundred years the family was prominent in public affairs. Charlemagne's Holy Roman Empire, which had struggled to maintain its existence for a thousand years without ever becoming fully coincident with political reality, and which had been the forerunner of that so strangely different Empire into which Dietrich Bonhoeffer was born, had been the cradle of one remarkably stable institution, the free cities of Germany.

These free cities, large and small, owned a history almost as long as that of the Empire itself. Traditionally unconcerned with the political life of Europe and comfortably preserved within their containing walls, they were seldom involved in the struggles for power which drained the resources and disordered the rule of the innumerable German principalities. While the fortunes of the princes and their subjects ebbed and flowed, life within the free cities took its even course, leaving the citizens at liberty to develop those traditions of culture and of civic responsibility which were to have so profound an effect on the character of succeeding generations. It was in the rich soil of these long-established cities that the solid burgher families who have made so large a contribution to the most valuable and enduring elements in Germany's culture, slowly grew to maturity.

The early history of the Bonhoeffer family is like that of many another which quietly blossomed through many generations in this worthy and not unfruitful setting. We have a short note on the family's beginnings in a memoir left by Dr. Karl Bonhoeffer, Dietrich's father:

"My grandfather, Sophonias Franz Bonhoeffer, born on May 29th 1797, was the last Bonhoeffer to be born in Schwäbisch Hall. In and around the church of St. Michael in Hall may be found numerous Bonhoeffer memorials and portraits of civic and ecclesiastical dignitaries of the free city. Originally goldsmiths, they are to be found during the eighteenth century in the academic, legal, theological and medical professions. The father and grandfather of my grandfather were doctors in Schwäbisch Hall, my grandfather himself was a pastor in Oberstetten, Neckarweihingen and Wildentierbach and finally retired to Schwäbisch Hall."[1]

[1] From an unpublished memoir written by Karl Bonhoeffer for his family in the years succeeding the second world war.

The connection of the family with Schwäbisch Hall, though weakened, was by no means lost in Karl Bonhoeffer's generation, and there is a page in the memoir which conveys with an unconscious vividness the particular flavour of visits to this city in which he had never lived, but which seemed nevertheless in a peculiar sense his home:

"Although I have not lived for any long period in Schwäbisch Hall, the little mediaeval town still gives me a strong sense that I belong there. This may be connected with my racial memories, but it is principally due to the fact that my father had retained his pride in our ancient patrician family and sought to further it in us boys by showing us the old houses of the Bonhoeffers with their arms over the entrances, the famous black oak staircase in the Bonhoeffer house in the Herrengasse, the monuments over the family graves and the portrait of 'the lovely Bonhoeffer woman' which hung in the church. I can remember also many fine ornaments, as for instance a watch set with pearls and small diamonds, which still survived from those days of patrician wealth. Also one met there many special confections, biscuits called 'Haller Printen', and other spiced delicacies which I have met nowhere else. The freedom of the city, which my father still possessed and which my brother secured, I was myself too late in applying for. An attempt to get it later failed, I could not fulfil the condition of owning property in the city. So the four-hundred-year-old family tradition of belonging to Schwäbisch Hall was lost."

Karl Bonhoeffer's grandfather was the first to leave the city, but affection for the place in which he had grown up drew him back to end his days there. His grandson had only a faint recollection of him, but he understood him to have been "a fine hearty parson, who drove about the district in his own carriage". "Politically," the memoir continues, "he was very unsympathetic to Prussia, which led to differences with his eldest son, my father."

In this family argument a controversy is mirrored which was to divide Germany for fifty years. In 1806, just a hundred years before Dietrich Bonhoeffer's birth, the moribund Empire had lain helpless at the feet of Napoleon. Napoleon had decreed its end, and then, turning his logical and impatient mind to the confusion which had been left behind, he had abolished the ecclesiastical states, merged the smaller principalities with the larger, swept away the rights of the free cities and reduced Germany's almost three hundred states to just over thirty, forcibly imposing upon them the liberal institutions which a whole generation of the French had given their lives to win.

Out of this arbitrary creation, only two states emerged as large and prominent enough in European affairs to be able to speak with the voice of Germany; these were Austria and Prussia. During the short-lived rule of Napoleon, only Prussia put up any resistance, and from this time onwards many Germans began to look to her for leadership. After Napoleon's fall, the unification of Germany became the aim of everyone who was concerned with politics, but while the *Kleindeutschen* favoured a union under the leadership of Prussia, with Austria excluded, the *Grossdeutschen* looked back to the days of the old Empire, for which the Austrian House of Hapsburg had provided an unbroken succession of Emperors for three and a half centuries, and mindful of the fact that Austria was a German state, hoped for the emergence of a German nation with Austria at its head. The Hapsburgs, however, were concerned to consolidate their new hereditary empire of Austria-Hungary and were only intermittently interested in Germany as a whole; whereas Prussia, strenuous, highly disciplined and full of expanding energies, appeared to many of the younger Germans as a more promising leader.

Karl Bonhoeffer's father, Friedrich Ernst Philipp Tobias, was an eminently hard-headed and realistic man, to whom the practical effectiveness of Prussia would make a persuasive appeal. He was a lawyer by profession, and moved from one post to another in Würtemberg as local judge. He ended his career as President of the Provincial Court in Ulm. He seems to have been an able and pleasant but rather taciturn man, a good father, but short-tempered and never a very intimate friend to his sons. They came nearest to him in the enjoyment of nature, which was perhaps his deepest pleasure, and which he shared with them to the full.

But it was their mother, who had been a Tafel, who was the strongest influence in the boys' lives; and she brought, besides wit and vivacity, a new streak of creative originality to leaven the solid Bonhoeffer tradition. Her father, Christian Friedrich August Tafel, was a lawyer, the second of four brothers, of whom Karl Bonhoeffer writes: "My grandfather and his three brothers were plainly no average men. Each had his special trait, but common to them all was an idealistic streak, with a fearless readiness to act on their convictions."

All these four brothers and their families were impassioned Liberals. The German Liberal Party laboured under the disadvantage of its unfortunate beginnings, when so many of the institutions for which it stood had been imposed by Napoleon as a condition of peace, so that

Germans had never struggled to secure them, and consequently the Liberal Party had more the character of a debating society than of a political party which must work for what it believed in and make what it believed in work. The German historian Treitschke, in his later years characterised the Liberals of the nineteenth century without much sympathy: "The purely political parties . . . were a direct product of literary concepts. German liberalism did not spring from the class-consciousness of wealthy and self-confident citizens, but from the theoretical ideas of scholars. An ill-defined historical yearning for the great days of the Empire, which had first arisen in the period of foreign domination, was gradually combined with the teaching of the Enlightenment concerning the natural rights of free personality; a few sentences culled from Montesquieu and Rousseau were combined with a fair proportion of educated prejudice. So arose a system of ideas to be based upon the rights of common sense, which it was hoped would raise our nation through freedom back to its ancient power."

It is not altogether surprising that this variant of Liberalism held little appeal for a writer who sympathised, as Treitschke did, with Prussian power politics. But though not perhaps cut out to form an effective political instrument, it provided, like Fabian Socialism in England, an admirable school for the intellect and emotions, and the brothers, flinging themselves with abandon into the Liberal cause, received undoubtedly much in return, their vivid lives gaining fire and purpose from their political enthusiasm. In her eighty-ninth year, Julie Tafel-Bonhoeffer wrote for her son a description of her father as she still clearly remembered him:

"She describes him as a lively attractive man with fine features, a high colour, grey hair and dark, glowing eyes. Her mother said of him that when he came into a small circle of his friends the atmosphere grew bright and warm as though the sun had risen. In their house there was much lively coming and going, a vivid intellectual life, acting, tableaux, and very strong political and social interests."[1]

It says much for Friedrich Bonhoeffer's humour and humanity that he was able to retain a warm affection for this lively and outspoken clan, who supported with so much energy and wit political opinions diametrically opposed to his own. Karl Bonhoeffer describes his needless anxieties with regard to a certain well-loved aunt, daughter of the politician, Gottlob:

"We liked it when she came to visit us, although I sometimes feared

[1] K.B.'s memoir.

that the heated political disputes which arose as a result of the collision between her freethinking and radical-democratic views and our father's support of Prussian leadership and the [Prussian] Empire might lead to a serious breach between them. This would have grieved us much, for we loved our aunt with her attractive vivacity, her unselfconscious nature, and her readiness to take us boys a little seriously . . . But in fact our fear was not justified, children take the impassioned arguments between grown-ups more tragically than they need, and I believe that my father particularly valued this aunt . . . little as his sentiments agreed with those of the democratic circle who frequented the house of Gottlob Tafel."

Julie Tafel herself, in the middle years of her marriage, contrived to make a considerable contribution to the social advance of Würtemberg. At this time her husband was established at the University town of Tübingen, where she found at least one friend who was sympathetic to her ideas. She concerned herself with the much-discussed subject of women's rights and so came into contact with Frau Weber, the wife of the Professor of Agriculture, who was making herself something of a laughing-stock through her writings on the subject. Julie Bonhoeffer wisely expressed herself rather in action than in words, concerning herself with the building of a home for elderly women and later in Stuttgart founding a domestic school for girls which earned her the distinction of the Olga Order, presented by the Queen of Würtemberg for distinguished social service. But though Julie Bonhoeffer entered with great spirit into national affairs, her deepest interest was for her children and grandchildren, and she took an active part in their lives until the day of her death.

By a curious coincidence, Julie's uncle, Gottlob Tafel, became acquainted with Dietrich's maternal great-grandfather, Karl August Hase, in the Hohenasperg fortress, where both were imprisoned for a time as a punishment for political activities regarded by the authorities as subversive. But in the case of Karl August political enthusiasm was no more than a transient phenomenon, and a few years after his youthful escapade he was respectably established at the University of Jena, where his marked literary ability became handmaid to his growing erudition and was the means of earning him an international reputation as an ecclesiastical historian. In recognition of his distinction he was granted the right to embellish the name of Hase with the coveted prefix "von". Some interesting historical and sociological research might be undertaken on the subject of this prefix. In the case of Hase it seems to have been awarded in view of the fact that his particular brand of success, which was simultaneously academic and popular, had made him acceptable in all ranks of society and, with the acquisition of the prefix, von Hase became *de jure* what he already was *de facto*, an accepted member of the German aristocracy. This was to have its effect upon the life of Karl August's eldest son, Karl Alfred, grandfather of Dietrich, who not only suffered for a time the uncomfortable distinction of being Court Preacher to William II, the third and last Hohenzollern Emperor, but was also able to marry the Gräfin Klara von Kalckreuth, second daughter of Graf Stanislas Kalckreuth, who was director of the grand-ducal art school in Weimar. With the von Kalckreuths a third and quite distinct element entered the converging streams of Dietrich Bonhoeffer's heredity.

The von Kalckreuths had owned large feudal estates in Posen, and could trace their descent back to the thirteenth century, when the Teutonic Knights had established the Christian faith in the heathen lands of Prussia and Pomerania by means of fire and the sword. In the history of Prussia's unique and isolated development, the von Kalckreuths had, with similar families, played their part. The curious circumstances which had kept alive in the state of Prussia to the end of the nineteenth century a variant of the feudal system, with its especial virtues and vices, had fostered in the families of the Prussian nobility on the one hand a sense of paternal obligation to their dependents, and on the other a sense of regal independence from the kind of restraints represented by constitutional authority. The grandfather of Reinhold von Thadden, creator of the Luheran Kirchenttage, could write when he was head of the family: "the landowner is in his own domain a minor king."[1]

Owing to their historical and geographical position, the Junker families never moved into the main stream of German life. Living and working largely upon their estates or in the immediate entourage of the Emperor, who remained for them first and foremost the King of Prussia, they felt for the most part only a limited enthusiasm for the headlong stream of events which brought first Prussia and then the whole German Empire under Prussian leadership into the forefront of European affairs; and the Junker Otto von Bismarck, the architect of Germany's fortunes in the nineteenth century, was regarded by many of his own caste as a renegade. While some took part in the moulding of national events, many remained in the background and, still deeply

[1] *von Oertzen, Junker*, p. 110.

rooted in the life of the land and of the peasantry, kept alive the mediaeval virtues. On their estates the sense of community lived on, when it was being lost in the rapidly changing society of nineteenth-century Europe; and in many of the old families there survived that simple intuitive wisdom which is the fruit of a life lived slowly with the land and with the seasons, and that rich general culture which is the outcome of well-used leisure. Their patriarchal life, already losing its place in modern Europe, was to meet its final end after the second world war, but it survived into Nazi Germany, and Dietrich Bonhoeffer, sent in 1935 to found a seminary for ordinands in the comparatively safe seclusion of Eastern Pomerania, was to find himself deeply and refreshingly at home in the atmosphere of rural culture and warm-hearted Christian piety which was the special climate of the families in whose comfortable country houses he soon became a welcome guest, for it was not only naturally attractive to him, it was also one of the converging elements of his rich and diverse heredity.

This outstanding heredity brought him distinguished parents, gifted brothers and sisters, and a home in which tradition and originality combined to create an altogether exceptional atmosphere of creative vigour. Few indeed come into the world with such a commanding prospect of a happy life. None could then have imagined the future in which that life would end.

CHAPTER II

Two years before Dietrich's birth, the Bonhoeffer family became established in Breslau, where Karl Bonhoeffer had been appointed Professor of Psychiatry and Neurology and Director of the University Hospital for Nervous Diseases. "We were lucky enough," he writes in his memoir, "to be able to rent a roomy house standing in a little birchwood in the neighbourhood of the clinic, which gave the five children plenty of freedom."

The five children already born were Karl Friedrich, Walter, Klaus, Ursula and Christine. Dietrich was born as the sixth of the family with a twin sister Sabine, from whom we have a recollection of him in early childhood: "My first memories," she writes, "go back to 1910. I see Dietrich in his party frock, stroking with his small hand the blue silk underskirt; later I see him beside our grandfather, who is sitting by the window with our baby sister Susanne on his knee, while the afternoon sun pours in in golden light. Here the outlines blur, and only one more scene will form in my mind: first games in the garden in 1911, Dietrich with a mass of ash-blond hair around his sunburnt face, hot from romping, driving away the midges and looking for a shady corner, and yet only obeying very unwillingly the nursemaid's call to come in, because the immensely energetic game is not yet finished. Heat and thirst were forgotten in the intensity of his play."[1]

There is one more glimpse from perhaps a year later. Dietrich is watching the terrifying splendours of a dragonfly, as it rides the air above a stream. "Look," he whispers to his mother, awestruck, "there is a creature over the water! But don't be afraid, I will protect you!"

After this Dietrich's individual life disappears for a time into the life of the family.

In 1912 his father was appointed Professor of Psychiatry and Nervous Diseases and Director of the Department of Psychiatry in the hospital of the Charité in Berlin. This meant a change from the setting of a quiet provincial university town to that of the capital of Germany, whose atmosphere of youthful vigour combined with intellectual and political ebullience gave it an air unlike that of any other capital in Europe. Berlin in 1906 was still intoxicated with its own success. Two

[1] *Begegnungen*, p. 12.

hundred years before, it had been a small undeveloped north German town whose name was seldom spoken outside Brandenburg; now it had become one of the greatest industrial and commercial cities on the Continent and the seat of an Emperor to whose court royalty and leading statesmen resorted from all over Europe. Its university commanded the best brains in Germany and its intellectual vigour was so intense as to survive the war and the Emperor's downfall, so that even in 1919 Klaus Bonhoeffer could write: "I think that at the present time it is intellectually the most lively town in the world, and we are at the right age to appreciate it."[1]

In the Reichstag in 1912, although Bismarck's blazing star had set, the Emperor William II pursued a course designed to rival that of his former Chancellor. Neither he nor his advisers were able to see the dangers that lay ahead, and when the Bonhoeffers moved to the capital, the sky above imperial Germany still seemed cloudless.

The family first inhabited part of a house in Bellevue a neighbourhood then very much sought after by wealthy Berliners. But Dr. Bonhoeffer describes this new home in his memoir without enthusiasm. "It had," he says, "with its usual 'Berlin room', entered from a long corridor, and the other rooms opening on to a court at the back, something of the character of a dungeon." It was a dungeon which however owned the distinction of sharing a wall with Bellevue Park, in which the royal children played. But it was neither the wealth nor the imperial magnificence of Berlin which attracted the Bonhoeffers. Battening on the spectacle of royalty was a pleasure rigorously discouraged, and when Sabine trotted in from the garden one day to announce, not without some satisfaction, that one of the little princes had contrived to poke her in the ribs with a stick, the information was received in a deflating silence. Ursula Bonhoeffer's most vivid recollection of this house is of breakfast on the verandah before school. Breakfast consisted of rye bread, butter and jam and hot milk, the latter so unpopular that the more adroit of the children contrived a surreptitious libation, received by the earth in the window-boxes. When this was discovered, cocoa was allowed as an alleviation. School was at eight o'clock. Dietrich's sister Sabine also remembers these mornings:

"Each of us had a lunch-packet (second breakfast) on its place, properly wrapped in greaseproof paper, which contained according to age three to six buttered sandwiches, with cheese or sausages on it. And I remember my mother saying that it was much work for the cook

[1] E.B. *D.B.*, p. 46.

25

getting forty sandwiches ready in the morning. We had 'breakfast bags' in which to put the second breakfast. We wore them round the neck, later put them in our satchel."[1]

It was with a general sense of relief that after four years of life in the Brückenallee, the family removed to a house in the Wangenheimstrasse in Berlin-Grunewald, a suburb known familiarly as "the academic quarter" and inhabited largely by families connected with the University. Here their neighbours included the great Adolf von Harnack, the historian Delbrück and many other scholars of international reputation.

The house which thenceforth was to be their home stood in an acre of garden and was very large by modern standards, so that the rooms in which the family lived and moved were spacious enough to be both gracious and eventful. The windows of the doctor's study rose some twelve feet into the ceiling; at their base his great writing desk, and upon the walls that flanked them his tier upon tier of books, were sacrosanct and not to be approached without permission. The character of the great drawing room was equally august; the children travelled about in it conscious of the need for dignity. Among its large groups of furniture the grand piano formed no more than an agreeable incident, while upon the generous expanses of wall vast mountain landscapes painted by Graf Stanislas Kalckreuth kept stately company with family portraits. Besides these there was room for smaller pictures painted by other members of the Kalckreuth family, of whom one, Leopold, had gained a national reputation, and also for several large Piranesis, brought from Rome by the Church Historian, Karl August von Hase. The dining room was on the same scale, and the great dining table round which a family of at least twelve regularly assembled, rose like a quite modestly-proportioned island out of a lake of shining parquet. The principal object of furniture in this room towered against the west wall. It was an immense edifice in solid oak executed to the design of Stanislas Kalckreuth, and consisted of a chest housed under a classical pediment rising upon serpentine pillars. It was possible to climb on to this chest and gaze out from its mythological depths as though from a protected lair, an activity discouraged but never wholly suppressed. The dining room was, in fact, regarded with a certain respectful familiarity, and one particularly intricate carved pedestal, which not only supported the bust of the illustrious Karl August, but also opened to reveal the cruet, was undignified by the name of "grandfather".

[1] Note to the author.

26

Upstairs the younger children had their domain, and here behaviour was still more relaxed. In this kingdom of their own the children moved into a world cut to their measure. The furniture of their play rooms had been designed by their mother and was plain and useful, with a charm all its own. Bright coloured curtains hung in the windows, and the walls sparkled with simple vivid paintings of the German country-side. Downstairs the children came and went as guests in an adult world, learning early to combine self-effacement with the gracious consideration for all comers which their parents peremptorily demand-ed, but upstairs in this territory of their own they were free. Their father seldom left the grown-up world, but when their mother came to them upstairs it was to join in their laughter and enter whole-heartedly into their games.

As the children grew older, their life expanded into other parts of the house. "The big sisters," Sabine tells us, "were given a room as a home for their dolls, where they might rule supreme. The boys had a workroom on the ground floor with a carpenter's bench, and an animal room in which turtle doves and squirrels in high cages lived together with snakes and lizards in the terrarium, and where their collections of stones, butterflies, beetles and birds' eggs were housed."[1]

This generous distribution of rooms to accommodate the family by no means exhausted the capacity of the house in Grunewald, and on the first and second floor large landings opened on to more rooms than the children had ever counted, so that the addition of visiting friends and cousins imposed no strain on spacial resources, while the children of the neighbouring families came and went without disturbing the easy routine of the family life. This firm and yet flexible routine and this rich-textured family life were the creation of Paula Bonhoeffer, of whom Sabine writes: "Our mother was a strong personality, intelligent, warm-hearted and unconstrained, gifted with organising ability and fine social talents. These were still the days when governess, nursemaid, house-maid, chambermaid and cook helped to keep the large household running, and so our mother was always ¦free and ready for essential things. With her spontaneity she brought surprises, fun and festivities into our nursery, and she had a large repertoire of songs and verses. But she also introduced us to life's serious side. She had taught all our brothers and sisters for one or two years; there was even a school room with desks in the house."[2]

[1] *Begegnungen*, p. 13.
[2] *Begegnungen*, pp. 12–13.

Their father, though he never lectured or scolded the children, had exceedingly high standards for their behaviour and performance. He demanded simplicity and integrity in all departments of life. Any affectation or melodrama was despised out of existence; the children were expected to ignore physical pain; clear thinking and straightforward expression of one's thoughts were demanded as a *sine qua non*. Burnt into the minds of all the children was the positive sinfulness of ever using a "hollow phrase". Dietrich, in the last year of his life, looked back to these exacting standards, and considered the difficulties they had set in his way and the achievement that these very difficulties had made possible. He writes in one of the letters from prison on August 14th 1944:

"I have often noticed how much depends on stretching ourselves to the limit. Many people are spoilt by being satisfied with mediocrity. It may mean that they got to the top more quickly, for they have fewer inhibitions to overcome. I have found it one of the most potent educative factors (I mean such obstacles as lack of relevance, clarity, naturalness, tact, simplicity, etc.) before we can speak freely of what is in our minds. I believe you found it so with us at first. It often takes a long time to leap over such hurdles as these, and one often feels one could have achieved success with greater ease and less cost if these obstacles could have been avoided . . ."[1]

Of secondary but very considerable importance in the creation of the family life were the two Horn sisters, who entered the family as governesses to the older children six months after the birth of Dietrich and his sister. Recent literature has consistently represented the governess as a negligible, or at least a neglected character; but neither the oppressed dependent immortalised by the Brontës nor the grotesque scarecrow occasionally depicted by a later generation bear any relation whatever to these two young women. The Horn sisters were intelligent, humorous and beloved. Sabine has given us a portrait of them:

"She [Fräulein Maria Horn] came from a community of the Moravian Brethren, and through her we learnt yet more songs. It is true that she was ornamented by a stiff collar, but her heart was in the right place, and so she soon became our mother's right hand and remained with our family for seventeen years, until her marriage. The stiff collar soon disappeared, and one morning she called out to the boys: 'boys, today we will wear our leather shorts!' Dietrich, I and Susanne were the special charge of her sister, Fräulein Käthe. She also gave us our

[1] *Letters and Papers from Prison*, new translation, p. 129.

28

first year's lessons. Dietrich loved her dearly. He voluntarily made himself her little helper, and when some favourite food of hers was served he cried, 'I have had enough', and emptied his plate into hers. 'When I am big I shall marry you, then you will stay with us always', he told her."[1]

Both these sisters, now in their eighties, remember the child Dietrich vividly. Fräulein Käthe Horn writes:

"I took care of Dietrich and his twin sister Sabine and their younger sister Susanne for a year. I also gave the twins their first lessons (Susanne was only three). There was never any difficulty with teaching or with their homework, both were gifted and ready to learn. All three were jolly children with whom it was a pleasure to play or to go for walks. They liked to play at being Heinzelmännchen, that is, they surprised me with some action that was meant to please me; for instance they would lay the table for supper, before I could do it. Whether Dietrich encouraged his sisters to do this I don't know, but I should suspect it. Dietrich was often mischievous and got up to various pranks, not always at the appropriate time. I remember that Dietrich specially liked to do this when the children were supposed to get washed and dressed quickly because we had been invited to go out. So one such day he was dancing round the room, singing and being a thorough nuisance. Suddenly the door opened, his mother descended upon him, boxed his ears right and left, and was gone. Then the nonsense was over. Without shedding a tear, he now did what he ought."[2]

Her sister adds: "Dietrich was, like his brothers and sisters, a high-spirited child. They played and romped in the large garden, but the children were *never* rude or ill-mannered."

As they grew up within this powerfully formative framework, the children began to show a wide variety in their individual natures. Klaus alone, though extremely able, did badly at school. He would not learn, and, as Sabine remembers, "hated some of his teachers from the bottom of his heart". Their father seems to have pinned particular hopes upon Walter, the second son. "He distinguished himself," Dr. Bonhoeffer writes, "when he was still a small child, by a surprisingly well-developed command of language and capacity for self-expression, and continued to show this in his further development. In his school-leaving report he received the top mark for German with the comment: 'has an exceptional capacity for expressing even difficult concepts in

[1] *Begegnungen*, pp. 17–18.
[2] Letter to the author, February 28th 1964.

clear and attractive language'. His greatest love was for nature and the woods. In our holiday house in the Harz mountains he was generally in the forest by sunrise, he knew all the birds and could attract them. He made friends with the foresters wherever he went and became an excellent shot. I once saw him bring down a circling falcon; but when he saw the bird dead at his feet he burst into tears."[1]

Walter, for a tragic reason, is the only one who is honoured with a character sketch in his father's memoirs. About Karl Friedrich there is only a passing mention of his early desire to become a physicist. He seems to have been the most studious of the brothers, a little quiet and withdrawn, but sensitive and warm-hearted, and greatly beloved by Dietrich as he grew older. Klaus had perhaps the widest gifts. He had a good academic brain together with artistic and social talents, and developed an early interest in politics, social reform and international affairs. Ursula, the sister who followed him, had the best practical capacity, and an unobtrusive firmness of character which may later have been the means of saving the sanity of her brother Klaus in the last critical months of his life. She was a beautiful girl, motherly and domestic, who was perhaps obscured a little in early years through the somewhat mordant nature of her younger sister Christine, who suffered from the possession of a highly critical brain which might have served a man better. She resented the fate which left her too often in the company of her sister, while she hungered for the companionship of the three elder boys, whose triumvirate was complete without her. Sabine needed no one but her twin brother, and her generous, selfless nature perfected their early companionship. When three years after the twins the last child, Susanne, was added, the children were already firmly grouped without her, and she suffered the difficulties of the youngest child in a large family not given to sentimentalising the baby. But the twins, self-contained though they were within their own relationship, were reasonably patient with their small sister, and responded to reminders from above to include her in their games. It was not however till many years later, when Sabine had married and gone away to Göttingen, that Dietrich would discover the joy of companionship with this youngest sister.

Among this vivid crowd of boys and girls Dietrich himself does not seem to have attracted much attention, although he must have been a child of startling beauty, with silver-fair hair and a ruddy skin, a heroic mouth and intensely gazing, deep blue eyes. They were in fact all hand-

[1] K.B.'s memoir.

30

some children, but physical appearance was never referred to in the Bonhoeffer family. The most extreme comment upon appearance which was ever permitted was that so-and-so had "a nice expression". Dietrich's expression hardly fell within so minor a category. Physically he was very strong, and a little pride in one's muscles was permitted; at any rate in the case of Dietrich it could not be suppressed. Sabine was always at hand to act as admiring audience while he bent his elbow and drew his splendid biceps like a small football along his upper arm. He had from the very beginning of his life ebullient health and immense vitality of mind and body. He played games to win, and whatever he did, he did it with his whole strength; but he was not quite free from fears. Concerning this his sister records:

"In 1913 Dietrich started school at the Friedrichs-Werder Gymnasium, and this caused some difficulty, as he was easily frightened and feared walking there alone, which involved crossing a long bridge. So at first he had to be taken there, his companion walking on the other side of the street so that he need not be ashamed in front of the other children. He eventually overcame this fear. He was also very frightened of Santa Claus, and showed a certain fear of the water when we twins learned to swim. The first few times he raised a terrific outcry and had to be taken off the 'line' again. When he saw that I learnt more quickly than he and without tears, he probably felt more confident and overcame this fear. Later he was an excellent swimmer."[1]

She also remembers that although he generally shone at school, he found difficulty in writing essays, and she often needed to help him. She believes this may have arisen from his fear that he might inadvertently employ a "hollow phrase", and so commit a sin against his father's inflexible standards of performance.

He does not appear to have shown any particular precocity. In his earlier childhood he seems to have read a few books repeatedly, until he knew them almost by heart. Of these *Rulamann*, the life story of a caveman, *Pinocchio*, and a translation of *Uncle Tom's Cabin*, were among his favourites. He seems to have begun reading the German classics, especially the works of Goethe and Schiller, when he was about ten years old, but this occasioned no surprise, still less any admiring comment, among the Bonhoeffers, and when he came storming down the stairs one day full of enthusiasm at having discovered Schiller's play *Fiesco in Genoa*, he was greeted merely with mocking laughter for having pronounced the hero's name as 'Fisco', unfortunately losing track of the 'e'.

[1] *Begegnungen*, p. 16.

The family often read plays aloud and sometimes embarked on productions. All were musical. Sabine describes Dietrich's musical beginnings and the combined musical activities of the family:

"When at eight years old he grew interested in music, our parents often encouraged him to play to us on Saturday evenings. He also became an accomplished sight-reader, and soon had to accompany the cello and violin and his sisters' singing. He loved to accompany our mother when she sang the Gellert-Beethoven psalms, or the songs of Cornelius on Christmas Eve. Dietrich was a very sensitive accompanist, and his natural kindness became evident here too, when he did all he could to cover up the mistakes of the other person and to spare him any embarrassment. With touching patience he would often spend hours in accompanying, so that sometimes he had not time to practise his own pieces. And this was in spite of the fact that he had thought for a time of becoming a professional musician, though he was later critical enough to realise that he had not enough talent for that. To begin with he played a great deal of Mozart and Beethoven, later more Bach. Generally on Good Friday we all listened to the Matthew Passion in church. But he also much enjoyed romantic music. The song *Gute Ruhe*[1] that the stream sings to the dead was such a favourite that he tried to set this Schubert theme as a trio."[2]

Dietrich was very much devoted to the annual festivals. "Here," writes Sabine, "our mother was in her element. On the Sundays in Advent we were all assembled with her round the long dining room table to sing carols. Our father also joined us on these occasions and read us the fairy tales of Hans Andersen and Volkmann-Leander. While the plate of Christmas biscuits went the rounds we sat working at our Christmas presents. Dietrich enjoyed carpentry, but was sorry that he could not draw. The gift for painting and sculpture which descended on our mother's side from the Kalckreuths and Cauers had missed him out.

"Christmas Eve began with the Christmas story. We sat in a large family circle, including the maids in their white aprons, all festive and expectant, until our mother began to read. She is unforgettable for me in her black velvet dress with the fine lace collar, her heavy fair plaits bound round her head, and below them her broad serious forehead. She had the pale skin of many blue-eyed people, but now she was flushed with the pleasure of the occasion. She read the Christmas chap-

[1] "Lullaby of the stream" from Schubert's song cycle "*die schöne Müllerin*".
[2] *Begegnungen*, p. 20.

32

Dietrich Bonhoeffer with his
sister Sabine about the year
1915

The house in the
Wangenheimstrasse

Bonhoeffer's grandmother,
Julie Tafel-Bonhoeffer

Bonhoeffer's mother,
Paula Bonhoeffer

Dr. Karl Bonhoeffer

ter in a firm, full voice. All signs of fatigue and exhaustion, caused by the Christmas preparations, which extended far beyond the confines of the family circle, seemed to vanish when Christmas Eve arrived. After the Christmas story she always set going the hymn: 'This is the day the Lord has made.' I remember that sometimes tears came into her eyes at the lovely verse:

> 'When I this glory contemplate
> My heart and soul in wonder wait,
> And worship God in heaven above,
> For His infinity of love.'

Also when she read those words in the Christmas story: 'but Mary kept all these things and pondered them in her heart'. Dietrich and I talked about this, it affected and oppressed us, and it was a relief when Mother's eyes grew clear again. Later we put the light out and sang carols in the dark, until our father, who had quietly left the room, had lit the candles on the tree and round the crib. When 'the Christ Child' had rung the bell, we three youngest children were allowed to go in first to the lighted tree, and there we sang, enchanted, 'Christmas tree, loveliest of trees'. Only then did the present-giving begin. At thirteen Dietrich and I were allowed for the first time to stay up with the grown-ups to see the New Year in. After a festive meal in the evening we first cast our fortunes with lead and played a family card game supposed to foretell the future. That was a family tradition, and another was that towards eleven o'clock the light was turned out, and we drank hot punch and lit the candles on the Christmas tree. When we were all assembled our mother read the 90th psalm: 'Lord, thou hast been our dwelling place in all generations . . .' The candles grew shorter and the shadows from the tree longer, and as the old year ended, we sang Paul Gerhardt's New Year hymn:

> 'Come now with praise and singing
> In joy our worship bringing,
> To God who till this hour
> Has given us life and power.'

When the sounds of the last verse had died away, the bells were already ringing in the New Year."[1]

---

[1] *Begegnungen*, pp. 21–22.

CHAPTER III

WHEN on August 2nd 1914 the first world war broke out, the distinguished inhabitants of the academic quarter shared the mental unpreparedness of the rest of Germany. Karl Bonhoeffer, looking back over the two years immediately preceding the war, writes in his memoir:

"We could not really believe that war was coming, even though we were aware of the sinister aspect of our encirclement by the Triple Entente. I do remember once in the winter of 1913–14, at a party with some members of the High Command, receiving the disquieting impression that they expected soon to have to reckon with a resort to war; but on the whole we consoled ourselves with the reflection that the Kaiser, in spite of his predilection for big words and rhetorical sabre-rattling, was at heart undoubtedly a man who wanted peace; and we clung to the superficial hope that the international interdependence of commercial interests might serve to prevent a conflict. But the murder in Sarajevo at last showed even the political innocents the seriousness of the situation for Austria and therefore for Germany."

At the hour when war was declared the younger children were with their governess at a garden fête in Friedrichsbrunn, where the Bonhoeffers owned a house for family holidays. The news spread like wildfire among the aimlessly wandering crowd, who at once fell into excited groups vociferously chattering. But Fräulein Horn stayed for no uninformed speculation; with a pale and anxious face which they still remember, she gathered the children and brought them on the next train home to Berlin.

On the day of Britain's entry into the war, Karl Bonhoeffer walked up Unter den Linden with the three older boys. "The elation of the crowds outside the palace and the government buildings which had been mounting during the last days had now given place to a dreary silence, which had an extraordinarily oppressive effect. The severity of the conflict which lay ahead was now evidently manifest even to the masses, and the hope for a speedy end to the war was extinguished for those who had insight, by Britain's entry into the ranks of our enemies."[1]

At first the war brought only quite pleasurable changes into the children's lives. It was in fact the prospect of food shortage which precipitated the move from the Brückenallee to Berlin-Grunewald.

[1] K.B.'s memoir.

Now goats and chickens came to inhabit the garden, and Dietrich in his enthusiasm saved up his pocket money to buy a hen of his own, and as food became more scarce, he became an expert forager, returning from school daily with news of where some extra sausage, milk or butter was to be found. Further interest was provided by a family of refugees from the Eastern borders who were billeted on the Bonhoeffers and received some distant rooms opening on to the hinder regions of the garden, where they lived in a primitive squalor which exercised a mesmeric fascination over the younger children. But though the children gathered at the door powerfully magnetised and gazed in with rapt attention, they never succeeded in penetrating the mysterious life of their visitors, which remained for them shadowy and remote. During the first two years of its course the war itself shared this insubstantial quality, but as it continued it began to press in harder upon the families in Grunewald, and its tragic aspects began to penetrate the children's consciousness. Sons of relations and fathers of classmates were reported killed or missing, a cousin came home from the front blinded, and stayed for a time in the Bonhoeffer family.

Now Dietrich and his twin sister had long conversations as they lay in bed in the evenings. They tried to imagine the experience of "being dead" and what eternal life might be like. They attempted to breach the defences of eternity by concentrating upon the word *Ewigkeit*, "eternity" and closing their minds to all other thoughts. They continued this spiritual exercise for many months.

In 1917 Karl Friedrich and Walter volunteered for the army. Karl Friedrich was determined to serve in the ranks, Walter was not averse to becoming an officer. In the spring of 1918 Walter was sent to the front. On the last evening Dietrich at the piano sang for his brother a farewell song: *Nun zu guter letzt, geben wir dir jetzt auf die Wanderung das Geleite.*[1] Next day all the children went down to the station to see him off. As the long military train slowly drew out of the station, their mother ran beside it crying: "Only space will divide us!" Two weeks later Walter Bonhoeffer was dead.

This drew the first line across the children's lives. The triumvirate of the older boys was broken. Their mother, till now a stranger to sorrow, was shattered by this first impact of it upon her life, and for more than a year she virtually dropped out of the family circle. Now the pattern which had seemed indestructible, rooted in the very nature of the world, was disturbed, and the heart of it seemed gone.

[1] "Now at last, as the end comes, let us bring you on your way."

It was at this time that Dietrich and Sabine were separated, Sabine sharing a room with Susanne, and Dietrich having for the first time a room of his own. For a time the nightly meditations on God and eternity continued, Dietrich beating on the wall when he and the girls were to begin. But soon he discovered that when he knocked the girls were often already asleep. After this his knocking ceased, and for the first time the boy was alone with his thoughts. It may have been now, in the discovery of loneliness and the bitter taste of grief, that Dietrich had his first experience of the mystery we call God, his first encounter with a reality which bursts the framework of language and is with the greatest difficulty communicated. If he did, we shall never know it now. All we have from himself, apparently referring to this period, is a curious fragment dating from the year 1932, which shows one aspect of his many-faceted nature which he himself despised and was later to suppress entirely: the temptation to religious heroics. Written on an odd scrap of paper, it starts without preamble:

"He liked to think about death. He had already as a boy liked to picture himself on his deathbed, surrounded by all who loved him, speaking his last words to them. He had often secretly considered what he might say at such a moment. Death was nothing strange or hard for him. He would have been quite ready to die young, a beautiful, devout death. They should all see and understand that death is not hard but splendid for one who believes in God. Some evenings, when he went overtired to bed, he had occasionally wondered if the moment had come. A slight giddiness often startled him so much, that he bit his tongue wildly, so that he might feel life and pain. Then he cried out in his ignorance to God and begged for a reprieve. These experiences confused him to a certain extent. So he obviously did not want to die; he was a coward after all; he felt nauseated by his theatrical imaginings. And yet he still prayed in hours of strength that God would at last release him, for he was really ready for death; it was only his animal nature that repeatedly made him despicable in his own eyes and that confused him in his own presence. Then one day he was seized with a grotesque idea. He imagined that he was a person who was in the grip of the only really incurable disease that existed, a crazy and uncontrollable fear of death. The knowledge that one day he would really have to die took such possession of his thoughts, that he stared at the unavoidable fact in dumb horror. And he knew that no one could heal him of this disease, for it was not a disease, but the most natural and self-evident thing in the world, because the most unavoidable. He saw himself rushing distractedly from one person to another, begging for help. The doctors shook their heads and could give no answer; the disease was that he had perceived the truth of this reality, the disease was incurable. He could only bear this thought for a few moments at a time. But from that day forward there was something buried within him about which for a long time he no longer spoke, no longer even thought. His favourite theme for discussion and fantasy had suddenly acquired a bitter taste. Now he was silent about the beauty of a devout death and forgot it."[1]

If this gives an unexpected glimpse into one secret area of his life at that time, it is not an altogether surprising revelation. It is hardly remarkable that when the seamless garment of his childhood was suddenly rent from top to bottom by his brother's death and his mother's retirement into grief, he overbalanced in an attempt to rediscover the stability which hitherto had seemed immutable. In the evening when he lay in bed alone, and Sabine no longer joined him in his meditations, he cannot have been invariably successful in confining his mind to the elusive thought of eternity. It must often have wandered away into the unexplored country of sorrow, and in these wanderings he evidently tried to master the new experience of death's reality, constraining it into the pattern of the lost happiness and so restoring the broken whole. But the stark reality of suffering was not to be dissipated by religious day-dreaming. Experience had cast the first shadow across the boy's life, and never after this was he unaware of the abyss. In the years that followed there was occasionally an outward sign of the inward change. In the midst of a light-hearted gathering of family and friends, when singing and laughter disposed all hearts to pleasure, Dietrich would sometimes fall speechless, quietly leave the party, and be discovered later sitting by himself alone and silent. No explanation was asked for and none given.

As the year 1918 advanced, the secure and even tenor of the Bonhoeffer family life will not have been shaken only by personal loss and anxiety. Throughout the whole of the Reich, tension and bewilderment were daily mounting. Until the later months of this final year, the possibility that Germany might be defeated had taken no serious hold upon the mind of the people, but then the news of reverses on every front could no longer be withheld. By August 8th it was known throughout the country that the gigantic last offensive launched against the West had failed, and the inevitability of a national disaster gradually penetrated the minds of the civilian population. Meanwhile disquieting

[1] E.B., *D.B.*, pp. 63-4.

37

rumours of disaffection among the troops began to filter back from the forward lines.

Karl Liebknecht and Rosa Luxemburg, leaders of the Spartakists, the original Communist movement in Germany, had been imprisoned for their political activities, but Rosa Luxemburg was contriving to smuggle out the famous "letters of Spartakus", which were circulated throughout the armies, profoundly affecting the spirit of the troops. Across the small intervening buffer of the Balkan countries there was the spectacle of Russia, where since 1917 the Revolution had been in progress, where the troops had disarmed and deposed their officers, where there now existed a people's army for whom officers were elected by the soldiers' councils, and where the principle of authority imposed from above seemed to have been swept away. Less than a year ago such a state of things would have seemed a fantastic impossibility; now the impossible had been achieved. Inspired by the news, the disillusioned German soldiers began to elect their own councils, modelled upon those of Russia, while at home in the factories workers' councils were formed on the same pattern. The comparatively small number of convinced and informed Communists were now able widely to disseminate the idea of revolution among a military and civilian population deeply dispirited by hardship and imminent defeat.

Finally, on October 23rd, President Wilson announced that if the Allies had to treat with: "the military authorities and the monarchical autocrats of Germany . . . they must demand not negotiations for peace but surrender". From that moment the Spartakists and the Independent Socialists, who were pressing for the removal of the monarchy and of the Imperial General Staff, raised their voices with redoubled conviction. These alone, as they contended, stood between Germany and a just peace. The Independent Socialists, anxious to avoid Communism on the Russian model, urged the need for a more moderate form of revolution upon the reluctant Majority Socialists. These however, well-tried in opposition but wholly inexperienced in government, were alarmed at the prospect of taking on responsibility for a defeated country from which the powerfully unifying element of the monarchy had been removed, and now joined the Liberals and the moderate right wing parties in desperately trying to shore up the tottering throne. It was thought that if the Kaiser and the Crown Prince were removed, a Regency more acceptable to the Allies might be arranged. Their efforts were however frustrated by the Kaiser himself, who obdurately refused to abdicate.

But now the disaffection in the armed forces began to mount threateningly. The mutiny which began in the Navy at Kiel spread into the ranks of the Army. At last, on November 9th, Prince Max of Baden announced from the Imperial Headquarters at Spar the abdication of the Emperor. It had been an agonising decision. Klaus Bonhoeffer, who was at that time attached to the Headquarters staff, saw General Hindenburg leave the conference chamber after his last conversation with the Kaiser. Hindenburg, he wrote, was: "lifeless as a statue in expression and gesture"; it was an impression, he added, which he believed he would never forget.

But the gesture of the abdication had come too late. On the same day, Karl Liebknecht announced from the steps of the Imperial Palace the establishment in Germany of a Soviet regime. The Majority Socialists, very much against their own wish, were forced into making a revolutionary gesture to forestall the reality of revolution on the Russian pattern, and before the day was ended Paul Scheidemann, leader of the Majority Socialists, had proclaimed the German Republic from the windows of the Reichstag.

Karl Bonhoeffer has described in his memoir his walk to the Charité Hospital on that memorable day:

"Detachments of troops marching in disorder, mingled with civilians who carried in their hands posters saying 'Don't shoot!', pale starved figures covered with sweat, who were addressing the soldiers with excited gesticulations and dragging their guns out of their hands, while others, taking no part in all this, hurried perhaps more quickly than usual to their places of business. There was no shooting. In my department of the hospital the porter came to meet me on the steps wearing a red cockade, evidently with the intention of barring the way to my office, or at least of embarking upon an argument. When I took no particular notice of him, but having greeted him as usual passed on into my room, he made no further resistance." Through this curious sub-revolutionary atmosphere the younger Bonhoeffer children will have been trotting daily to and fro to school.

But the basic prerequisites for a violent revolution were not present. The historian of the German army, John Wheeler-Bennett, makes a concentrated and lucid comment upon the situation which now prevailed:

"The change of regime did not come as the result of any long-planned revolutionary movement. It did not represent any basic change of heart on the part of the German people themselves. It was brought about without any great, deep-seated conviction or willingness on the part of its progenitors, who would certainly at the time have preferred to retain the monarchy. It occurred in very great measure because those in power believed that by this means alone could Germany comply with President Wilson's preliminary prerequisite for peace, and partly because of the fear of Bolshevism; both courses being the result of pressure from outside rather than from within Germany."[1]

Out of this confusing and self-contradictory situation, the unhappy Weimar Republic was born. Not whole-heartedly desired, even by its creators, Germany's first democratic government had no means of inspiring enthusiasm among the disillusioned masses of the people. The enlightened and liberal-minded intelligentsia, among them the Bonhoeffer family, saw in it the best hope for their country and willingly supported it. But among the nation as a whole no interest could be aroused. Political bewilderment was accompanied by profound spiritual depression. Parties of the extreme left still campaigned for revolution on the Russian model, while the violent nationalists of the right obstructed the government by all possible constitutional and unconstitutional means, invented and popularised the legend that Germany would have won the war if she had not been stabbed in the back by the Socialists (Hitler was to add "and the Jews"), and did not hesitate to use violence in the support of their cause. Meanwhile an unexpected blow from without was to fall upon the staggering infant republic.

The government confidently supposed that, since President Wilson's demands had been met by the abdication of the Kaiser and the establishment of a democratic regime, they might now look forward to a peace treaty based upon Wilson's fourteen points. Neither the government nor any elements in the German nation had any sense of special responsibility for the war. They considered that both sides had entered it on the strength of treaty obligations and that their invasion of neutral Belgium could be justified on the grounds of military necessity. In May 1919, the news of the vindictive terms of the treaty they were to be offered exploded like a bomb. Horror, despair and furious resentment spread like a running fire through the length and breadth of the country. Germany, bankrupt and beaten, accepted the terms of the treaty, but with a sense of burning injustice.

It was into a nation in which despair and resentment struggled against the natural pressure towards recovery that Dietrich Bonhoeffer must now grow up. He was, however, affected by the prevailing atmosphere much less than most of his contemporaries. In the Bonhoeffer

[1] Wheeler-Bennett, *The Nemesis of Power*, p. 19.

family an imperturbable sanity and liberality of outlook steadily rode the waves of this restless political sea. Dietrich, more interested in philosophy and religion than he was in politics, armed himself with the eminently reasonable attitude of his parents and went on his way. But now his loneliness, first intensely felt at the time of his brother's death, began to grow. At school he was popular and admired as well for his ability as for his physical prowess, but he had made no intimate friends. His deep affection for his elder brothers had in early years been the somewhat removed affection of the youngest son in a large family, who was relegated to the ranks of "the little ones" while the elder brothers lived in a world of their own. His distance from them was increased by the fact that he had never shared their interest in natural science. The animals, plants and chemical experiments which had their being in the "boys' room" had no special attraction for him. "Dietrich has no interests," had been the elder brothers' wholly unfounded verdict. Finally his brothers' participation in the war raised another barrier between them. While Dietrich had been still going to school, Karl Friedrich had stood in the midst of violence and death, and Klaus had seen with his own eyes the downfall of his Emperor. Meanwhile, the girls developed their own interests, and as Dietrich grew up towards manhood he was increasingly aware of his life as being separated by various factors from the life of the others.

His intention of reading theology at the university, which seems to have been present for some time, was one more isolating factor. Christian ethical standards were deeply established in the Bonhoeffer family life, elementary religious instruction had been given by Paula Bonhoeffer with simple piety, and Bible reading and choral-singing were associated in particular with the festivals of the Christian year, but there was virtually no church-going, even at Christmas and Easter. Confirmation was regarded as an important formality, but not apparently associated with subsequent participation in the Communion service. For Dietrich's decision to enter the Church there was some precedent among his ancestors, but no occasion whatever from his family life or from the influence of family friends. All we have from Dietrich himself, obliquely referring to the decision, is another curious fragment from the year 1932, a companion to that in which his religious day-dream was confessed. Once more he plunges into the narrative without introduction:

"He blushed when one day in the Sixth Form he replied quietly to a question from his master that he wanted to study theology. He had not even stood up, so quickly had the answer escaped his lips. The surprised experience of finding the attention of the master and the whole form focused upon his person and not simply upon his performance, and now of suddenly having to give a personal answer, moved him to something between vanity and humility, so that this disregard of classroom etiquette was a measure of the consternation into which question and answer had thrown him. His master evidently felt it in the same way; he only allowed his gaze to rest upon him a moment longer than usual, and then quickly and kindly released him.

" 'Then you have some surprises ahead,' he said almost as quietly and shyly as his pupil. He had the question 'how long?' on the tip of his tongue, but as though this touched the secret of his own theological studies, once passionately begun and then quickly abandoned, and as though he felt dissatisfied at his own failure to say anything better to the boy whom he had long known and loved, he became embarrassed and clearing his throat he took up the Greek text which was the subject of the lesson.

"The boy had drawn this short moment deep into his consciousness, something unusual had happened, and he enjoyed its unusualness and felt ashamed, both at the same time. Now they all knew. Now he had told them all. Now the riddle of his life must be solved. Now he stood solemnly before his class and before his God. Now he was the centre. Did he now look as he would have wished to, his features marked with seriousness and determination? This thought pleased him, although he rejected it at once, while he impressed upon himself the high seriousness of his confession and of his task. Nor could it escape his attention that the master was suffering some embarrassment on his account, and that at the same time he regarded him with favour. The moment was suffused with pleasure, the classroom expanded to an unlimited field. There he stood in the middle of the world as the prophet and teacher of his knowledge and his ideals, now all must listen in silence, and the favour of the Eternal rested upon his words and upon his head. And then he was ashamed again. For he knew of his despicable vanity.

"How often he had already tried to master it! But it always crept in again, and now it spoilt the enjoyment of this moment. Oh, he knew himself well at seventeen. He knew all about himself and his weakness. And he knew also this very thing, that he did know himself. And through the small crack in this very knowledge, his deep-seated vanity leaked back again into the chamber of his spirit, and he was alarmed.

"It had made an incomparable impression upon him when he had read in a work of Schiller's, that a man needed only to mortify in himself a few small weaknesses, in order to become like the gods. Since then he had been on the watch. He would emerge from this battle as a hero, this was the thought in his mind. He had just made a solemn undertaking to do it. His way had been foreordained, at fourteen he had already known with certainty that he would have to follow it. But what if he refused? If the fortunes of battle went against him? If he failed to hold out?

" 'You have some surprises ahead,' suddenly rang in his ears. About what? What did this voice mean? What was the meaning of his classmates' gaze, inquisitive, mistrustful, bored, disappointed and mocking? Did they not believe he could do it? Did they not quite believe in the sincerity of his intention? Did they know something about him which he did not know himself?

"Why do you all look at me like that? Why are you embarrassed, sir? Stop looking at me! Shout at me that I am a conceited liar who does not believe what he is saying! But do not stand so considerately silent, as though you understood me! Laugh openly, but do not stand there useless, dumb, it is not to be borne!

"Then there is the crowd. He stands in the midst of them and speaks, speaks, glowing, inspired. He corrects himself. Upon the crowd rests a leaden silence, a sneering silent scorn. No, this cannot be. He is not the man they take him for. He is in earnest. They have no right to despise me. They do me an injustice, all of them. He prays.

"God, tell me yourself if I am really in earnest with you. Destroy me in this moment if I lie. Or else punish them all; they are my enemies and yours. They do not believe me. I know myself. I am not good. But I do know it, and God, you know it! I do not need the others. I, I will gain the victory. Do you see, how I am winning? Do you see, how they retreat? How they are discomforted? I am with you! I am strong. Oh God, I am with you!

"Are you listening? Or are you not listening? To whom am I speaking? To myself? To you? To the others here?

"And who speaks? My faith? My vanity?

"God, I will study theology. Yes, I have said it. They have all heard. There is no way back now. I will . . . But if . . . ?

"And as he was ready to turn back again, he heard the voice of his master, as though from far away. 'Are you not well? You look pale.' Then he pulls himself together, stands up—and translated as usual the difficult Greek text . . ."[1]

[1] E.B., *D.B.*, pp. 65–6.

This cannot be a recollection of an actual occasion, since Dietrich's classics master knew of his decision to take up theology some time before he entered the sixth form. But that it was basically an autobiographical reflection seems virtually certain. For here, more blatantly exposed than it would ever be again, was Dietrich Bonhoeffer's arch-enemy — vanity, the self-loving, self-admiring vanity which placed him, heroic and virtuous, at the centre of his own stage: "There he stood in the middle of the world." Already he had recognised it and was fighting it, fighting it with the weapon of his own determination, but infinitely subtle, insidious and tyrannical, it held him in its grip. "How often he had already tried to master it! But it always crept in again, and now it spoilt the enjoyment of this moment. Oh, he knew himself well, at seventeen! He knew all about himself and his weakness. And he knew also this very thing, that he did know himself. And through the small rift in this very knowledge, his deep-seated vanity leaked back again into the chamber of his spirit." It was an impasse. The better he did, the better his vanity would like it, and the more shining his virtues became, the more powerful would be his pride. This was a situation which he could not master, but out of which he could only be redeemed.

While these struggles were beginning in the boy's heart, his brothers came back from the war. Both had been profoundly affected by their experiences and were searching for ways into a more human future. Karl Friedrich, who had been devoted to the cause of the common soldiers and had given his support to the workers' councils, was disposed to see some hope in Marxism; Klaus was more concerned with practical efforts to secure social justice within the existing political framework. Both now continued their interrupted education, Karl Friedrich in natural science, Klaus in law.

As Dietrich grew up to meet them, he was more in their company. They discovered the disconcerting intensity of their younger brother's mind, and now they would gladly have drawn him into their orbit, enclosing him in a three-sided fellowship as intimate as theirs with Walter had been. But a divisive factor entered; their brother's declared intention of becoming a theologian led to passionate arguments between them. These arguments were to have a strong formative influence on Dietrich, both negative and positive. Klaus, the fastidious artist in living, struggled to impress on him the feeble and provincial character of the Protestant Church in Germany, grieved that a brother of his should resolve to devote his life to so peripheral a phenomenon. To this

44

Dietrich stoutly replied: "If the Church is feeble, I shall reform it!" The answer, meant as a joke, yet carried the germ of a real intention, and Dietrich was led by Klaus to an interest in sociology, with the idea that a study of social patterns might be a first step towards improving them.

The effect of his arguments with Karl Friedrich was less happy. An established sceptic, Karl Friedrich feared that his younger brother was deliberately turning his back upon the world of verifiable truth in order to bury himself in fruitless metaphysical speculation. With painstaking precision he spread out before him the map of the universe that science was revealing, but Dietrich would have none of it, and resolutely closed his mind to this aspect of reality. At this stage he felt that his God must be defended against any scientific interpretation even of the physical universe. "*Dass es einen Gott gibt, dafür lass ich mir den Kopf abschlagen*" was his final comment, which means, freely translated, "You may knock my block off, but I shall still believe in God." The words expressed better than he realised his unwillingness at that time to face the facts which science was revealing, and it may have been at this time that there began in the deeper layers of his mind an unconscious flight from this aspect of reality which was only halted in the very last years of his life. It seems probable that this final turning at bay to face the facts of science and appreciate their value was one of the elements which has lent the theological letters from prison their startling quality. To one who had for a longer time appreciated scientific fact as a primary ingredient of truth this recognition could hardly have come with the force of a revelation. That it did so come to Bonhoeffer is perhaps, by a curious inversion, the result of these early talks with Karl Friedrich. At the time, however, they showed no apparent effect, and his determination to read theology remained unshaken.

His parents made little comment on his resolution. His mother accepted it loyally, though without enthusiasm. His father, always scrupulous in leaving his children free to follow the direction in which their gifts and interests led them, never showed disappointment at his youngest boy's choice of a profession. Nevertheless Dietrich, who by this time knew his father's agnostic-humanist attitude, must have been well aware that his father could not enter far in heart or mind into the life which he had chosen. But if Dietrich had misgivings, they were caused by purely interior conflicts; exterior criticism, spoken or unspoken, had no power to move him.

CHAPTER IV

WHEN Dietrich left school in 1923, the rich and vivid family life of the Bonhoeffers, damped down for some years after Walter's death, had once more burst out into a cheerful blaze.

Evenings of chamber music with friends were frequent, and Dietrich had become an outstanding pianist. He also wrote plays and produced them and organised fancy dress parties which were becoming famous in the neighbourhood. Invention in connection with these parties was rich and exuberant, and the sight of Karl and Paula Bonhoeffer, dressed as Wotan and Freya, and somewhat inappropriately framed within the neo-classical portico of Stanislas Kalckreuth's gargantuan sideboard, is remembered by a few to this day. Though politics were never a main interest, a distinguished group which included the Bonhoeffers was for some time in the habit of gathering at the house of the historian Delbrück to discuss the prospects for the new republic. A moderately conservative outlook was expressed by some, a consistently liberal one by the Bonhoeffers. From this charmed circle the restless and disordered life of post-war Germany seemed far away, yet the young Bonhoeffers could not but be aware of it. In his last year at school, Dietrich had heard from his classroom the shots which killed the Foreign Minister Rathenau, and in the same year Klaus wrote in a letter to his future brother-in-law Hans von Dohnanyi:

"I have now got to know them [i.e. his fellow law-students] from their political aspect. But when I think of it I feel sick. The other day we had a meeting at which Professor Goetz from Leipzig spoke on 'the student in the modern world'. He spoke excellently and in a way quite free from personalities or party politics. *But* . . . on a democratic basis. So the students groaned, shouted and insulted him. Our historian Haller also made a spectacle of himself when he attacked his colleague blatantly, like an ugly demagogue. Then the mob of students cheered. People must have noticed how horrified I was. Anyway I had some trouble with one supporter, an asinine be-monocled Lieutenant . . . It is depressing when one sees how the people on whom we have to build for the future . . . think backwards with their eyes on the days of 1870-1, and even that only as an empty affectation. Hans, what a thought it is, that these are the people we shall have to do with

46

later . . ."[1] Appallingly prophetic words! It was at the hands of men like these that Klaus and Hans von Dohnanyi were to die.

Meanwhile Germany had been staggering from one political crisis into another. An attempted counter-revolution from the right had followed the Allies' demand for the surrender of an indiscriminate list of war criminals. The failure of this *coup d'état* had been followed by a series of political murders. Now a further blow was to fall. At the Allied Conference in Paris on January 4th 1923, Germany was found to be in default in respect of her reparations payments. Britain was disposed to consider a reduction in the amount demanded, France remained adamant. The inevitable clash occurred and Britain withdrew, leaving the way open for unilateral French action. Upon this France and Belgium, at the direction of Poincaré, occupied the Ruhr. The German government, unable to retaliate, announced a policy of passive resistance, and the whole country, including parties of the extreme right and left, fell in behind them. All work ceased in this vital area of coal and steel production. Fully justified as this gesture may have been, in making it Germany dealt the final blow to her own tottering economy, and the inflation already well on the way, now surged forward and gathered a momentum which no purely political measures could stem. A complete standstill of the national life seemed imminent, but the situation was retrieved by the intervention of the President, who now called forth out of comparative obscurity in the German People's Party a man who was to prove himself the outstanding European statesman of the postwar years, Gustav Stresemann. Stresemann represented the indestructible liberalism which was to go on living steadily in such families as the Bonhoeffers through the barbarous period of dictatorship which now lay only ten years ahead. Stresemann, and the men he gathered round him, very nearly rescued his country for sanity; it will remain one of the blackest tragedies of history that irrational forces in the end prevailed.

The new Chancellor brought to his task an acute mind, detached, far-seeing and wholly free from national resentment; and, with the rise to power of this quiet man, the Bonhoeffer's Germany began to be born. He saw clearly and from the outset of his career that co-operation between the nations of Europe, based upon mutual understanding and genuine good will, was essential not only for the future of his own country but also for the future of Europe and indeed of the world. He was determined to see Germany great, perhaps even the leading nation

[1] E.B., *D.B.*, p. 58.

in Europe, but this was to be through co-operation and economic re-covery. His policy was *Erfüllung*, fulfilment, not obstruction. A recovery which began with the end of passive resistance in the Ruhr now led Germany steadily forward by way of the Dawes and Young Plans, the Locarno Treaty, her entry into the League of Nations, and the Kellogg Pact, until by the end of the 1920s her place in Europe was once more established.

But in 1923 all this and what was to follow it lay hidden within the secrets of time, and meanwhile the inflation galloped on its way. Karl Bonhoeffer describes the difficulties of life at that time:

"The personal life of the family was affected in the first years after the war by the shortage of food and the inflation, which reached its peak in 1924 when the mark stood at one billion to the pound. On the first of every month one went home with one's brief case full to bursting with paper money. The problem was to spend all of it as quickly as possible on commodities, that is to say food, because it was probable that, because of the progressive devaluation, within a few weeks or even days, the money would be worth nothing. Into this period fell the repayment of my two life insurance policies, each worth 50,000 M. I had promised the children that we would spend the money on a bottle of wine and some strawberries. In fact however it turned out that the bottle of wine had to be abandoned—there was only enough to pay for the strawberries!"[1]

But in spite of the fantastic financial situation, the family contrived to continue their normal life. Karl Friedrich completed his course at the university and became "Assistent" in Physical Chemistry at the Kaiser Wilhelm Institut. Ursula was married to Rüdiger Schleicher, and Christine to Klaus' friend, Hans von Dohnanyi; both were lawyers. Maria Horn was also married from the house to Dr. Czeppan, Classics Master at a local boys' High School. And Dietrich in the same year went up to Tübingen to begin his theological studies.

Almost imperceptibly among the crowd of elder brothers and sisters, Dietrich had grown to manhood. In appearance he was an altogether Germanic type, and to the eyes of those who look instinctively for fine bones and a certain spare leanness of the flesh that covers them, his exterior beauty would seem to have been gone. But to his fellow-countrymen, whose visual demands are for something more robust and substantial, he now began to appear a magnificent figure. Standing over six feet tall with immense shoulders, and thighs and forearms wreathed

[1] K.B.'s memoir.

48

in muscle, he had a massive head crowned with a shock of unruly yellow hair, and a forehead which bulged over intensely blue penetrating eyes in a face whose strong regular features commanded attention. Only his hands were thin and sensitive, unexpected accompaniments to so formidable a body. But when all the salient facts of his physical appearance have been enumerated, one suspects that some vital factor has contrived to escape. Pictures of Bonhoeffer as he was at this time plainly do not reveal him. His apparently rather ungainly body was evidently irradiated by an interior quality which lent him something that had the effect of beauty. This indefinable quality was accompanied by immense vigour of mind, practical energy, and health so vigorous as to constitute a natural force. But below these masterful elements there lay a deep-seated sensitivity. The delicate hands told one side of the story as accurately as the great expanse of forehead and the solid thighs told another. Bonhoeffer would prove to be a man of innumerable dimensions and, as his rich and complex nature expanded, he was to develop a bewildering diversity of intellectual and moral qualities. As first one facet of his character and then another turned uppermost, his friends and associates, whose own more moderate equipment of gifts was easier to organise and render obviously coherent, were often to find themselves asking what manner of man this was.

But now the full scale of these developments lay many years in the future, and Dietrich went up to Tübingen in 1923 still little more than a boy. The University of Tübingen, like other German universities, still ran largely upon the mediaeval pattern. The system of Colleges and Halls of Residence developed in England and carried over to America was unknown. An undergraduate was not assigned to tutors or expected to fulfil any requirements with regard to residence. There was little official supervision of his work. A young man went up to the university with the intention of learning, and he was responsible for doing so. One particular characteristic of German university life is the fact that a man is not expected to spend the whole of his student life at one university; it is common to move from one to another, attracted perhaps by this or that particular lecturer, or simply in order to gain a wider breadth of experience.

Bonhoeffer went for his first year to Tübingen because of family connections with the university. It had been his father's, and both Karl Friedrich and Klaus had studied in Tübingen after the war, and Christine was now established there reading biology. Tübingen was also at that time the home of his Bonhoeffer grandmother, the vivacious and lively-minded daughter of Christian Friedrich Tafel. Now at the age of nearly eighty she had added wisdom to vivacity and lost none of her intense interest in life and people. The brilliant young man and the brilliant old lady appreciated one another to the full, and Bonhoeffer was to keep up a steady correspondence with her till the day of her death.

No particular course of study was laid down for the theology students, and he devoted his time to gaining a general view, exploring in particular the territories of Religious Philosophy and Church History, and attending a course of lectures on Dogmatic Theology given by Karl Heim. The only theologian at Tübingen who had a permanent influence on Bonhoeffer was Adolf Schlatter, from whom he gained an appreciation of the Jewish background to the New Testament, which he was to defend in later years against anti-Jewish pressures in German scholarship.

His social activities at Tübingen were mostly associated with his membership of the *Igel*,[1] a student society to which his father had belonged, and which was a product of the later years of the nineteenth century. The semi-political societies known as the *Burschenschaften*, to membership of which Bonhoeffer's great-grandfather Karl August von Hase had owed his imprisonment, had been succeeded by others, whose members wore brightly coloured pillbox hats and went in for duelling with naked swords, so that to have one's face criss-crossed with scars was regarded by many as a mark of distinction. The *Igel* had been formed as a protest against the duelling societies, and to symbolise their revolt its members had chosen for their colours light grey, middle grey and dark grey, and for their hat a hedgehog skin.

In the *Igel* Bonhoeffer made many friends, but the friendships did not survive the rise of Hitler's regime, when the *Igel* failed to make any protest against Nazi demands, and Bonhoeffer ceremoniously resigned. It was as a result of his membership of the *Igel* that Bonhoeffer had his first and last experience of military service, when he went to camp for a fortnight with "The Black Reichswehr", a postwar territorial training organisation which was technically illegal but generally recognised as necessary, in view not only of the explosive internal situation of the postwar years, but also of the pressure upon Germany's borders. In this very year of 1923, France had crossed over the Rhineland frontier and occupied the Ruhr, unopposed because of Germany's military helplessness, and it was feared, not without reason, that Poland

[1] "Hedgehog".

might attempt a similar incursion on Germany's eastern border. At home, nationalist and anti-democratic rumblings were to be heard in the dangerous hinterland of intrigue whose existence continually complicated the task of the Weimar Republic, and it was in November of this year that Hitler made his first irruption into the political limelight.

The Putsch in the Bürgerbräukeller was in many respects a highly successful failure, for the treason trial which followed it gave Hitler a platform from which to inform all Germany of his nationalist sentiments and to make a bid for the support of the Reichswehr, many of whose leaders shared his views. He was sentenced to five years' imprisonment, but released after six months and bound over, after which, according to one optimistic historian writing in 1929, he "faded into oblivion".[1] When the small, black-haired agitator disappeared from the scene after the trial, most Liberals would have shared this comfortable view; and at the time the year 1923 appeared no more portentous than others. For Bonhoeffer it had been uneventful, but it was followed by an experience which was to be of profound significance to him, and which gave body and colour to his dawning sense of the significance of the Church in the world; for in the spring of 1924 Dietrich and his brother Klaus set out on a three months' visit to Rome.

Since the eighteenth century Italy has been the Mecca of cultured Germany. Touched with magic by the burning heart of Goethe, it became a land which Germans longed for with a peculiar passion, and in the discovery of which they seldom seem to have been disappointed. For young Englishmen of Goethe's day, making the Grand Tour, Italy did not contain this indefinable magic; they obediently admired it, adding it to the collection of European countries visited, and returned home with their education only quite generally extended. But for young Germans it was not so; Italy seems to have had then, and to have now, particular power to awaken in them dormant faculties of the mind, and to effect a spiritual and emotional enrichment which is never afterwards wholly lost.

To both the Bonhoeffer brothers, in different ways, this minor miracle occurred. The impact of Rome upon them was immense. The artist Klaus was swept up immediately into the city's visible splendours. His sensual vision caught fire in the vivid streets, among the rich colours and under the hot blue skies; he was filled to overflowing by the visual riches poured out before his eyes with prodigal abandon wherever

[1] From the *Diaries of Lord D'Abernon*, footnote by the editor.

he went: classical majesty, renaissance majesty, sturdy simplicities escaped from the middle ages, fountains exploding in transparent spray out of an inexhaustible prodigality of inventions in carved stone, steps flowing down from splendid porticoes with a grace invariably unique. All this was enough for Klaus, and he gazed transported upon the Forum and the Colosseum, the city wall and the Pincio Gardens, and was content to bathe in the architectural beauty of the seven churches without concern for the life within them. But upon Dietrich a different revelation had broken: his first vision of the Church's glory.

Until now, church-going had played little part in Dietrich's life. The provincial Church of Lutheran Prussia was a phenomenon virtually ignored in the Bonhoeffer pattern of life. His father never spoke of it; his brothers frankly despised it, even his mother seemed to think it of small significance. Dietrich's own concept of the Church was as yet wholly unformed. Upon the few occasions when he had hitherto taken part in a religious service, it had been in one of the plain and severe churches of Protestant Berlin. But now before his dazzled sight there blazed out the visible symbol of the Church Universal; the Church of Rome, the Church at the heart of the world. Without prejudice or anxiety, Bonhoeffer gave himself up to this new experience.

His first High Mass was the Mass of Palm Sunday in St. Peter's. The vast concourse of worshippers and the assembly of priests from all the corners of the world made a deep impression upon him; he noted their variety in his journal: "Seminarians, monks . . . white, black, yellow faces, the sense of the Church's universality is immensely powerful." The same day at evening came Vespers sung with piercing sweetness by the novices in Santa Trinita del Monte. The comment in his journal reads: "The day has been wonderful, the first day on which something of the reality of Catholicism dawned on me, nothing to do with Romanticism etc., but I believe I began to grasp the concept of 'Church'." Next morning he spent an hour in Santa Maria Maggiore. It was the main day for the Holy Week confessions.

"All the confessionals occupied and thronged about with praying people. One sees here such a pleasing number of serious faces, around whom all that one says against Catholicism falls wide of the mark. Children too confess with real earnestness, this is very touching to watch. For many of these people, confession is not a duty any longer but has become a need. Confession does not have to lead to scrupulosity, even though that may often happen and does, especially with the most serious believers. Confession is not only what they are taught, but it is for primitive people the only way of speaking to God, and for those who see further it is the actualisation of the idea of the Church, which is fulfilled in Confession and Absolution."

On Good Friday he stood four hours in ·St. Peter's with the grieving throng and finally shared in the great ceremonial of Easter night. In the end he observed with a detachment remarkable in a boy who was not yet eighteen:

"A reunion with Protestantism, good as it might be for both sides—at least in part—seems impossible to hope for. Catholicism can get on for a long time without Protestantism. The faithful remain entirely devoted, and often during the celebrations in these mighty surroundings the Protestant church seems like no more than a small sect."

Dietrich's exploration of Rome was not confined to the Church. With Klaus he explored the Roman antiquities and made an expedition to Naples and Sicily and even crossed over to North Africa and spent a fortnight wandering in the Libyan desert. In a letter to his parents appears a note on the Mohammedan religion: "In Islam everyday life and religion are a single whole, as also in general they are in the Catholic Church. As for us we just go to church and when we come back a quite different life begins . . ."[1]

After two months Klaus returned and Dietrich stayed a few weeks longer attending lectures, possibly at the Papal University. Early in June he returned home.

The Roman term had had a profound effect upon him. It was to lend colour and depth to his concept of Christian life; and to determine his preoccupation with the idea of the Church during his student years. In 1927 he wrote for a small discussion group a note on the Roman Catholic faith which sums up the observations that he had been making:

"The services which the Catholic Church has rendered during the course of her history to European culture throughout the world are hardly possible to overestimate. She has Christianised and civilised barbarian nations and was for a long time the only preserver of science and art. Her monasteries were distinguished for this. She has developed a spiritual power second to none and to this day we admire the way in which she combines the principle of Catholicity with that of the single saving Church, of tolerance with intolerance. She is a world in herself. Endless multiplicity of life has gathered in her, and this many-coloured

[1] Quotations from the Rome and North Africa Journal appear in E.B., *D.B.*, pp. 86–9.

picture gives her her irresistible charm (*complexio oppositorum*). Seldom has any country brought forth such a varied progeny as the Catholic Church. With astonishing power she succeeds in maintaining her unity within all this variety, and in winning the love and reverence of the masses and in awakening in them a strong sense of community.

"But it is just because of this greatness that our uncertainties arise. Is it possible that she has ceased to be a signpost to God and become a barrier on the road? Has she not perhaps built an obstruction across the road to salvation?

"But no one has yet obstructed the way to God. She still has the Bible and so long as she has that, we may still believe her a Holy Christian Church. *God's* word will never return unto him void (Isaiah 55; 11), whether it is preached by us or by our sister Church. We repeat the same creed, we pray the same 'Our Father', and we have many customs in common. That unites us, and as far as we are concerned we will gladly live in peace beside this unequal sister, but we will not let her take anything from us which we have recognised as the word of God. We are not concerned with the name Catholic or Protestant, but with the word of God."[1]

[1] E.B., *D.B.*, pp. 52–3.

CHAPTER V

DIETRICH came back from Rome hugging an antique guitar for his sister Sabine. She returned from a term at Breslau a few days afterwards, and he met her on Berlin station with the guitar and a kiss. In an emotionally reserved family, the kiss was an unusual event, but this was a special moment in both their lives, for Sabine, at eighteen, had become engaged to Gerhard Leibholz, a brilliant young lawyer who was to distinguish himself in academic circles. Even in these early days, Leibholz's deep and generous nature, combined with his intellectual gifts, gave him a quiet distinction, and he was to win the hearts of all the family. But there was one circumstance which was to prove a bitter misfortune in the years to come; Gerhard Leibholz was Jewish by birth.

Now, however, all was joy, and Dietrich received the news of his twin sister's engagement with unaffected delight, warmly welcoming her husband-to-be into the family circle. But this regrouping of relationships, happy and natural as it was, cannot have come to him entirely without a sense of loss. The devotion between the twins, so deep as seldom to need any expression, was for both an element in life almost as inevitable as the air they breathed. During the early years of childhood neither had needed any other intimacy, and to that day Dietrich had found no other. But now, though their mutual affection was never to wane, he must in another sense part with Sabine, and the sense of ultimate isolation which had begun to take hold of him as he grew up into, and yet separated from, the world of his brothers, was deepened and intensified.

When in the summer term of 1924 he went up to Berlin University, he continued to live at home, and the affectionate, undemonstrative relationship with his brothers and sisters continued to enrich him. It was at this time, when Sabine was removed, that his relationship with his youngest sister, Susanne, was pleasantly extended. She alone among his brothers and sisters took part in the practical activities of his Christian life as they developed, and Susanne has never lost the memory of work and recreation with this loved elder brother. But still at heart Dietrich remained alone, never truly intimate with his family or with his teachers at the university, though they were to serve him well.

His formation within the Lutheran framework was rigorous and thorough, different in character from any that he might have received in England or America. It is an effect of the unique historical conditions under which the Anglican Church came into existence that, while Anglican theology owes much to the teaching of Luther and to a lesser extent Calvin, continuity with the Catholic tradition has never been wholly lost. In Germany however the Reformation's break with the Catholic tradition was more nearly complete. It is as though the view down the Christian centuries were blotted out by the gigantic figure of Martin Luther, to whom German Protestants look back as though to the beginning of Christian Europe. For many Germans to this day Martin Luther seems to have a power of inspiration which is second only to the power of Christ himself, and Bonhoeffer too experienced this dynamic force. Soon to grow restless within the limitations of Lutheranism, he would never cease to be devoted to the man who created it. In his book, *The Cost of Discipleship*, written many years later, we catch a glimpse of that concept of Luther by which he was inspired:

"When the Reformation came, the providence of God raised Martin Luther to restore the gospel of pure, costly grace. Luther passed through the cloister; he was a monk, and all this was part of the divine plan. Luther had left all to follow Christ on the path of absolute obedience. He had renounced the world in order to live the Christian life. He had learnt obedience to Christ and to his Church, because only he who is obedient can believe. The call to the cloister demanded of Luther the complete surrender of his life. But God shattered all his hopes. He showed him through the Scriptures that the following of Christ is not the achievement or merit of a select few, but the divine command to all Christians without distinction. Monasticism had transformed the humble work of discipleship into the meritorious activity of the saints, and the self-renunciation of discipleship into the flagrant spiritual self-assertion of the 'religious'. The world had crept into the very heart of the monastic life, and was once more making havoc. The monk's attempt to flee from the world turned out to be a subtle form of love for the world. The bottom having thus been knocked out of the religious life, Luther laid hold upon grace. Just as the whole world of monasticism was crashing about him in ruins, he saw God in Christ stretching forth his hand to save. He grasped that hand in faith, believing that 'after all, nothing we can do is of any avail, however good a life we live'. The grace which gave itself to him was a costly grace, and it shattered his

56

whole existence. Once more he must leave his nets and follow. The first time was when he entered the monastery when he had left everything behind except his pious self. This time even that was taken from him. He obeyed the call, not through any merit of his own, but simply through the grace of God."[1]

Almost immediately following this passage is an indictment of Lutheranism which shows that Bonhoeffer's for many years uncritical admiration of Luther was not extended to all his followers:

"Luther had said that grace alone can save us; his followers took up his doctrine and repeated it word for word. But they left out its invariable corollary, the obligation of discipleship. There was no need for Luther always to mention that corollary explicitly for he always spoke as one who had been led by grace to the strictest following of Christ. Judged by the standard of Luther's doctrine, that of his followers was unassailable, and yet their orthodoxy spelt the end and destruction of the Reformation as the revelation on earth of the costly grace of God."[2] It was then with a mind in which the capacity for generous enthusiasm would be tempered by a strong and independent critical faculty that Bonhoeffer went up to the University of Berlin.

In the generation which was then drawing to a close, the theological faculty had been brought to the highest point of its distinction by Adolf von Harnack, under whose leadership the great school of liberal theology had developed. Immense cultural riches had been gathered round the faith, and scholarship had developed critical techniques and made historical explorations from which the whole of European theology had been able to benefit. When Bonhoeffer arrived in 1924, Harnack, though already in semi-retirement, was still the presiding genius and continued to lecture and to hold a seminar in Church History for selected students. Bonhoeffer became a member of this seminar, and it seems at first sight surprising that, having the opportunity to do so, he did not put himself into the hands of this towering scholar, who would have been ready to become his principal teacher. But Eberhard Bethge has remarked Bonhoeffer's unwillingness at any time in his life to give himself up to a mind so great that it might have overshadowed his own, casting his in its own mould, and perhaps robbing him of the freedom and independence of judgement which were for him the very stuff of life.

There remained the choice between Reinhold Seeberg and Karl

[1] Dietrich Bonhoeffer, *The Cost of Discipleship*, 1964 ed., pp. 39-40.
[2] *C. of D.*, p. 41.

Holl. Holl was of a calibre to appeal to Bonhoeffer; a profound scholar, uncompromising, hard-thinking and tough, and having a personal enthusiasm for Luther which matched Bonhoeffer's own. But he died before the young student had been up more than a year, and so the choice fell upon Seeberg. Seeberg was an accomplished lecturer with a smooth academic facility which did not attract his new student, who was soon arguing hotly against his too comprehensive approach. He attempted to combine philosophy with theology and the Idealists with Martin Luther in a way which Dietrich found unconvincing. Nevertheless he learnt much from Seeberg. It was from Seeberg that he received a thorough grounding in the mechanics of his trade. He acquired a sound grasp of the theological teaching of his predecessors, and he learnt from him a theological language, complex and somewhat bloodless, but which provided him with a useful technical apparatus for the next few years, and after a year or two he had gained enough solid and detailed theological knowledge to believe that he might now begin to trust his own judgement. In the expert hands of Seeberg and the powerful hands of Harnack he was trained to think with a discipline and precision which were to serve him so well in the years to come, when far from the stimulus of acute minds or the comfort of spiritual inspiration, he was to follow God in the wilderness of a proscribed and persecuted Church.

Thus in Berlin Bonhoeffer was equipped with his theological apparatus, but ultimately the decisive influence came from another quarter. In the University of Göttingen a prophetic voice was being raised, the voice of Karl Barth. The liberal theologians of Berlin were concerned to know everything possible about the Christian faith, but Karl Barth was concerned with the Christian faith itself. No matter what it cost, he would return to the heart of the matter. With assertion and counter-assertion, with parable and paradox, he strove to convey the blinding vision of the God who, purely as an act of divine mercy, and for no conceivable works of righteousness which they might have committed, revealed himself to men.

The Berlin school were up in arms. Harnack was deeply distressed. This seemed to him to be an abandonment of all the riches which scholarship had been accumulating around the faith during the whole of the last century.

"The theology of today," he wrote, "is good (and that is a great thing) in that it is serious and that it goes straight to the point. But how weak it is as a science, how narrow and sectarian its horizon . . . how optimistic its method and how short-sighted its conception of history . . . and what threatens to disappear altogether is the connection of theology with culture and the *Universitas Litterarum*."[1]

Meanwhile Barth was demanding from Göttingen: "Should not the theologians find the courage to let our theology begin with a perhaps fundamentally sceptical, but yet clearcut, reminder of what is admittedly unacceptable, incredible and admittedly a cause of dissent, namely the claim that God himself has said something and done something, something which is new and outside the normal correlation of all human words and things, but which yet, in its newness, has been set within this correlation, one word and one thing among others, but yet specifically this word and this thing."[2]

So the battle was on between the discursive, research-loving, culture-broadening school of the Liberal theologians and Karl Barth's so-called dialectic school, with its intensive, single-minded search for ways of apprehending and expressing the burning central truth.

There was no doubt where Bonhoeffer would stand. In a choice between wide culture and the white-hot single-hearted passion for this truth, there was in effect no choice at all. A man of a different temper from Bonhoeffer's might have pulled up his roots in Berlin and gone to sit at the feet of Karl Barth at Göttingen. Bonhoeffer preferred to stay and maintain his own convictions at Berlin. Thus it was in the fires of this controversy that his theology was forged. The experience of discovering how to learn all he could from a group of able men, while staunchly upholding the insights of their most brilliant opponent, provided an admirable intellectual formation. But from the point of view of immediate academic success it was by no means an advantage.

Harnack and Holl were delighted with the young student's handling of religious history, but when Seeberg had to mark an essay on dogmatics it was another matter. The essay came back criss-crossed with severe comment, question marks and "No!" frequently interspersed. This was all seditious Barthian stuff not to be tolerated! At the foot of the essay he had appended the laconic verdict: "Fair, Seeberg 31.7.25". Dietrich was disturbed by this reaction, but in no way deflected from his opinions. A fellow student, Helmuth Goes, remembers him at one of Harnack's seminars in the winter of 1925:

[1] Letter from Adolf von Harnack to Martin Rade, quoted by A. von Zahn-Harnack in *Adolf von Harnack*, 1st edn., p. 536.
[2] A. von Zahn-Harnack, *Adolf von Harnack*, p. 530.

"What really impressed me was not just the fact that he surpassed almost all of us in theological knowledge and capacity; but what passionately attracted me to Bonhoeffer was the perception that here was a man who did not only learn and gather in the *verba* and *scripta* of some master, but one who thought independently and already knew what he wanted and wanted what he knew. I had the experience (for me it was something alarming and magnificently new!) of hearing a young fair-haired student contradict the revered historian, his Excellency von Harnack, contradict him politely but clearly on positive theological grounds. Harnack answered, but the student contradicted again and again. I don't any longer remember the content of the discussion—the talk was of Karl Barth—but I remember the secret enthusiasm that I felt for this free, critical and independent judgement in theology."[1]

This note is interesting not only for the light which it throws on Bonhoeffer's capacity, even then, to swim against the stream, but also for its reference to the "passionate attraction" which he was already beginning to exercise. The result of this not entirely enviable gift was that he was now continually surrounded by admiring friends of lesser calibre. He seems to have had a particular fascination for many who were unhappy, incomplete or entangled in their own difficulties, and he already devoted many hours of his day to battling with their problems, somehow fitting it in among his many other activities. When his cousin, Hans Christoph von Hase, once reproached him for wasting his time with such people, he answered simply, "If I can help them it isn't wasted."

Dietrich indeed still seemed to have time for everything, and Helmuth Goes remembers that when the seminar which so much delighted him was ended, Dietrich asked casually, "Herr Goes, will you come and dance at our house this evening?"

The evening, like the seminar, was unforgettable, all grace and gaiety, with the young people of the family pleasantly doing the honours, theology students, law students and young scientists happily mingling, and Dietrich himself now dancing, now most beautifully playing the piano, while all this mobile pattern of music and laughter was gathered into one with a web of conversation which was as light as it was brilliant.

These informal evening parties continued to be a feature of the family life throughout the children's student years. Besides this there were

[1] E.B., *D.B.*, p. 96.

expeditions into the surrounding country, concerts, opera, visits to the theatre where the productions of Max Rheinhard were at their height, lectures at the Kaiser Wilhelm Gesellschaft, and much else besides. Dietrich worked with immense speed and concentration and never seemed too much burdened or too busy to take part in these pleasures. For the family was still the centre to which his life returned.

But for a single factor, these years when he lived at home and studied at Berlin University may represent the period of the most unclouded happiness that Bonhoeffer was ever to know. During these years he developed to the full the capacity to live simultaneously at a number of different levels which he describes later in the *Letters from Prison*.

But throughout these rich and vivid years of near-fulfilment he still in his deepest experiences remained alone. It was not until many years later, when the outward pattern of his life would soon be destroyed and the normal roads to effective action barred against him, that he was to receive the gift of a friendship through which the deepest springs of his creative energy were to be set free.

Now he forgot the sense of personal need in intensive activity, in the living at many levels of which these crowded years were making him master. At home he moved in the world of liberal culture and of light-hearted family affection which since his childhood had been his native element; at the university he was receiving an intellectual training which was strenuous and demanding to the highest degree; and simultaneously he found time to give himself up with whole-hearted enthusiasm and enjoyment to leading a children's service on Sunday mornings in the church in Berlin Grunewald.

This children's service, which he began to hold in 1925, continued for two years. It was a requirement of the Konsistorium which governed the Provincial Church of the Mark Brandenburg that some exercise of this nature must be undertaken by men who were preparing for ordination. But in view of the demanding nature of his theological studies, Bonhoeffer could have passed muster by producing evidence of some largely nominal parochial activity. Nothing was further from his intention.

He immediately threw himself heart and soul into the work, co-operating with the newly-arrived Pastor K. Meumann. On Friday evenings the small group responsible for the work met for discussion, and on Sunday mornings they held classes for the children which had

61

generally been prepared beforehand. Some of Bonhoeffer's lessons were prepared with great care; he presented the required Bible story in his own vivid and dramatic words, learning to live in the lives of the children, so that the lessons he had to teach them caught fire in their hearts in a way that many of them never forgot. Not content with teaching on Sundays, Dietrich gathered the children together for games and took them for expeditions into the country, and after a time the "Thursday Group" came into being, in which a number of the older boys gathered at the Bonhoeffer's house in the Wangenheimstrasse for discussion. Under Dietrich's leadership a wide area of ground was covered, the boys discussed religious, cultural, political and ethical subjects, each in turn producing an introductory paper, and for this group Dietrich wrote, among many others, that essay on the Roman Church which was the fruit of his enriching visit to Rome two years before.

It is to the later years at Berlin University that another event belongs, which perhaps only through the accident of circumstances remains a minor one. For now Dietrich, in a youthful and unpractised manner, began to fall in love. The girl was a distant cousin, and is said to have borne a shadowy and indefinable resemblance to Sabine. Dietrich was evidently quite seriously in love, but had no gift for expressing his sentiments; the girl was apparently in an identical condition. The result was an awkward and unrewarding relationship, which almost petered out in 1928 when Bonhoeffer left Berlin for a year, but which lived on obscurely, ready to blossom again later.

Meanwhile he continued to work for his degree with immense speed and concentration. At the end of 1927, six weeks before passing his first theological examination for the Church Board, he presented the thesis for his Ph.D. under the title *Sanctorum Communio* and defended it in public debate. This work is an immense *tour de force* for a young man of twenty-one. Turgid and overloaded though the style may be, it is redeemed by the concentration of creative thought which drives it forward. It is the work of a man who is not only concerned to show what he knows; he is above all passionately concerned with the subject in hand. He is concerned because he is a theological student, but more still because he is a Christian.

"The nature of the Church," he states roundly in his introduction, "can be understood only from within, *cum ira et studio*, and not from an indifferent standpoint. Only by taking the claim of the Church seriously, without relativising it alongside other claims or alongside one's own reason, but understanding it on the basis of the Gospel, can we hope to see it in its essential nature."[1]

In the thesis which follows he attempts to understand the relationship of the Church in its sociological aspect, as a group of sinning and stumbling human beings, to the Church in its divine aspect as the body of Christ on earth, and at the same time he attempts the impossible task of reconciling the empirical approach to the subject which he found at Berlin with the Barthian concentration upon the Church as an aspect of God's self-revelation.

The attempt is not wholly successful, but the thesis stands now not only as a monument to his precocious erudition, but also as a means by which we may follow the workings of this powerful and strenuous mind in its search for the identity of the Church. Bonhoeffer emerged from this first full-scale engagement with the subject having gained certain convictions about the Church's essential nature which were not merely theories assembled for the purpose of presenting an impressive thesis, but which he believed with passion and integrated firmly into his Christian life.

This vision of the Church, first glimpsed during his visit to Rome, and worked out with relentless thoroughness through the almost three hundred pages of his thesis, was set forth with warmth and vividness in one of his first sermons, written a few months later:

". . . it is perhaps the most serious calamity of the present time that we do not know what 'Church' means, that which burned so passionately in the heart of Jesus at the time of his farewell, and about which Paul has written to us with such incomparable beauty in the letter to the Ephesians . . . but it is not just that we need to understand this, but that we need ourselves to become the Church . . . Paul calls it being the body of Christ. Paul writes to the Christian community at Corinth, to people who are tormented with all kinds of questions . . . to a community in which sin is at work, as it is today in us and in which faith is weak, to such a community Paul writes the words: 'You *are* the body of Christ.' Not 'you shall be' no, just this, '*you are*'. That is the whole point for him, that they belong to the body of Christ, whether they are sinners or not. '*You are*', and so the words speak clearly to us too: 'You are the body of Christ', you must only recognise it, you need not add anything to it; God has already done everything; he has given us participation in the body of Christ as a free gift of grace, but that means that he has drawn us all together into a single life, whose power, and

[1] Dietrich Bonhoeffer, *Sanctorum Communio*, p. 20.

63

whose honour, whose blood and whose spirit are Jesus Christ. God has drawn us into the ranks of his own nation, he has chosen for himself a community in the world, whose Lord is Jesus Christ, and to whom we belong . . . The body of Christ, the nation of God on earth, the holy community which God has chosen, that is the Church about which we are to speak . . . And God has made us members of this nation, as truly as we love Christ. We live within this nation perhaps without knowing it, we are buttressed and borne up by it and live by its love. We are not alone on our homeward journey, no, we are surrounded by many companions who help us, support us and carry us forward and who show the way. But wondrous as the nation itself, as the Church of God which is the body of Christ, are the means by which it helps us.

"There are three powers at work in it which are greater than human strength, they are the gifts of God to his Church, and only through them can the Christian community live, and through them the greatest might on earth is entrusted to the Christian, entrusted to us.

"The first is that we can sacrifice ourselves for each other in faith, for our life is only a life when it is an offering made for God and man, a visible or invisible offering, no matter which. The power of the offering is in the power of our fellowship, and because the people of God sacrifice themselves for one another, they are the mightiest in the world.

"The second is—secret and wonderful, known to only a few, but the power without which not one of us would have a spark of faith left— that we can pray for each other, and that millions of hearts are praying for us, for our faith and our power. Let us but think of this: that the world is an altar, from which prayer rises to heaven a millionfold, that no second passes when this nation are not raising their hands to heaven and beseeching grace for us, for each of us, and that for our salvation the hearts of the whole community are trembling and praying, and that perhaps one or another from among the intimate circle of our friends is daily lifting our soul to God and interceding for us. Which of us would not grow humble and small at such a thought; who knows whether this man or another may not be the saviour of his soul; or whether there is not one who keeps night vigil for him on his knees before God, for it is not our own merit which preserves us, but God's unfathomable grace and love to our neighbour and to us . . .

"But the third is the highest, most divine, most wonderful and most mysterious and holiest of anything that is to be found among men. That we may mutually—I for you and you for me—forgive one another's sins and lift the burden of guilt. This is the great mystery of confession, of willing confession which one may make to another.[1] . . . Sacrifice, intercession, absolution, those are the wonderful powers of the Christian community, which are all contained in the word Love, Love as God has shown it to us, in becoming Christ to the other person. These three powers are the blood in the body of Christ, which holds all in one. One body, that means one life, and so it is. All the members live one single life, breathe one single air, are fed with a single food, the word of God, and drink from a single cup, the blood of the Lord Jesus. Where one is, there is the whole community, not one is alone, not one is forsaken, not one is homeless, the community is with him in love, that is to say in sacrifice, in intercession, in absolution . . . Therefore come into the community, come into the nation of God; you *are* the body of Christ, you *are* the Church of God, you *are* his sanctified community. Behold and wonder and be thankful.

"There is only one hope for our age, which is so powerless, so feeble, so wretchedly slight and pitiable, and with all this so forlorn—return to the Church, to the place where one man bears up another in love, where one man shares the life of another, where there is fellowship in God, where there is home, where there is love . . . Church, that is our faith—I believe in a holy Church; Church, that is the significance of our human society; Church, that is our hope for the present and the future. In the words sung once by an ancient Father of the Church: God our Father, the Church our Mother, Jesus Christ our Lord, that is our Faith. Amen."[2]

These words must have rung in the ears of his pedestrian congregation with an intensity which may have seemed to some exaggerated. But for the young man who delivered it they represented a passionately realised truth, a truth moreover which was to be lived out in uncompromising practice in a life of unforseen difficulty and danger that lay now only a few years ahead.

[1] The doctrine that any member of the Church was entitled to hear the confession of another and absolve him had been pronounced by Luther, but the practice had fallen into disuse in the Lutheran Church. Bonhoeffer was to revive it seven years later in the seminary at Finkenwalde.

[2] From an unpublished sermon on I Corinthians 12: 26 and 27, preached at Barcelona, July 29th 1928.

CHAPTER VI

BONHOEFFER had now secured the equivalent of a doctorate at the university, and completed the first stage in his preparation for ordination. The next stage required in his progress towards becoming a pastor was to spend a year as curate under a parish priest. A place was offered him under Pastor Olbrich, Chaplain to the German Lutheran Community in Barcelona, and after some hesitation Bonhoeffer accepted it.

When he left Germany in February 1928, the country was in a state of apparent stability, in the years which preceded the Depression, It was reaping the benefits of Stresemann's policy of "fulfilment". By his able statesmanship he had secured the Dawes Plan by which the burden of reparations was reduced; on this had followed the Locarno Treaty and Germany's entry into the League of Nations. With her position in Europe re-established prosperity increased, bolstered by foreign loans. How precarious was this state of equilibrium future events were to show, but few intelligent Germans, and least of all the perennially optimistic liberals, saw cause at that time to be anything but hopeful; so it was in a mood unclouded by any political anxiety that Bonhoeffer set out for Barcelona.

This journey was his first excursion outside the range of his family life. For by far the greater part of his twenty-two years, he had lived at home in the charmed academic circle of Berlin-Grunewald. During the year at Tübingen he had lived within the orbit of his sister Christine and his Tafel grandmother. His excursion to Rome had been in the company of Klaus. Now he set out alone.

If Bonhoeffer had been less gifted in the human qualities, the entry into the German community at Barcelona might have proved a profound disappointment to him. He had lived till now in a world of exceptional erudition and brilliance, able to minister richly to his temperamental needs; in Barcelona he found himself thrown into a circle of expatriate small business men, in the parish of an elderly pastor who had established its religious and cultural requirements at a conveniently low level. Into this comfortably dormant society Bonhoeffer strode, shining with his characteristic blaze of intellect and spirit.

One might have supposed that a young man of his calibre, entering upon his first practical assignment in surroundings of such entrenched mediocrity, might either have rejected it and fled to a field of more congenial opportunity, or else flared up into a dramatic rebellion which would have gained him some excited followers and many implacable enemies, tearing the little community in two. Bonhoeffer did neither of these things. He took in the situation with clear-headed detachment, gave polite and friendly co-operation to the elderly chaplain, and to the little group of German families, men, women and children, he simply and warmly gave his heart.

His eruption into the small community acted like a kiss for the Sleeping Beauty. Life flowed again around the church. The congregation doubled. Parishioners whose religion had lain for many years submerged were startled into discovering the Christian faith as a living reality. But Bonhoeffer did not only arouse the Christian zeal of the little community, he took an active interest in the variety of problems which faced its members. This young man of twenty-two, never hitherto associated with business, now gave his mind to his new friends' business anxieties, and without any personal experience of marriage and parenthood he was able to enter into the hopes and fears of parents bringing up children, and of the children who benefitted and suffered from their concern. He started a children's service, and a study circle for sixth form boys. He embarked upon the adventure of awakening their minds and of trying to interpret their difficulties to their schoolmasters. On behalf of his older compatriots he soon became active in the *Deutsche Hilfsverein*[1] a society designed to help with problems of unemployment, business failures, vagrancy and other disorders. He would have done more to extend the work of the church, if his pastor had not firmly contained his energies, not wishing to be left in charge of a large number of new undertakings.

But within the permitted framework, Bonhoeffer contrived to extend himself to the full, and he was soon enduring the effects of his resultant popularity. He never refused invitations to social gatherings, but gracefully bore with the banalities of the conversation and accompanied on the piano the orgies of sentimental singing, to the delight of all but himself.

The glowing country of Spain itself, hot and alien, tragically poor and romantically rich, formed no more than a background to these German days, but it was a background that Bonhoeffer explored with interest whenever opportunity offered. He made one or two friends among the

[1] German Friendly Society.

Spaniards, and was especially attracted by their gracious ease, and their ability to "make nothing of themselves". The Catholic Church, in its Spanish manifestation, proved to be a disappointment, lacking the numinous splendours of the Church in Rome, but he enjoyed the vigour of the popular religious festivals. On leave from the pastorate, he visited Toledo, Cordoba and Seville with Klaus, fell in love with El Greco and bought with Klaus' help what might have been a Picasso. Klaus, returning with it in triumph to Berlin, was offered 5,000 marks for the picture; but when a photograph was sent to Picasso, he commented non-committally that his work had often been faked by a friend in Madrid. The enthusiasm of the buyers waned, and the picture remained with Klaus, a sensational memento of Spain.

Bonhoeffer has not left much record of his impressions of Spain itself, a diary begun when he first arrived was soon abandoned. But we can gain some impression of his life in the German community from a letter written to his friend Helmuth Rössler:

"Every day I am getting to know new people, at any rate their circumstances, and sometimes one is able to see through their stories into themselves—and at the same time one thing continues to impress me: here I meet people as they are, far from the masquerade of 'the Christian world'; people with passions, criminal types, small people with small aims, small wages and small sins—all in all they are people who feel homeless in both senses, and who begin to thaw when one speaks to them with kindness—real people; I can only say that to me it seems that these people stand in God's grace rather than in his anger, and that it is much more the Christian world which stands in his anger rather than his grace. 'I am sought of them that asked not for me . . . I said, behold me, behold me, unto a nation that was not called by my name' (Isaiah 65:1). This summer, in which I am on my own for three months, I have to preach every fortnight . . . and I am thankful that I have success in it. It is a mixture of subjective pleasure, let us call it self-satisfaction, and objective gratitude—but that is the judgement upon all religion, this mixture of the subjective and the objective, which one may possibly ennoble, but which one can never fundamentally uproot, and the theologian suffers doubly from this—but again, should one not rejoice at a full church, or that people are coming who had not come for years, and on the other hand, who dare analyse this pleasure, and be quite certain that it is free from the seeds of darkness?"[1]

It is worth stopping to read that sentence again. "Who dare analyse

[1] Dietrich Bonhoeffer, *Gesammelte Schriften*, volume I, pp. 51–52.

this pleasure and be quite certain that it is free from the seeds of darkness?" Here for one moment the curtain is twitched aside, and we catch another glimpse of that secret world in which Dietrich Bonhoeffer's deepest battles were being fought. For him the temptation to say in his heart "I think I made a good impression" was no light matter. It was real temptation, Luther's *Anfechtung*, which means not merely trial, but attack. The letter continues: "On Sunday I am going to preach on Matthew 5:8; I have never approached any sermon with such beating of the heart."[1]

This sermon begins:

" 'Blessed are the pure in heart, for they shall see God.' As in ancient Israel any man who touched the ark of the covenant forfeited his life, because a divine power went forth from it against which he could not stand, so likewise the man who approaches too near to the word of our text today, must lose his life before it. Such wonderful powers go forth from it, it shines with such wondrous and quiet radiance, that we cannot turn our eyes away; we are like the merchant in the parable of Jesus who could not turn his eyes from the costly pearl that he had found, and gave all that he had so that he might gaze on it for the rest of his life. So I bring you today this word in my text, and I know that the best thing we can do in the face of it is to be silent. To gaze and be silent, to let the word pierce us and master us, to lose our life to this word and to let it lift us into eternal heights and distances."[2]

It is a characteristic opening. Bonhoeffer set himself a hard task in these sermons; he was striving to speak to the hearts of the congregation, to impress upon them basic theological truths and to find words with which to express insights which were struggling for form within his own mind. Fourteen of the sermons have been preserved and three lectures which he delivered in the Christmas holidays, and they tell us a good deal about the young man who wrote them. We discover his sensitive awareness of the many layers of consciousness, his discernment of the particular griefs and poverties of the modern world, his deep understanding of the meaning and demands of friendship and of the value of many human experiences to which few have the capacity to give themselves fully.

"Waiting is an art which our impatient days have forgotten. We expect to pick the ripe fruit when we have only just planted the sapling;

[1] *G.S.*I., p. 53.
[2] Sermon preached in Barcelona, August 12th 1928.

greedy eyes too often find themselves deceived, when the fruit that looked so delicious turns out to be green inside, and careless hands fling away ungratefully the thing which has caused them such disappointment. The man who does not know the austere pleasure of waiting, that is of abnegation in hope, will never discover the perfect blessing of fulfilment."[1]

"Work is a means by which man makes something of himself. All work must be ultimately work on oneself."[2]

"If you would find eternity, give yourself to time. This seems like a tremendous paradox: if you desire the eternal, give yourself to the temporal. If you desire God, hold fast to the world."[3]

"Our whole being pants for solitude, for silence. For at some time or another we have all tasted what silence is, and we have not forgotten the fruit of such hours."[4]

He is not ashamed to describe his own experience of temptation for the benefit of the hearers, whom he longs to touch and awaken.

"We all know those hours in our lives in which we have been disgusted with ourselves, in which we loathed ourselves, in which the whole miserable feebleness of our way of living was apparent to us, we all know too the hours when we fall, go back on our own intentions, the hours of shameful defeat, the hours when we despise ourselves . . ."[5]

In these youthful sermons, Bonhoeffer revealed much more of his personal life than he would do later, and we have a reference to his private prayer, whose rarity makes it precious:

"Our relationship with God must be practised, otherwise we shall not find the right note, the right word, the right language when He comes upon us unawares. We have to learn the language of God, learn it with effort, we must work at it, if we too would learn to converse with Him; prayer too must be practised as part of our work. It is a grave and fatal mistake, if one confuses religion with a heightening of the feelings. Religion means work, and perhaps the hardest and certainly the holiest work that a man can undertake. It is pitiable to be content with the remark 'I am not naturally religious', when there is a God who desires to possess us. It is an excuse. Certainly, some find it harder than others do, but no one, and of this we may be sure, has achieved it without effort. And here is the reason why being silent in God's presence

[1] Sermon, August 12th 1928.
[2] Address to the Sunday School, Barcelona.
[3] Sermon, September 23rd 1928.
[4] Sermon, July 15th 1928.
[5] Sermon, August 12th 1928.

requires work and practice: it takes daily courage to expose oneself to God's word and to allow oneself to be judged by it, it takes daily energy to delight in God's love. But this brings us to the question: What shall we do, in order to penetrate into this silence before God? Well, about that I can only tell you, in all humility, just a little from my own experience. Not one of us lives such a hectic life that he cannot spare the time, even if it is only ten minutes in the morning or the evening, to be still and let the silence gather round him, to stand in the presence of eternity and to let it speak, to enquire from it about our condition, and to gaze deep into himself and far out, beyond and above. It may be done by taking up a few words from the Bible; but the best is to abandon oneself completely and let the soul find its way to its Father's house, to its home, where it finds rest. And whoever attempts this, working at it seriously day by day, will be overwhelmed by the riches which will flow from these hours. Of course, all beginnings are difficult, and whoever sets out upon this undertaking will find it at first an unaccustomed experience—indeed it may be quite an empty one. But it will not be long before his soul begins to be replenished and revitalised and to receive strength, then he begins to know the eternal quiet which rests in God's love; stress and anxiety, hurry and restlessness, noise and clamour are stilled within him, he has become silent before God who is his help. 'My soul is silent before God who is my help'."[1]

This is a revealing passage, and so is the opening outburst in his sermon on the nature of the Church:

"There is one word that, for a Catholic who hears it, kindles every feeling of love and blessedness, that stirs to the depths in him every religious perception from horror and fear of judgement to the sweet sense of God's presence, but which quite certainly awakens in him the affection which the child feels for its mother, gratitude, reverence and devoted love, feelings which possess a man when he sees again, after many years, the home of his childhood. And it is a word that has for Protestants the ring of something endlessly banal . . . alas for us if this word, the word 'Church', does not very soon become vital again and a matter of deep concern in our lives. Yes, 'Church' is the word whose sense we have forgotten and whose splendour and greatness we shall consider a little today."[2]

[1] Sermon on Psalm 42: 1, which Luther has translated in words that may be rendered 'My soul is silent before God, who is my help', preached July 15th 1928.
[2] Sermon, May 23rd 1928.

In these vigorous sermons, themes which will become familiar are already beginning to appear. There is the insistence on man's utter dependence upon God's grace, there is the reminder that the Christian must not forsake the world—"If you want to find God, be faithful to the world." There is the concern for the Christian's relationship with his fellow man, "this enigmatic, impenetrable 'thou', it is God's call, it is God Himself who meets us".[1] There is the victory of Christ crucified, when Bonhoeffer speaks of the battle "in which God seems to be defeated, on Good Friday, and in which he is victorious through his defeat, on Easter Day";[2] and already in these sermons a word is beginning to appear, often with a particular significance which needs to be understood, the word "religion". Bonhoeffer dramatises his meaning himself with characteristic vividness:

"Religion is the most ambitious and the most subtle of all men's efforts to escape from the fear and restlessness of their own hearts and to reach out to eternity. The eternally mysterious and disturbing is sought and found and brought into a permanent relationship, a secret converse with the soul, until the soul herself gains access to the eternal. Here human spirituality, born of restlessness, achieves its finest flower, here if anywhere must the way to the eternal be found, here, where man abandons himself to eternity, here surely he must have discovered and earned his way to the eternal. Out of darkness and fear, out of all that is enigmatic, the transitory and temporal, man has found the way to light, to joy, to the eternal. Mankind could point with pride to this fine flower of the human spirit—if it were not for one thing: namely that God is God and that grace is grace. At this point begins the destruction of our illusions and of our cultural enthusiasm, the great destruction which God himself effects, and which the ancient myth of the tower of Babel typifies. 'And if by grace, then is it no more of works; otherwise grace is no more grace.' Our way to the eternal is interrupted and we are plunged back into the depths from which we came, with our philosophy and art, our morality and religion. For another way now opens, the way of God to man, the way of revelation and grace, the way of Christ, the way of justification by faith alone. 'My ways are not your ways,' that is the answer now. It is not we who go to God, but God who comes to us. It is not religion that sets us right with God, for God alone can do this; it is his action on which we must depend."[3]

[1] Sermon, April 15th 1928.
[2] Sermon, April 8th 1928.
[3] Sermon preached on Romans: 6, March 11th 1928.

Here it is, an impassioned exposition of Karl Barth's understanding of the term. Barth had dragooned the word into intensive service and set it as a sign above everything in religious practice which could conceivably be understood as an abandonment of faith and a recourse to the arch-enemy "works", but the pejorative use of the word was by no means new with him. Ever since Luther had written, "Religion also is one element of our fleshliness," it had tended to be suspect to continental Protestantism. For Bonhoeffer himself the entirely negative meaning of the word was all the more readily accepted since his own most powerful temptation was a religious one. For him the battle against "religion", understood in this particular way, represented the battle against his own besetting sin, the sin of self-righteousness. Thus the idea of the tension between religion and Christianity begins to arise:

"The Christian religion as a religion is not of God. It is on the contrary another example of a mortal road to God like the Buddhist or any other, although of course different in form. Christ is not the bringer of a new religion, but the bringer of God, therefore as an impossible road from man to God the Christian religion stands with other religions; the Christian can do himself no good with his Christianity, for it remains human, all too human, but he lives by the grace of God, which comes to man, and comes to every man, who opens his heart to it and learns to understand it in the Cross of Christ; so the gift of Christ is not the Christian religion, but the mercy and love of God which culminate in the cross."[1]

We have now arrived at the three lectures given in the Christmas holidays and particularly intended for the boys in the sixth form of the German school, for whom Bonhoeffer felt an especial concern. The first of these is a vivid essay on the life of the Old Testament prophets, which reveals in the intensity of its subjective force, the intuitive understanding which was already dawning in Bonhoeffer of the particularly painful nature of the prophetic gift. It was a pain which would become an integral part of his own experience in the years that lay ahead. The two lectures which followed it, though not so well suited to the modest intellectual equipment of his audience, are of considerable retrospective interest because of the amount that they reveal of the thoughts and attitudes of the young man who wrote them. The material used is ill-digested and inexpertly handled. Profound insights flash out from among an interesting mêlée of serious con-

[1] Unpublished lecture—Jesus Christ and the nature of Christianity.

siderations imperfectly understood and superficial ethical conventions not yet discarded. So, at the end of a facile justification of nationalist aggression, a single sentence leaps out to command our attention: "Love your neighbour more than your own timid conscience." Other powerful phrases stand out from the general background: "The man who gives up his freedom, gives up his Christianity" . . . "In ethical decision, we are led into the deepest loneliness" . . . "That we have not the task of choosing between good and evil, but between one evil and another." On the hard subject of moral decision, we find a first definition of his concept of the essence of the Christian existentalist situation, which is already becoming a part of the fabric of his life: "Sparks do not fly in a vacuum, but when hard stones strike upon one another; thus the Holy Ghost does not spark in ideas and principles, but in the needful decision of the moment." Finally there is an expression of what for Bonhoeffer already represented the Christian root of all ethical convictions: "The effect of all the ethical teaching of Jesus is to say: You stand before the face of God, God's mercy rules over you, but you stand with others in the world and have to act and be effective, so remember in all action that you act under the eyes of God, who has his will, which he desires should be done. What this will is, the occasion will tell you; it is only necessary to understand that one's own will must always be abandoned to the divine will, that one's own will must be given up, if the divine will is to be manifested."[1] The insistent motive of man's total dependence upon God's grace runs powerfully through these lectures as it does through the sermons, and we are left with the expectation that to learn to live more and more fully in this total dependence will be the task of Dietrich Bonhoeffer's life. Thus we already find in the papers remaining from this period in Barcelona many of the ideas and insights which were to be defined and developed more fully as his experience grew. At the same time it is possible to detect indications of two aspects of Bonhoeffer's intellectual condition whose significance becomes more clearly evident as his development continues.

The first is the fact that his exceptional capacity to enter and understand human situations was not accompanied by an equal ability to enter imaginatively into the life of nature. The vast and challenging realities of the universe, the fascinating complexities of the world of plants and animals, the solid yet changing structure of the landscape, these had not the power to speak to him in depth, they had not the

[1] Lecture: "Basic Problems of a Christian Ethic."

74

power to wound and constrain, distress and delight him as could the inexhaustible spectacle of human life.

The small indications which begin to suggest this are negative, like the condition itself. It was a Bonhoeffer with his sensitivity anaesthetised and his awareness concentrated on one aspect only of the scene before him, who could enjoy the drama of bull-fights. To the surprise and horror of his twin sister, he could describe them enthusiastically in his letters home. The surging emotion of the crowd, the splendour of the spectacle, the courage and skill of the matador evoked a ready response from him. The sight of the horses, often ripped to pieces by the bull, of the bull himself, tortured to death with sophisticated barbarity, left him not quite, but very nearly, unmoved.

A clue to the character of this indifference is perhaps provided by a passage in his farewell sermon to the congregation at Barcelona:

"Man knows that a flaw runs through the world, a flaw that becomes visible in mankind and that disappears where man is not, in nature. Man wanders through God's world as a stranger, nay more as one cast out and fallen away, he sees paradise lying before his eyes and himself driven out."[1]

It is hard to imagine Bonhoeffer making such a purblind comment upon the human scene. His sense of alienation from nature can hardly arise from the palpably erroneous supposition that nature is perfect whereas man is not, but rather from a failure to understand man and nature as involved in the same catastrophe, the whole creation groaning and travailing *together*, together waiting for redemption. The most elementary biologist, the most simple-minded naturalist cannot possibly be unaware that what we see around us is no nearer to being paradise than what we see within us. No one can perceive the splendour and significance of creation who cannot suffer its grief. But for Bonhoeffer at this time nature represented no more than a decorative backdrop to his thoughts, which were about quite other matters.

The child who had felt no interest in the pigeons, snakes and lizards of "the boys' room", the student who had not cared to hear about the discoveries of science, was growing up now into the young man who could cheerfully follow Luther in a virtual abandonment of the spectacle of creation, in order to fix his gaze on the redemption of man. A theology in which God's authority could become, in John Todd's phrase, "that which can practically obliterate all created reality", seemed to him at that time to present no constricting limitations. If he did begin to sense

[1] Sermon on Phil. 4: 7, undated.

75

any limitation, it was perhaps in the conventional Lutheran understanding of prayer. For he was already feeling constrained by a powerful inward pressure to explore the vast territory of the spirit, of which so large an area had been wiped off the map of Protestant theology. Without any guidance, or any knowledge of the long history of Christian prayer, Bonhoeffer was already beginning to feel his way forward towards that interior world where meditation of many kinds may lead on into that deep expectant silence in which the spirit becomes alert to hear God's voice. This, the second aspect of Bonhoeffer's condition at that time, was clearly related to a strong desire which now began forming in his mind. Finding little in the traditions of his Church to help him in his search, he now turned his thoughts to India. Soon after his arrival in Barcelona his remarkable grandmother had written: "In your place I should really try, when the opportunity offers, to see the complementary world of the East. I am thinking of India, Buddha and his world."[1]

For the next five years the dream of India lay just below the level of his conscious thought. From time to time it would break surface, and he would begin preliminary investigations regarding a journey to the East. Of India as a geographical entity he had a curiously ill-defined notion, one which was perhaps related to his unrealistic picture of nature as a whole; but of India as representing all that he had not, he now began to build up a strong symbolic representation, and within this picture were entwined some of those deep religious insights which insisted upon expression, and for which he found little response in his own world. In 1932, in Berlin, with only a few more months to run before Hitler's rise to power, he described for the students of the Technical High School this India of his imagination:

"This world, in which the hand of man's work has only to be opened in order to receive the earth's fruits bountifully, creates in its inhabitants a deep quiet of heart; and the soul breathes in that life which surrounds it with plenty, it penetrates into this full and bountiful process of life, unites with it, searches out and broods upon its rhythms and its depths, which are ultimately the depths of the soul itself, and the wide reaches of the Indian soul are the wide reaches of all that lives. So the contemplative soul finds its own image again in all that lives, as in a thousand mirrors, from every natural form it receives the silent answer—*tat tuam asi*—that art thou, thou myself. And then comes over it the eternal awe at the holiness of all life. It is wounded, when nature

[1] E.B., *D.B.*, p. 138.

suffers violence, it is torn when a living thing is wounded . . . Learn to suffer, learn to pass away, learn to die, all this is better than to assert oneself, to do violence and live. Only so will your soul, which is the soul of the All, remain immaculate and holy. Through love and suffering we find our way to the All and overcome it."[1]

That was a last cry of longing, for Bonhoeffer was never to see India, but the rich interior world which he once hoped to discover there he would to a great extent discover in his own solitude, by wholly other means.

When this curious meditation was written, and delivered to what must, one feels, have been a fairly mystified audience, India was already moving out of reach. In only a few months then, the National Socialists were to spring the trap. But when Dietrich left Barcelona, that still lay hidden in the future, and now, happy and free and innocent of any foreboding, he set his course for home.

[1] *G.S.* III, pp. 261–2.

CHAPTER VII

BUT when Bonhoeffer went back to Berlin in February 1929 the power of the Weimar Republic to survive was plainly declining. It was beginning to fall a victim to its own inherent weaknesses as well as to a widespread distaste for democracy which the circumstances of its establishment had increased, together with the peculiarity irrational nature of the Conservative opposition. The Conservative party in Germany had been, ever since the end of the 1914–18 war, less a political party than the expression of a national neurosis. The self-pity, resentment and despair felt by many Germans after the Treaty of Versailles combined with the confused recollections of grandeur of many among the older generation to draw together an element among the nation who were ready to use violence and demagogic agitation with a view to discrediting the whole idea of German democracy, and to reinstating the monarchy and an authoritarian regime. It is not altogether surprising that the German Conservatives were not by any means proof against the tireless intrigues of the National Socialists, and it is characteristic of the two parties that the political pact which gave Hitler the support of the Conservatives in 1929 was occasioned by the Conservatives' desire to raise a popular petition for a bill to be brought before the Reichstag "Against the Enslavement of the German People" which the luckless Republic were said to be implementing by the acceptance of the Young Plan, an agreement which had been negotiated for the express purpose of relieving the country of the economic load of the postwar reparations, and of giving her again a more effective place among the nations of Europe. But the irrational nature of the rebels' case might still have destroyed their chances of success if it had not been for the second factor in the situation, the collapse of the postwar period of prosperity and the beginning of the economic depression which, by 1929, was settling down like a dead weight upon the whole western world, and which brought in Germany as elsewhere a wave of unemployment that the nation did not hesitate to lay at the door of the Weimar government.

Against the depression the government took the classic and classically unpopular step of recession; in the international field they continued their policy of steady co-operation. It was the road of Liberal common sense, and the Liberals blindly pinned their faith to it. It is an illustration of the unfounded optimism of the doomed republic that even a year later, when matters had already gone from bad to very much worse, a man as well-informed as Karl Bonhoeffer could still write to Dietrich, by this time in New York: "You write that the news from Germany sounds disturbing over there. It is certainly not pleasant, and the endless brawls between the Nazis and the Communists are a sign of the tension which exists. But at present the rumours of a putsch do not look like being substantiated. I think the Reichswehr is standing firm under Gröner, so that no party is likely to be able to bring off a successful putsch . . . from what you write about New York, economic and social conditions do not sound much better there. Anyway I do not think that we need fear any disturbances here before you return."[1]

At the beginning of the summer term, Bonhoeffer settled back again into his life at the university. Seeberg having retired, his ex-student now became "voluntary assistant" to his successor Lütgert, a post which gave him a status at the university, as well as some research and routine work to do. In hours of leisure he now set to work on the thesis for his "Habilitation". He worked with his usual speed and concentration, and in February 1930 the paper was handed in.

In this thesis, to which he gave the title *Act and Being*, he is concerned to do several things. First, he demolishes the attempt often made in German academic religion to press philosophy into the service of theology and to treat them as complementary disciplines. Bonhoeffer held to the Barthian view that philosophy, of whatever colour, is man's attempt to arrive at truth through his own thought, and that therefore it remains irredeemably self-centred. Theology is different in kind from philosophy because, as he later expressed it, "the christian theologian must know the proper and stable premise of his whole thinking which the philosopher does not recognise: the premise of the revelation of God in Christ, or, on the subjective side, the faith in this revelation."[2] Theology is rooted and grounded in this central fact of Christian faith: that it is not I that can go to God, but God who in mercy and in his own complete freedom, comes to me. So my knowledge of him can never be the fruit of my own reflection; it is always and at every stage the sole gift of God, and when God in his mercy wills to reveal himself to me I become a new man, born again through his grace. Thus far Bonhoeffer

[1] E.B., *D.B.*, p. 185.
[2] *G.S.* III, p. 111.

79

follows Karl Barth, but then he goes on to ask Barth himself some searching questions. If man's being in truth depends entirely on God's act of self-revelation, how is continuity in truth provided for? And, in his effort to ensure that God is never degraded to become an object of man's search, is Barth in danger of lifting him into regions which become too theoretical and remote?

"It is a fateful error on Barth's part to replace the Lord and Creator with the concept of the subject. In the first place it means that I have God always at my back, with the result that I must be content with dialectical theology's permanent reflection on its own faith instead of having direct recourse to Christ . . . But the ultimate reason for the inadequacy of Barth's explanation is the fact that it fails to understand God as Person. From this failure arises a defective definition of the Being of revelation, whence a defective concept of knowledge. When we come to ask what truth remains in the interpretation of the act which underlies the non-objective concept of knowledge, we must extract our answer from defining the being of revelation as personal, accepting whatever consequences may follow for the concept of knowledge itself."[1]

For Bonhoeffer, the experience of revelation as personal, the "direct recourse to Christ" must be through the Church, which is "Christ existing as community". Through the Church the word of revelation is mediated to me in the Sacrament, in preaching and the Scriptures, and I encounter Christ in the other person, while it is my privilege and duty to "become a Christ" to him. Only through the Church is the revealed truth to be found, concrete and living. In this second thesis, Bonhoeffer carries forward his concept of the Church from the place where he left it in *Sanctorum Communio*.

This second work shows more economy and discipline of thought than the first. It begins slowly, employing the highly technical philosophical language which its author had learnt from Seeberg. But as he proceeds, Bonhoeffer warms to his subject, and his passion drives him forward with a gathering impetus, till gradually we are drawn with him into his own intense search, his search for the concrete reality of the life in Christ. For this is it, this is revelation, this is truth itself.

"Where the 'I' has truly come to the end, truly reaches out of itself, where its grasp is more than a final 'seeking of the self in the self', there Christ is at work. However, certainty about this is never to be won by reflection on the act . . . but only in the direct contemplation of Christ

[1] *Act and Being*, pp. 136–7.

80

and His activity upon me, within me . . . It is all-important to know that self-understanding is possible only when and where the living Christ approaches us, only in his contemplation."[1]

On July 8th Bonhoeffer passed his second theological examination before the Church Board, which opened the way to his ordination, and on July 18th his thesis *Act and Being* was formally accepted for his habilitation at the university, which marked the completion of his formal studies. On July 31st he delivered his inaugural lecture in the great hall of the University of Berlin, "The Enquiry into Man in Contemporary Philosophy and Theology"; it was well received, and now Bonhoeffer was launched on what might have been a distinguished but uneventful academic career. During this year the main personal event for Bonhoeffer was to be provided by the ripening of a friendship which was to mean much to him, and the warmth of which was to lend a note of particular intensity to his struggle on behalf of the Jews and of Christian "non-Aryans" in the years to come.

The theological student Franz Hildebrandt was the son of Hildebrandt the art historian, and of a Christian-Jewish mother. They had met first on December 16th 1927, the day before Dietrich was to defend his first thesis *Sanctorum Communio* in public debate. "On that Friday night," writes Hildebrandt, "we found ourselves arguing, and continued arguing ever since through twelve years of unbroken friendship, till the outbreak of the war made contact between England and Germany impossible. But having talked theology with him (and indeed, not only theology) meant that one could never talk like that to anyone else again since he is gone. He was my senior in age and training by exactly three years; I did not know then how many years, how many dimensions, he was ahead of our whole generation."[2]

The stimulus of this friendship lent spice to what might otherwise have been almost a humdrum year. Bonhoeffer, burning with a theological zeal for the most part unshared by others, observed the Church which he proposed to serve with a somewhat depressed and critical eye. The parish church at Berlin-Grunewald was not often honoured with his presence; if he did attend a service it was generally at the church of Berlin-Moabit, of which Günther Dehn the Christian Socialist, was pastor. But he did not join the religious movement of the Christian Socialists, or any other of the active groups who were concerned to

---

[1] *Act and Being*, pp. 160-1.
[2] From a paper on Dietrich Bonhoeffer broadcast by Franz Hildebrandt, March 13th 1960.

explore the practical realities of the Christian life. He still saw theology as the most vital foundation of the faith.

"From the standpoint of [theology] everything must be judged, grasped and if possible altered. Authority depended—so he certainly believed—upon the thoroughness and piercing accuracy of theological formulations. With this was associated a certain contempt for the official Synodical or Presbyterial daily business of the Church which was native to Germany. Even in this field he hoped to gain most through theology."[1]

It was in the second half of this year that the idea of a visit to America began to arise. Bonhoeffer, anxious to spend some time in the New World, hesitated in the fear that he might find himself marooned at some remote State University. But when he was presented with the opportunity to spend a year at the Union Theological Seminary in New York, he grasped it without hesitation. A year's sabbatical leave from Berlin was granted, and he left Germany in September 1930 armed with the Sloane Fellowship and a curious little notebook filled with English idioms and arguments against Germany's war guilt. It was to be the only lengthy excursion he ever made into an entirely non-German world.

Three days after Bonhoeffer's arrival in New York, a general election in Germany produced a surprising result: the number of National Socialist representatives in the Reichstag leapt from twelve to a hundred and seven. But Bonhoeffer was too much involved in his discovery of the New World to perceive the horrifying significance of these unexpected figures. The extreme contrast presented by the Union Theological Seminary to almost every aspect of the University of Berlin engaged his full and fascinated attention. Bonhoeffer was astonished by the American students' ability to live cheerfully in a crowd day and night, by what he called their "social courage" referring in particular to the ease with which any student could approach any professor or lecturer, uttering what the young German observer described as "the thousandfold hello" and treating the august personage as an equal, and finally by the way in which individual mental effort could at any moment fall a victim to general conversation. This way of living led to a friendly openness which made a strong appeal to him, but he commented solemnly that in his opinion, as a result: "In a conflict between the will to speak the truth with all its consequences, and the community spirit the latter would win the day."[2] He himself entered

[1] E.B., *D.B.*, p. 162.
[2] G.S. I, p. 85.

into this wholly novel community spirit with a ready grace. The beautiful formal manners which were current coin at the University of Berlin were temporarily laid aside and Bonhoeffer made himself master of a polite bonhomie which must have been entirely captivating.

Meanwhile, of the study of theology, as he had learnt to know it in Berlin, he found virtually no trace in New York. To Superintendent Diestel, Dean of the district of Lichtenfelde, he wrote: "A theology is not to be found here. I attend what are theoretically lectures and seminars on dogmatics and religious philosophy, but the impression remains annihilating. They chatter till all is blue without any factual foundation or any criteria of thought becoming visible. The students, who are mostly twenty-five to thirty years old, have not the faintest notion what dogmatic theology is about. They do not know how to ask themselves the simplest questions. They intoxicate themselves with liberal and humanistic expressions, laugh at the fundamentalists, and basically they are not even a match for them. They are interested in Barth, and make now and then a small excursion into "pessimism". That is worse than ever. In contrast to our own liberalism, which was undoubtedly in its best representatives a powerful phenomenon, over here it has all been fearfully sentimentalised, and this with a truly naïve dogmatism. Often it goes through and through me when here in a lecture they dismiss Christ, and laugh outright when a word of Luther's is quoted on the forgiveness of sins."[1]

But in spite of the absence of theological substance, Union Theological Seminary owned one virtue which was not conspicuous among the learned members of the theological faculty at Berlin—a burning concern to bring what they knew of Christianity into contact with daily life at every point. For more than fifteen years the need for Christians to learn a practical concern for the community had been preached by the exponents of the "Social Gospel", and this was still the formative influence upon Union in the 1930s.

As long before as 1917, Walter Rauschenbusch had written: "The new thing in the Social Gospel is the clearness and insistence with which it sets forth the necessity and possibility of redeeming the historical life of humanity from the social wrongs which now pervade it and which act as temptations and incitements to evil and as forces of resistance to the powers of redemption."[2] With this in mind the course of studies had been designed to open students' eyes to the social and political

[1] *G.S.* I, pp. 76–7.
[2] Walter Rauschenbusch, *A Theology for the Social Gospel*, p. 95.

problems of the day, to train them to look with a Christian and critical eye at contemporary literature and to give them some opportunity to begin to use their energies in the service of the community. Dietrich's course of study during his year in America fell under the following heads: "Religion and Ethics—Religious Aspects of Contemporary Philosophy—Church and Community; the co-operation of the Church with Social and Character-building Agencies—Ethical Interpretations —Ethical Viewpoints in Modern Literature—Ethical Issues in the Social Order—Theology I, the idea of God in His Relations to the World and Man—Seminar in Philosophical Theology—Brief Sermons —The Minister's Work with Individuals."[1] These subjects were handled by many distinguished lecturers, among them Reinhold Niebuhr, John Bailie, James Moffatt and Henry Emerson Fosdick.

Having abandoned the expectation of learning anything valuable in the field of theology, Bonhoeffer threw himself into this unexpected form of religious education with zest. The subject was Life, so Life it should be, and Dietrich began both to live and observe the life of Christian America with all his native intensity. First came the investigation of Social Problems, to which the effects of the economic depression were beginning to lend an immediate urgency. Upon this subject, Bonhoeffer has left an appreciative note:

"In connection with a course of Mr. Webber's (Church and Community) who is the one-time minister of the Church of All Nations, and by this means has become familiar with almost all the social institutions in New York, I paid a visit almost every week to one of these character-building agencies: settlements, Y.M.C.A., home missions, co-operative houses, playgrounds, children's courts, night schools, socialist schools, asyls [sic], youth organisations, Association for advance of coloured people. Here I got some insight into the attempts at voluntary social work. . . . It is immensely impressive to see how much personal self-sacrifice is achieved, with how much devotion, energy and sense of responsibility the work is done."[2]

Guided by his own anxiety and concern for the life of the Church, Bonhoeffer explored the activities of the churches in New York and came to a disappointing conclusion:

"One may hear sermons in New York upon almost any subject; one only is never handled, or at any rate so rarely that I never succeeded in hearing it presented: namely, the gospel of Jesus Christ,

[1] E.B., *D.B.*, p. 197.
[2] *G.S.* I, p. 101.

84

of the cross, of sin and forgiveness, of death and life. . . . But what do we find in the place of the Christian message? An ethical and social idealism which pins its faith to progress, and which for some not quite evident reason assumes the right to call itself Christian. And in the place of the Church as a community of believing Christians stands the Church as a social institution. Anyone who has seen the weekly programme of one of the large New York churches, with its daily, almost hourly events, tea parties, lectures, concerts, charitable events, sports, games, bowling, dancing for people of all ages, anyone who has heard the efforts to persuade a new arrival to join the Church on the grounds that it will give him a special kind of entry into society, anyone who has observed the painful anxiety, with which the pastor advertises and presses for membership, is able to make some estimate of the character of such a Church. . ."[1]

Always on the lookout for the reasons for theological convictions on the one hand, and for their effects on the other, Bonhoeffer made, under the guidance of Professor Lyman, a careful study of the pragmatic philosophy which seemed to be generally accepted in America, and of which William James and James Dewey had been the most distinguished exponents. On this subject he observed:

"In them [i.e. the pragmatic philosophers], and especially in James, I found the key to understanding the modern theological language and thought forms of the liberal and enlightened American. The destruction of philosophy as an enquiry into the truth, in favour of a positive empiricism with practical objectives—which is pursued in its most radical form by Dewey—fundamentally alters the concept of knowledge; and truth, as the absolute form of all thought, is reduced to the proportions of that which shall establish itself as 'in the long run useful'. . . It is not truth that counts, but works, and this is the criterion. Manifestly here, thought and life accomplish their tasks in close proximity to one another. For theology this has various consequences. It is no longer in danger of talking about God in a way unrelated to life. Even God is not actual but 'working' truth, that is to say, he is active in the process of human life or he 'is' not at all . . . James' theory of 'the growing God' was greeted with amazing enthusiasm and is constantly repeated at the Union Theological Seminary and throughout the whole of enlightened America. It combines in a masterly manner religion and the belief in progress, so that one receives from the other support and justification . . . Pragmatism and Instrumentalism as a philosophy of

[1] G.S. I, p. 95.

life has undoubtedly released forces which could be used for a recasting of the established order in education, politics and social work in the spirit of the great idea of social progress, and it has fallen on fruitful soil."[1]

Here the note ends, and the inexorable "But" remains for once unspoken.

With the same objective desire to understand the mechanics of American life and thought, and stimulated by his literary seminars, Bonhoeffer dived energetically into American literature. He discovered in American novelists as a whole a further illustration of the superficial attitude which he found disturbing in all departments of American life, and which seemed among the current writers to lead to cynicism on the one hand and an easy sentimentality on the other. But there was one notable exception. In the novels of young negroes he found repeatedly the deep-rooting intuitive insights, what he described as the "very productive power and warmth," which other American writing seemed to lack. He wrote to his grandmother that this "always awakens in one the wish to get to know the man himself."[2]

There is no record of his ever having met one of these American negro novelists, but a strong desire of Bonhoeffer's to gain some real knowledge of American negro life was fulfilled through his friendship with a remarkable man. Frank Fisher, one of the very few negro students at Union Theological Seminary, was a Christian of outstanding calibre. The single-hearted passion for their Christian faith drew the two young men together. Frank Fisher recognised in Dietrich Bonhoeffer a man who could be trusted with the secrets of his people's suffering. He took his new friend to his home in Harlem and introduced him to negro family life, a privilege which he would have ventured to accord only to very few. But his friend was equal to the occasion. The delicacy of the true aristocrat and the observant "consideration" which had been insistently taught him at home since his earliest childhood, stood Bonhoeffer in good stead now. He knew how to value and guard the sensitive pride which would have erected a barrier against a less responsive visitor. And his natural warmth and exceptional insight into the human condition wherever he had an opportunity to enter it made him deeply aware of the true qualities of this oppressed world within a world. His negro friends found that they could honour him with the truth, and they took him to their hearts without reserve. Bonhoeffer for his part entered into the life of these outcasts of society with a remarkable intensity and depth, until he learnt to observe the pheno-

[1] *G.S.* I, pp. 91–3.
[2] *G.S.* I, p. 80.

menon of white America from the black American point of view. Meanwhile he took an active part in the Christian life of the Harlem community.

"For more than six months," he writes, "I went almost every Sunday at 2.30 to one of the large negro Baptist churches in Harlem, and together with my friend, or sometimes in his absence, I led a group of young negroes in Sunday School; I also led the negro women in Bible classes, and at one time helped weekly in a weekday Sunday School. Thus I not only came to know a number of young negroes very well, but also had an opportunity to visit them in their homes. This personal contact with the negroes was for me one of the most pleasing and significant events of my American visit."[1]

A remarkable feature of Bonhoeffer's life at every stage was the amount that he contrived to pack into his days. He lived not only in depth but in an astonishing breadth, and it was a conspicuous aspect of his achievement that, while he rejected the humanist ideal as a philosophical basis for religion, he contrived to live the broad and rich life which humanists admire with what was little more than the overflow from his deeper spiritual energies. Built upon the foundation of daily prayer and meditation, which he was attempting to practise in the quiet of his own solitude, rose a remarkable superstructure. Bonhoeffer was able to be, at one and the same time, a variety of different people, or rather to be himself in a bewildering number of different aspects. He was the hard-thinking, critically observant European theologian, he was the reader, the writer and the ready speaker at the Union Theological Seminary, he was the easy though selective conversationalist, he was the hail-fellow-well-met among the students and lecturers which every member of Union had to be, he was the devoted student of the negro problem. And, in addition to all this, he found time to enjoy the pleasures of the ordinary disengaged sightseeing visitor to a new country.

In addition to a visit to Philadelphia, where he made the acquaintance of an American branch of the Tafel family, and a visit to Washington with Frank Fisher, he made a Christmas journey to Havannah, where the beloved governess of his childhood, Käthe Horn, was now teaching in a German school. The delights of New York he enjoyed principally in the company of a Swiss friend, Erwin Sutz, a fellow musician and Barthian, and of the young American theologian Paul Lehmann, who has written a vivid recollection of Bonhoeffer as he appeared to intelligent American eyes:

[1] *G.S.* I, pp. 96–7.

"Bonhoeffer was the most un-German of Germans. He was German as regards the furnishings of his mind and spirit. This meant a conspicuously thorough schooling in language and letters, in philosophy and theology, and an uncommon competence at the piano. He was German, too, in the intensity and methodical precision with which he tackled every fresh problem, whether in the academic world, with which he was familiar, or the new world of the United States, with which he was to become astonishingly familiar in an uncommon minimum of time. He was German in his passion for perfection, whether of manners or performance, or of all that is connoted by the word *Kultur*. Here in short was an aristocracy of the spirit at its best.

"But at the same time Bonhoeffer was the most un-German of Germans. His aristocracy was unmistakable yet not obtrusive, chiefly, I think, owing to his boundless curiosity about every new environment in which he found himself, and his irresistible and unfailing sense of humour . . ."

This reference to Bonhoeffer's humour is to be noted. It is universally remembered by his friends, but it is not often to be discerned in his writing. This must be understood from the fact that he is practically always writing, even in letters, upon serious subjects, and the capacity to treat a grave subject lightly and still say something serious about it seems to be a specifically Anglo-Saxon characteristic. For most Germans, humour belongs strictly in its own department, and the English tend to accuse the Germans of humourlessness, because their learned treatises are not enlivened by wit, whereas Germans suspect the English of levity, precisely because theirs are. Since these seem to be the facts and, in this respect at any rate, Bonhoeffer was characteristically German, readers of his work have to resign themselves to taking his humour to a great extent on trust; that it constituted a vital ingredient of his charm seems to be established. Lehmann's reminiscences continue:

"What the paradox comes to is that he [Bonhoeffer] was unique among his countrymen in achieving what the German spirit at its best seeks but does not in like measure succeed in, namely the capacity to see oneself and the world from a perspective other than one's own. This paradox of birth and nationality in Bonhoeffer has seemed to me increasingly, during the years since, to have made him an exciting and conspicuous example of the triumph over parochialism of every kind."[1]

To this triumph over parochialism, the year in America made a

[1] Paul Lehmann; given on the B.B.C. February 12th and March 18th 1960.

88

very considerable contribution. The de-parochialising influences were numerous, and one of the most powerful was contributed by a young Frenchman, Jean Lassère. Jean Lassère was a pacifist and an intensely concerned participant in the Oecumenical Movement. Bonhoeffer, before meeting him, had been content to repeat the conventional opinion with regard to a Christian's duty in war, and had accepted a view prevalent at the time in Germany, that the Oecumenical Movement was a rootless upstart, with which no serious theologian or loyal patriot should have anything to do. Lassère, shy, undogmatic, but passionately convinced, quietly challenged these opinions, and he was a man who could not be easily dismissed. He was equipped with a sound theological training on the European model, and moreover he had thought deeply and rigorously about his subject. Bonhoeffer found himself unexpectedly outclassed. A man commanded his respect and attention who could say: "Do we believe in the Holy Catholic Church, the Communion of Saints, or do we believe in the eternal mission of France? One can't be a Christian and a nationalist at the same time."

Bonhoeffer was not wholly converted to pacifism, nor persuaded to abandon altogether his critical attitude to the Oecumenical Movement, but his mind had been opened and began to be strongly exercised in two wholly new directions, while his narrow nationalism fell off like an abandoned disguise. With this growing insight into the possible demands of his faith in national and international affairs, he began to consider his own country's problems with more detachment. But he was all the more deeply disturbed by a letter which arrived at the end of February from a friend who was a pastor in a country parish in Brandenburg:

"Because my heart," so the letter ran, "is so passionately concerned with the titanic struggle of national self-assertion and will to the future, which has been so powerfully gaining ground especially in the country . . . I often find myself sorely put to it not to betray the Gospel for the benefit of 'the holy possessions of the Nation', especially as thus the way of the Cross which the Church must tread today . . . can be eased very much through outward success . . . the quiet work of the Stahlhelm, continued through many years, the more recent loud and able agitation of the National Socialists, have had an effect upon the younger population of the countryside which before one would not have believed possible. War of Liberation, renewal of Prussian Nationalism, purity of the race, struggle against the Jews and the Young Plan, death to Marxism, the 'Third Reich' of German freedom and justice

. . . these are the ideas that move the rural population of today, who are in a highly excited condition. And in the midst of all this to preach the Cross! It is indeed . . . hard in such conditions not to betray the *Theologia Crucis*, and to go on valuing the Kingdom of God more highly than our tortured fatherland . . .

"At the moment I see the great tragedy for our Church and Nation in this; that in this powerful popular movement a purified and glowing nationalism is combined with a new heathenism, which is more difficult to expose and condemn than the religion of the Freethinkers, not only because of one's own feelings, but also because it parades in a Christian dress. The basis of their neo-pagan religion is the demonstrable unity of religion and race, specifically of the Aryan [nordic] race . . . Acceptance of the Church depends upon her services to race and national culture . . ."[1]

The letter continued in this vein throughout a total length of some fifteen hundred words. Bonhoeffer translated it and read it aloud to a group of Union students, striving to convey to them some understanding of the situation it depicted. Its dangers for the life of the German Protestant Church were appallingly obvious to this clear-thinking, single-hearted young theologian; how radically it would affect his own life the coming years were to show.

Meanwhile there was to be one more journey before he left the States to return home. With his friend Jean Lassère, he set out in an ancient Oldsmobile, and with many breakdowns and various camping adventures, the pair made their way to the Mexican border. Here the Oldsmobile retired from the fray, and the friends went on into Mexico by train. For a week they explored the mysteries of Mexico's strange intermediate culture, with its Spanish Catholic and native Indian elements so curiously and provocatively combined. They covered fifteen hundred miles of Mexican railway line, giving themselves up whole-heartedly to discomfort and discovery, and crowned their journey with a peace talk to the students of the Victoria Teachers' Training College in Mexico City. After spending a week there and encountering a mild contretemps at the border, they were re-admitted to the States and reunited with the Oldsmobile, in which they returned to New York, sunburnt and dust-encrusted and immeasurably enriched.

So ended a year which had brought to Bonhoeffer much experience and enlargement of outlook, a year on which he would look back with appreciation and gratitude to the end of his life.

[1] *G.S.* I, pp. 56–7.

Part II

ACTION

Daring to do what is right, not what fancy may
                              tell you
valiantly grasping occasions, not cravenly doubting—
freedom comes only through deeds, not through thoughts
                              taking wing.
Faint not nor fear, but go out to the storm and
                              the action,
Trusting in God whose commandment you faithfully
                              follow;
freedom exultant will welcome your spirit with
                              joy.

Dietrich Bonhoeffer.

CHAPTER VIII

"THE Old Testament tells us the strange story of Jacob, who, falling into enmity with his brother, has fled from his home in God's promised land and lived many years in exile. But at last that life can hold him no longer, he is determined to go home to the land of promise, home to his brother. He is on the journey. It is the last night before he is to enter the promised land. Only one small river flows between. When he is about to cross he is prevented; there is one who wrestles with him; he knows not who; it is night. Jacob is not to return to his home; at the entrance to the promised land he is to be overcome, to die. But to Jacob immense powers are given, and he holds his ground against his assailant and gains a hold upon him; he does not let him free until he hears him say: 'Let me go, for the dawn is breaking.' Then Jacob gathers the last of his strength, still he grasps him: 'I will not let thee go except thou bless me.' To him it is as though the end had come. So strong has been the hold of his powerful assailant. But in this moment he receives the blessing, and the stranger is gone. Then the sun rose upon Jacob . . ."[1]

It was with this arresting paraphrase of the story of Jacob at Peniel that Bonhoeffer ended a public lecture given at Potsdam–Herrmannswerder in the year after his return from America, and the story was to appear again many times in notes and sermons during the period which followed. For him this year was to be a period of intense and fruitful activity in a variety of fields, but inwardly it was the time of his first wrestling with the angel. His personal life was crowned with success and crowded with interest and opportunity, but the conflicts and contradictions which surrounded him on every side asked him inexorable questions which must be faced and battled with at the deepest level if his religious calling and with it his very faith itself were not to fall to the ground. For he returned to a country crushed under the economic depression which had hit all Europe and America, where democratic institutions were in an advanced stage of disintegration, and where the final battle between the diseased nationalism and the forces of international Communism was being fought out on a violent and mindless level. Bonhoeffer, returning to his first academic post at Berlin, wrote to his friend Erwin Sutz of the difficulties of the situation, and added:

[1] *G.S.* III, p. 284.

"One is made particularly conscious of these problems by the unprecedented state of our public life in Germany. Matters really look exceedingly serious. There is literally no one in Germany who is able to grasp the situation, even remotely. But one cannot escape the strong impression that we are facing a major turning point in world history. Whether it will lead to Bolshevism or to a general magnanimous understanding, who shall say? Who knows finally what is best? But the coming winter can hardly leave anyone in Germany unaffected. Seven million unemployed, that is to say fifteen or twenty million people hungry, I do not know how Germany or how individuals can survive this. Well-informed people from the world of commerce have told me that to all appearances we are racing towards a situation which no one can foresee or prevent. Can our Church survive a catastrophe? Or will it be all over with us, unless we change fundamentally and at once? Unless we speak quite differently, live quite differently? But how? Next Wednesday there is to be a meeting of all the pastors of Berlin to discuss the problems of the winter; we shall see what they think these problems are! I fear the worst for this meeting. And yet no one knows how to do better. And this, in times like these! What is the use of all our theology?"[1]

Here Bonhoeffer touched what was for him the heart of the matter: the Christian community seemed inert, almost indifferent, and in this situation of unparalleled suffering and need, the Church showed itself unwilling to speak or act with authority. Bonhoeffer poured out his concern in a letter to Helmuth Rössler:

"About one thing I believe we agree: that our Church is today incapable of proclaiming God's commandments in any concrete form. The only question is whether this is connected with her essential character . . . or whether it is a result of degeneracy and loss of substance. Either way one can agree that it is a question of the Church's mandate to teach and to speak with authority. But—is it not a characteristic of the Church's authority (distinguishing it from all other authority) that the Church does not have the authority first and then act upon it, but that she gains it through proclaiming God's commands, and to the extent that they are accepted as being his commands, and that with every word spoken she puts her authority at risk? The authority of the state does not rest in concrete decisions, but the authority of the Church does, entirely. But she must not fail to make decisions through fear of this risk and of possible chaos . . . And this quite apart from the

[1] G.S. I, pp. 23-4.

fact that, in a case where by some catastrophically mistaken decision the Church's authority may really be lost, a quite different authority becomes visible, which is that of God's mercy."[1]

But Bonhoeffer's voice only cried in the wilderness of his own distress, and another letter to Rössler uncovers for a moment his inner turmoil:

"There is one great country that I should like to visit, to see whether it may not be from there that the great solution is to come—India; for otherwise all seems to be over, and the great dying of Christianity to be at hand. Is it possible that our age is past, and the Gospel entrusted to another People, perhaps to be preached with quite other words and deeds? What do you think of the immortality of the Christian faith in the face of the world situation and our own way of living?

"It seems more and more incomprehensible that for the sake of one righteous man 'the city should be spared'. I am now chaplain to the Technical High School, how can one preach such things to these people? Who is there who still believes them? The invisibility kills us. If we cannot find the presence of Christ in our personal lives, then perhaps we may find it in India, but this eternal desperate fact of being thrown back upon the invisible God himself—there is not a person that can stand it any longer."[2]

Bonhoeffer had some cause at this time to feel desperation, for the Church was not only weak and ineffectual, she was also torn by the beginnings of a deep internal division. Working upon confused emotions, National Socialists inside the Protestant denominations were beginning to distort the faith in order to accommodate within its framework the semi-religious mystique of National Socialism. Out of these politically oriented distortions, the so-called "Faith Movement" was beginning to arise, whose members, later to be called the "German Christians", were to play a disruptive part in Church politics after Hitler came to power. The upholders of the Faith Movement declared that every nation should develop its individual form of the Christian Faith, for religion is rooted in the "soil" of the country and the "blood" of its people. The national faith of Germany was strong and heroic, God intended the Germans to unite under a powerful leader, to pour out their energies for the national good, and to keep the "Aryan" race to which they belonged free from any taint of alien blood. Those who were later to become the "German Christians" found a considerable attraction in these doctrines, which accorded so well with

[1] *G.S.* I, p. 63.
[2] *G.S.* I, p. 61.

95

contemporary political emotions. In a sermon preached in Berlin, on May 8th 1932, Bonhoeffer gave a sketch of the particular kind of religious militancy which attracted these people. He chose the text from II Chronicles, "Neither know we what to do, but our eyes are upon thee," and after telling the story of Jehoshaphet, King of Israel, whose speech at a council of war was converted into this prayer, he continued with bitter irony:

"But we are used to something better than this, we know better how one ought to speak on such an occasion. Our plans and programmes do not melt into prayers, instead they go on to become, amid the blaze of enthusiasm, shining standards and banners proclaiming the virtue of our cause. Now determination does not change into despondent humility, but into the irresistible claim to our own power and our own audacity. No, on the contrary, now it is the prayers that turn into programmes, the requests into orders, and finally at the end of the programme, we must append the name of God, so that he too may be pressed into the service of the programme, of the clever plan, of our own determination, and then—well, then the Christian Council of War is ended; this is what we like to hear, and what we have heard, for better or worse, a hundred times."[1]

But bitterly distressed though Bonhoeffer was by conditions in his country and in his Church, he was not one whom anxiety or interior turmoil had any power to paralyse. Since his appointment as lecturer at the University of Berlin and as Chaplain at the Technical High School did not go into effect until October, he had a few months to spare, and he used them to do two things. The first was to visit Karl Barth, who was now at the University of Bonn, and to whom he had received an introduction from Erwin Sutz. A letter written to Sutz at the time gives a vivid picture of an experience which was very nearly a great one:

"You can well imagine, that I have often wished for you here, sometimes especially, in order to have a good laugh occasionally in this circle of dedicated disciplines. I don't quite like to risk it here, or only rather diffidently (that sounds improbable, doesn't it!), but with my bastard theological origin I have not much excuse, as I realise quite clearly. They have a nose for thoroughbreds here. No nigger passes for white, even his fingernails and the soles of his feet are examined. To me hospitality has hitherto been accorded as to an unknown stranger. But of course everything is very, indeed completely

[1] G.S. I, p.134.

different when it is a case of Karl Barth himself. One can breathe again and no longer be afraid of suffocating in the rarefied atmosphere. I don't think I have ever regretted an omission in my theological past so much, as that I failed to come to him sooner. Now I can spend only three weeks here, lectures . . . seminar, society, an Open Evening, and yesterday a few hours, lunching with Barth. Then one really hears and sees something! There is no sense in my describing to you what you have seen much better for yourself. But it is important, and a very pleasant surprise, to find that Barth stands beyond his books. There is with him an openness, a readiness to accept an objection if it is to the point, and with it an intense concentration and urgent striving for the mark, for the sake of which one may speak proudly or modestly, arrogantly or quite tentatively, which is certainly not concerned in the first place to serve his own theology. I am understanding better and better why Barth is so tremendously difficult to follow in his books. More even, than by his books and lectures, I am impressed by his conversation. In it he is entirely present. I have never seen anything like it before, and should not have believed it possible . . . We very soon arrived at the problem of ethics and discussed it a long time. He did not agree with me where I expected it. Barth said that besides the one great light in the darkness there were other lesser lights, what he called 'relative ethical criteria', whose sense and right to exist he could however not make clear to me; we got no further than his resort to the Bible. Finally he suggested that I was making grace into a principal, and killing off everything else with that. I of course disputed his first proposition, but still I should like to know why everything else may *not* be killed off . . . but I was glad to hear Barth's position clearly expressed . . . Here is indeed a man, from whom one might learn something . . ."[1]

Bonhoeffer found it hard to tear himself away to go back to Berlin. It was the beginning of a fitful association which was never quite to ripen into a friendship. Their minds never completely met, but passed by one another repeatedly, a hair's breadth apart. The two minds, powerful, single, intense, recognised one another over the heads of the theological academics, they felt a mutual regard, but it was never to warm into complete confidence. Perhaps Bonhoeffer was too ready to believe that he was Barth's equal; perhaps Barth was too ready to believe that he was not.

The second event of these leisured months was to affect the course of

[1] *G.S.* I, pp. 19 and 20.

97

Bonhoeffer's life more profoundly than the meeting with Barth. Since the meeting with Jean Lassère in New York, his somewhat conventional patriotic sentiments had given place to the conviction that a Christian had the duty to promote peace and international friendship, and that this meant, at the very least, co-operation between the divided Churches. In October he wrote to Helmuth Rössler:

"My sojourn in America and since then in England has made one thing clear to me: the absolute necessity of co-operation, and at the same time the inexplicable division, which seems to make such a joining together simply impossible."[1]

It was thus with a sense of urgency tempered by scepticism that Bonhoeffer decided to take another look at the Oecumenical Movement, which till now he had been ready to dismiss as theologically unjustified and politically unsound. As soon as his interest became apparent, he was seized upon by the minority in the Berlin Faculty who were concerned with the movement, and Superintendent Diestel appointed him a member of the Youth Delegation to the World Alliance for Promoting International Friendship through the Churches, which was meeting in Cambridge from September 1st to 5th. The mandate of the World Alliance had been expressed in a statement of policy adopted at the Conference of Prague in 1928:

"The work of the World Alliance for International Friendship through the Churches rests upon the readiness of its National Councils and of the Churches working together in them to use their influence with the peoples, parliaments and governments of their own countries to bring about good and friendly relations between the nations . . .

"Among the international questions which affect moral-religious or Church interests, the following are the most important:

(a) The securing of religious freedom and of the rights of Churches, groups or sections of people in any country.
(b) The prevention of every oppression, injury or obstruction of any Churches, congregations, schools, institutes and other works in any sphere of religious activity.
(c) The elucidation of other political or church events which are calculated to endanger good relations between the Churches.
(d) The promotion of positive relations between Christians, congregations and Churches of the different lands.
(e) Endeavours towards the conciliation of class and race antagonisms which become of international importance.

[1] *G.S.* I, pp. 60-1.

(f) Support of proposals and measures calculated to promote justice in the relations between the peoples."

A general statement of good intentions such as this was not likely to commend itself to so rigorous a theologian as Dietrich Bonhoeffer, but the central aim of the Alliance was to promote peace on a Christian basis, and by reason of its broadly-based constitution, it was, of the three main oecumenical groupings, the one least dependent upon purely ecclesiastical elements, and best able to secure the interest and support not only of priests and theologians, but also of Christian laymen. These characteristics seemed to Bonhoeffer to give it the best chance of being effective. So, with a mind fairly equally divided between hope and critical uncertainty, the newcomer to the movement set out for Cambridge.

From the point of view of Bonhoeffer's gaining quickly effective personal influence, no better conference could have been chosen. Bishop Ammundsen, the President, expressed his opinion that the World Council was beginning to be overweighted with middle-aged distinction, and proposed that the youth delegates should be accorded full membership of the Conference. This, after a certain amount of discussion, they received. The youth delegates thereupon asked to be given more opportunity for effective participation, and made three concrete proposals:

1. That the Youth Commission be enlarged.
2. That a permanent secretary for the Youth Commission be established in Geneva in the person of H. L. Henriod.
3. That the honorary youth secretaries be appointed as co-ordinators for the work of the youth commission; and these were to be: F. W. Tom Craske for the British Empire, U.S.A. and the Far East, P. C. Toureille for France, Southern Europe, Poland, the Balkan countries and Czechoslavakia, and Dietrich Bonhoeffer for Germany and Northern and Central Europe.

The proposals were accepted by the World Council and ratified by its Management Committee, and at the same time the three youth secretaries were co-opted as members of the Management Committee.

Bonhoeffer did not speak publicly at this first conference, but he must have been active behind the scenes. On the international stage, Germany's friendship with England and America was already far advanced, while with France it still hung fire; but after his experience with Jean Lassère, Bonhoeffer was not surprised to find that in his attitude to oecumenical work he was theologically much more in

99

sympathy with the French than with those whom he was disposed to dismiss as "the Anglo-Saxons". One of the French delegates wrote at the time for a French periodical:

"There was . . . another German, a young don. After ten minutes' conversation we discovered that our theological position was the same. Suddenly the certainty arose in us that the secret of our approach to one another was to be found here, in the religious necessities. Security? Revision of Treaties? Pacifist propaganda? Perhaps . . . but in fact we are being constrained to show forth the truth of Christianity and to make the Church visible."[1]

The young don was Dietrich Bonhoeffer, and no doubt his friendship with the French was cemented by a common distaste for the attitude of the "Anglo-Saxons" who saw it as their task to address themselves to the immediate problem of furthering peace, without waiting to underpin their work with a solid theological foundation. In Bonhoeffer's view this was to build the house on sand.

The Oecumenical Movement meant for Bonhoeffer the Church in the international field. It was vital, in his view, that here as elsewhere the Church should speak with authority, not making mild proposals, but daring to command. Plainly the Church could only do this if the theological foundation of her work for peace was clearly understood and expressed. Bonhoeffer's views emerge clearly in an article written for the German periodical *Theologische Blätter*:

"We shall not escape the comment from various directions that on the one hand too much and on the other too little has been said . . . We will not evade this criticism . . . the 'too much' is to be found particularly in the theological formulations, which are effectively controlled by Anglo-Saxon theology, which sees the problem of war, for instance, only as that of how to realise an ideal which is already established, that is to say as a practical problem and not as the problem of discovering essential truth. This is what so often gives international ecclesiastical resolutions a grandiloquent sound which to our ears tends to ring hollow. The 'too little' lies undoubtedly in what has *actually* been said. When at the end of the main session an Indian called upon the assembly with powerful words to say something more that was definitive, to say in fact what would be the attitude of the Church if the point of catastrophe was reached, this was surely the expression of the hope, justified but again disappointed, that at last, at last, the Churches would speak out definitely . . . It is worth noting that the

[1] Quoted E.B., *D.B.*, p. 244.

Youth Conference which was attached to the World Alliance could not feel justified in publicising a resolution . . . Criticism of the whole undertaking from the most varied standpoints has nowhere been louder than in the circles of the Youth Conference. Here too the intellectual division between the French and Germans (also the Danes) on the one side and the English and Americans on the other became plainly evident. The young Frenchman saw many of the vital points very much as we did, in particular theologically. In three youthful circles the serious obstructions which stand in the way of a completely uninhibited relationship between us were faced with great honesty. But we saw our common need and responsibility not only in this, but also in the failure to establish a firm theological foundation for our work, for which the Anglo-Saxon basis, till now generally accepted, is not in fact sufficient."

Bonhoeffer returned from Cambridge to prepare for his first term at Berlin University. Apart from the fairly nominal post as Assistant to Lütgert, which assured him of a small income, Bonhoeffer had, as *Privatdozent* somewhat the position of a lecturer at a mediaeval university. He depended for his audience, and so for his income, entirely upon his ability to attract the voluntary attendance of students. At first students came to his lectures largely from curiosity. One of those who attended these lectures has written recently:

"He looked like a student himself when he went to the desk. But then our attention was so much riveted by what he had to say, that we no longer came for the sake of the very young man, but for the sake of his subject."[1]

In this first term Bonhoeffer was offering a series of lectures on "The History of Systematic Theology in the Twentieth Century", and a seminar on "The Idea of Philosophy in Protestant Theology". His own comment on the two was given in a letter to Sutz, written early in 1932:

"The term is ended. The lecture course is finished—it was dull enough—at least to me. However the Seminar was really pleasant and interesting. I had a couple of quite lively chaps from Barth and Gogarten in it . . ."[2]

But Bonhoeffer was out of his element in the faculty of theology at Berlin, not only as a follower of Barth, but also as a virile, independent thinker. After the death of Harnack the theological faculty had fallen

[1] Quoted E.B., *D.B.*, pp. 65–6.
[2] *G.S.* I, p. 26.

into an aftermath which left its members politically impressionable and intellectually flaccid. Without having the vitality to carry theological Liberalism any further, they yet remained resolutely insensitive to the wind of change which was blowing from Bonn, and the epithet "Barthian" remained in Berlin a term of unmitigated reproach. It is small wonder that in this dreary and censorious atmosphere Bonhoeffer was out of his element. He spoke of his "cold solitude" and wrote to his friend Sutz:

"My theological affiliations make me somewhat suspect here, and people are evidently beginning to get the feeling that they have been nursing a viper in their bosom. I hardly ever see any of the Professors, not to my inconsolable regret. Since my return from Bonn [Barth] I am more than ever struck by the feebleness up here."[1]

A visit of Barth to Berlin at the invitation of the faculty still further increased Bonhoeffer's sense of academic desolation. Once more it is described in a letter to Sutz:

"The meeting of Barth with our local Princes of the Church was typical in every way, and as depressing as might have been expected. There still exists in these people an inquisitorial spirit, which is content with the symptoms and does not go to the roots of a problem—so little to the point and so much fumbling. It was not a pretty picture—the faculty and the General Superintendents [of the Church] were invited to a lecture at Richter's—where Barth like a prisoner at the bar, sitting on a little chair, had to give an account of himself to these great men of the Church. Then, on his request that the questions might begin, there followed a long uncomfortable silence, because no one wanted to be the first to make a fool of himself, and at last, when the silence began to be oppressive, Herr Knak began with a question as to what in Barth's view was the difference between the Swiss and the German national sense. With that the level of the questions was set, once and for all. They were agonising hours, from which Barth returned home somewhat shattered, but the churchmen very well satisfied with the discovery that Barth was a charming man."[2]

Bonhoeffer's ordination, which took place in November, seems to have ranked as a comparatively minor event, but it constituted him a fully-fledged pastor, with the right to be considered for a parish. In the same month another event took place which was to fill the next half-year with a vital new experience. He was asked to take over a con-

[1] *G.S.* I, p. 24.
[2] *G.S.* I, p. 30.

firmation class of about fifty boys in Wedding, one of the toughest districts of working-class Berlin. Eberhard Bethge recollects the description Bonhoeffer gave him of his arrival on the scene:

"The aged pastor with Bonhoeffer mounted the stair of the many-storeyed school building. Above, the children were hanging over the banisters and dropping all manner of rubbish on to the heads of the two men as they slowly climbed the winding stair. Having arrived at the top, the old pastor attempted with shouting and force to push the crowd into the classroom. He tried to tell them that he had brought a new pastor to teach them whose name was Bonhoeffer. As soon as those nearby had heard the first syllable they began a chant: 'Bon, Bon, Bon!' The old man left the scene, resigning it. Bonhoeffer remained silent, leaning against the wall with his hands in his pockets. Minutes passed. The unmoved composure of the new arrival made the shouting suddenly less fun. Then Bonhoeffer began to speak a few words very quietly. Only the boys nearest to him could hear anything. What was he saying? Suddenly the whole class stood silent. Bonhoeffer only said that they had put up a remarkable performance for him, told them one short story about Harlem; and said that if they would listen, he would tell them more next time. He dismissed them, and the boys' attention was secured."[1]

Not only had Bonhoeffer secured the boys' attention, they had also secured his. The second half of the term was more and more completely devoted to them. Early in the new year he rented a room in Berlin Wedding, so that he might devote his time still more fully to them and their families. On December 25th he wrote to Sutz:

"Recently I spent two days with some of them in the country, tomorrow I shall take another group. We enjoyed the time together. As I am keeping the boys until their confirmation, I must visit all of their fifty families, and so I am moving into the district for two months. I am looking forward to the time very much. This is real work."[2] On February 26th he wrote:

"Tomorrow I examine my confirmation candidates. Their confirmation is in a fortnight. The second half of the term has been almost entirely given up to the candidates. Since New Year I have been living here in the north, so as to be able to have the boys here every evening, in turns of course. We have supper together and then we play something—I have taught them chess, which they now play with the greatest

[1] E.B., *D.B.*, p. 273.
[2] *G.S.* I, p. 25.

enthusiasm. Everyone is actually free to come unannounced. And they all like to come. So I don't push them all that much. At the end of each evening I read something out of the Bible and after that a little catechising, which often grows very serious. The experience of teaching them has been such that I can hardly tear myself away from it."[1]

In accordance with the normal practice in the German Evangelical Church, Bonhoeffer himself confirmed his fifty candidates. The sermon that he preached to them has been preserved, and it shows a gentleness which is rare in the sermons of this period, which were more often burning and intense. He took for his text the story of Jacob's wrestling with the angel, which had so deep a symbolic significance in his own life at this period, and then, quietly and warmly, he began to talk to his boys, every one of whom had become dear to him, and the trials and temptations of whose hard lives he by now knew only too well:

"Dear Confirmation Candidates! When in the last days before your confirmation I asked you many times what you hoped to hear in your confirmation address, I often received the answer: we want a serious warning which we shall rememember all our lives. And I can assure you that whoever listens well today will receive a warning or two by the way; but look, life itself gives us enough and too many serious warnings today; and so today I must not make your prospect for the future seem harder and darker than it already is—and I know that many of you know a great many of the hard facts of life. Today you are not to be given fear of life but courage; and so today in the Church we shall speak more than ever of hope, the hope that we have and which no one can take from you."[2]

And then he spoke of hope, quietly, simply, clearly, the hope that Christ gives freely through the medium of the Church. The sermon ended with Jacob, where it had begun:

" 'I will not let thee go except thou bless me.' 'If God be for us, who can be against us?' "[3]

A few days after their confirmation, Bonhoeffer took the whole crowd of candidates to stay with him in his parents' house at Friedrichsbrunn. He left them with regret and sooner than he wished to, to attend a conference of the Youth Commission of the World Alliance in Epsom. Evidently this conference was "Anglo-Saxon" dominated, and Bonhoeffer described it as "fairly superfluous". A Franco-German con-

[1] *G.S.* I, p. 27.
[2] *G.S.* IV, pp. 44-5.
[3] *G.S.* IV, p. 50.

ference in the Westerburg which followed three months later was more deeply concerned with theology and impressed him as having more substance. For a conference which met only ten days later at Cerno-horske Kupele, he wrote his most important address on the theology of the Oecumenical Movement for Peace. In it he described the basis upon which he believed the movement was to be supported. This was not on the grounds that peace as opposed to war was in itself an absolute law. The only absolute law of peace was the law of God's revelation of himself to man in the forgiveness of sins. But war should be absolutely rejected by the Church today on the grounds that it had reached propor-tions in which it had the power to obscure the revelation of God.   On these grounds and on these alone, it should be rejected. The address was delivered to the Conference and well received, but Bonhoeffer himself remained critical of it. "It was an attempt to salve my theo-logical conscience," he observed in a letter to Sutz, "but many question marks ought to be added." August brought two more conferences of the World Alliance, the first in Geneva, followed by a meeting of the Youth Delegation in Gland. The chief importance for Bonhoeffer of the Geneva Occesion lay in the fact that in the simultaneous meeting of the Oecumenical Council for Life and Work, Bishop Bell of Chichester was elected President, and it was now that Bonhoeffer first made his acquaintance, an acquaintance which would later ripen into a friendship that was to be not without consequence in Bonhoeffer's life.

Meanwhile he continued to lecture at the University, and his main contribution in the summer term was a series of two-hour lectures on "the Nature of the Church", based on his thesis *Sanctorum Communio*. We have a vivid recollection of this series and of the young man who delivered them, from his pupil Wolf Dieter Zimmermann:

"A young lecturer walked to the desk with a quick, light step. Fair, rather thin hair, broad face, rimless glasses with a gold bridge. There followed the opening words of greeting and a short outline of the aim and structure of the lecture, all in a firm, rather throaty voice. He opened his manuscript and began his lecture. He first pointed out that nowa-days we often ask whether we still have a use for God. But this is to put the question the wrong way round. The Church exists and God exists, and we are the ones who are being questioned. We are being asked whether we ourselves are ready to be used, for God can use us. What fascinated me from the outset about this man was the way in which he saw things, the way he 'turned them round', away from the positions in which they had been arranged for everyday use, and back to the place which God had ordained for them. And in the process there occurred—as though of itself—a transformation of the values which had seemed to us so obvious and so well-established. To tell the right question from the wrong one was among the most vital tasks of theology."[1]

By means of his seminars, and through informal evenings of discussion, Bonhoeffer was getting to know his students, and many were becoming his devoted disciples. Unawares, he was gathering together a nucleus of men who would later rally round him in the struggle of the Church against Hitler. Some discussions took place in the house of Wolf Dieter Zimmermann, who also participated in another venture. In May 1932, Bonhoeffer rented a piece of land in Biesenthel, on the outskirts of Berlin, where he and his students and some of his ex-confirmation candidates spent weekends together, making a first experiment in Christian community living.

At the same time Bonhoeffer was preaching at regular intervals at the University Church. He took preaching intensely seriously. For the Lutheran it represents the central function of the Church, the human means by which God's word is revealed. Bonhoeffer's sermons at this time were intense, daring and prophetic. They were delivered in a cool, concentrated, undramatic manner, and neither their style nor their content rendered them very popular.

But the most powerful and uncompromising of all was probably preached before a packed congregation, among whom Hindenburg may have been present, for it was delivered on Reformation Sunday, when German Protestants gather to remember with a glow of pride the magnificent achievements of Luther. But this was to be a Reformation Sunday which the Congregation in the Kaiser Friedrich Memorial Church would remember with more pain than pleasure. The opening text was already a little ominous:

"Revelation 2: 4, 5, 7: 'Nevertheless I have somewhat against thee, because thou hast left thy first love. Remember therefore from whence thou art fallen, and repent, and do the first works; or else I will come unto thee quickly, and will remove thy candlestick out of his place, except thou repent . . .

" 'He that hath an ear let him hear what the spirit saith unto the Churches; to him that overcometh will I give to eat of the tree of life, which is in the midst of the paradise of God.' "

And then the sermon began:

[1] *Begegnungen*, pp. 45–6.

"Our Protestant Church has reached the eleventh hour of her life; we have not much longer before it will be decided whether she is done for or whether a new day will dawn—it is high time we realised this."

It is a strange, disturbing picture. The great sombre Church, the large middle-aged distinguished congregation and the fair-headed young man still looking like a student, raised above them in the soaring pulpit, and delivering with controlled urgency a sermon of whose formidable content a few passages may serve to give some impression.

"And another thing we ought to realise, that a fanfare of trumpets is no comfort to a dying man, much less does it bring him back to life; a fanfare of trumpets belongs to a state funeral. It belongs at that point in which one shouts down the cold silence with a still colder clamour, at that point where graveyard wreaths and funeral marches must cover the rot of mortality . . . such fanfares, which can only show that death has already come, such fanfares of death are known to all of us who still take part in the life of the Church. Reformation Sunday—that is the dreadful day which has made us most familiar with this kind of thing . . . The Church which celebrates the Reformation cannot leave our ancient Luther in peace, he is called in to support all the fearful practices which go on in our Church today. We prop up this dead man in our Church, cause him to stretch out his hand, point to this Church and say, with dramatic conviction, over and over again: 'Here I stand, I cannot do otherwise;' and we do not see that this Church is no longer the Church of Luther, and that it was in fear and trembling, driven by the devil into his last stronghold, that Luther spoke in the fear of God his 'here I stand'; and we do not see that these words are singularly inappropriate for our use today. It is simply not true, it is unpardonable frivolity and arrogance, if we dig ourselves in behind these words. *We can do otherwise*; at any rate we should be able to, and it would mean a poor state of things before God and the world, if we could act only so and not otherwise. Not one of us has taken up that final position, from which he can only say to God in prayer, 'I cannot do otherwise, so help me God!' A thousand times today it will have rung out from the pulpits: 'Here I stand, I cannot do otherwise'—but God answers 'I have somewhat against thee . . ."

". . . No, this is no longer the time for such solemn Church festivals, in which we strike attitudes before ourselves, that is not how we should celebrate the Reformation. Leave the dead Luther in peace at last, and listen to the Gospel, read his Bible, hear the actual word of God. In the day of judgement God will surely not ask us 'Have you celebrated the Reformation in a representative manner?' but 'Have you listened to my word and kept it faithfully?' Let us then accept these words: 'I have something against these, because thou hast left thy first love' . . .

"But now let us think of the Church as a whole; where are now the days of God's first grace . . . where is the time of which we read: 'and the multitude of them that believed were of one heart and of one soul, neither said any of them that ought of the things which he possessed was his own; but they had all things common. And with great power gave the apostles witness of the resurrection of the Lord Jesus; and great grace was upon them all.'[1] Where is this multitude who, because they knew one of God's miracles, the resurrection from death to life, believed all things possible to him who had faith, through the power of grace and the power of our love to God? And who even believed that men might love one another, and that they might enter into another's need and in all humility help him? Where is this community of the first love, which shone with the light of God like a lamp for the world? . . .

" 'Remember therefore from whence thou art fallen and repent, and do the first works.' This last passage is necessary, without it the first has no significance. It may sound unsuitable, especially on Reformation Sunday, to speak of works. But it would be a horrible misunderstanding of the Gospel if one were to suppose that faith and repentance were only for pious evening and morning hours. Faith and repentance mean letting God be God—and to be obedient to him in our actions too, especially in our actions. Do the *first* works—how important it is to say that, no one who knows the Church of today will wish to complain that she does nothing . . . but do we do the *first* works, which are ultimately the whole point? To love God and to love one's brother with that first passionate burning love that will risk everything for him except God? Do we really let God be God, do we entrust ourselves and our Church completely to him? *If we did, then things would surely look different, surely something would come burning through* . . .

"But now it grows serious: 'or else I will come unto thee quickly, and will remove thy candlestick out of his place, except thou repent.' Here God speaks with the utmost gravity. The hour is at hand for our Church . . . how might it come about? Today we had better make no grand speeches about our acts of heroism in the event of such a collapse —let God be the Lord.

"The avenging Lord before whom we bow is also the Lord of promise. He alone knows his people, he is here, perhaps in the midst

[1] Acts 4: 32 and 33.

of us. He alone knows to whom he is speaking when he says, 'to him that overcometh will I give to eat of the tree of life, which is in the midst of the Paradise of God.' Will this be ourselves, shall we overcome, shall we have faith to the end? The future makes us afraid, but the promise comforts us. Blessed are those to whom it is spoken.

"And now, when you leave the Church, do not think that was a good or a bad Reformation festival, but let us go forth soberly and do the first works. So help us God. Amen."[1]

In this great sermon the bitter interior struggle boiled up to the surface, but more often it was concealed; only occasionally in a private conversation a sign of it might here or there appear and be observed by one or another of his students.

"He seemed less quiet and collected in a *tête-à-tête*. Then one noticed at once how complex a character he really was, and how much was fermenting in him and how much tormented him."[2]

These, and no others, were the years when his faith was at breaking point, and when a weaker, a less heroic spirit might have left the Church. But Bonhoeffer responded to the challenge in exactly the opposite way. Now, for the first time in his life, he went regularly to the Sunday morning service, and he began to take Holy Communion as often as he could. His spiritual concentration, austerity and self-discipline served him as well tempered instruments, and now in his deep but controlled agony of mind his prayer was immeasurably deepened and enriched.

"And he said 'let me go, for the day breaketh.' And he said 'I will not let thee go except thou bless me.'"

It was a long struggle, dark and secret and nowhere recorded, but we may discover a little of the outcome from three letters. The first extracts are from a letter written to Ursula's husband, Rüdiger Schleicher, in answer to what was evidently a critical enquiry:

". . . How can I live a Christian life in this actual world, and where is the final authority for such a life, which alone is worth living?

"First of all I will confess quite simply—I believe that the Bible alone is the answer to all our questions, and that we need only to ask repeatedly and a little humbly, in order to receive this answer. One cannot simply *read* the Bible, like other books. One must be prepared really to enquire of it. Only thus will it reveal itself. Only if we expect from it the ultimate answer, shall we receive it. That is because in the Bible God speaks to us. And one cannot simply think about God in

[1] *G.S.* IV, pp. 93 *et seq.*
[2] *Begegnungen,* pp. 56–7.

one's own strength, one has to enquire of him. Only if we seek him, will he answer us, Of course, it is also possible to read the Bible like any other book, that is to say from the point of view of textual criticism, etc.; there is nothing to be said against that. Only that that is not the method which will reveal to us the heart of the Bible, but only the surface, just as we do not grasp the words of someone we love by taking them to bits, but by simply receiving them, so that for days they go on lingering in our minds, simply because they are the words of a person we love; and just as these words reveal more and more of the person who said them, as we go on, like Mary, 'pondering them in our heart', so it will be with the words of the Bible. Only if we will venture to enter into the words of the Bible, as though in them this God were speaking to us who loves us and does not will to leave us alone with our questions, only so shall we learn to rejoice in the Bible . . .

"If it is I who determine where God is to be found, then I shall always find a God who corresponds to me in some way, who is obliging, who is connected with my own nature. But if *God* determines where he is to be found, then it will be in a place which is not immediately pleasing to my nature and which is not at all congenial to me. This place is the Cross of Christ. And whoever would find him must go to the foot of the Cross, as the Sermon on the Mount commands. This is not according to our nature at all, it is entirely contrary to it. But this is the message of the Bible, not only in the New but also in the Old Testament . . .

"And I would like to tell you now quite personally: since I have learnt to read the Bible in this way—and this has not been for so very long—it becomes every day more wonderful to me. I read it in the morning and the evening, often during the day as well, and every day I consider a text which I have chosen for the whole week, and try to sink deeply into it, so as really to hear what it is saying. I know that without this I could not live properly any longer. And I certainly could not believe . . ."[1]

The following is from a letter to his eldest brother, Karl Friedrich:

"It may be that in some respects I seem to you a little fanatical and mad. And I am afraid of it myself sometimes. But I know that if I were more 'sensible', I should honestly very soon have to pack up my theology altogether. When I began with theology, I pictured something different—perhaps a more academic affair. But now it has turned into something quite different. But at last I begin to think that I know, or

[1] *G.S.* III, pp. 26 *et seq.*

at least that I am on the right track—for the first time in my life. And that often makes me very happy . . . I think I know that I should be for the first time inwardly clear and truly genuine, if I began really to be in earnest with the Sermon on the Mount . . ."[1]

And finally a biographical note in a letter written in circumstances which demanded a degree of self revelation rare for Bonhoeffer:

"I flung myself into my work in a most unchristian manner. Ambition, which some have observed in me, made my life difficult . . .

"Then something new entered, something which to this very day has changed my life and turned it upside down. I found my way for the first time to the Bible . . . I had already preached often, I had already seen a great deal of the Church and talked and preached about it—but I had not yet become a Christian . . .

"I know that in those days I used the cause of Jesus Christ to my own advantage. I pray God that I may never do so again. Also I had never really prayed, or only very little. Forsaken though I was, I was nevertheless quite pleased with myself. From this condition the Bible has released me, and especially the Sermon on the Mount. Since then everything has changed. I have been clearly aware of this and so have others who have had to do with me. That was a great liberation. Then it became clear to me that the life of a servant of Jesus Christ must belong to the Church, and the extent to which this must be so became clearer step by step."[2]

The three letters, written some time later, all look back to the two hard years which preceded Hitler's advent. Plainly for Dietrich there had been a victory.

"Then Jacob gathers the last of his strength, he does not let him go. 'I will not let thee go except thou bless me.' To him it is as though the end had come. So strong has been the hold of his powerful assailant. But in this moment he receives the blessing, and the stranger is gone. Then the sun rose upon Jacob, and he halted upon his thigh, but he entered into the promised land. The way lay ahead, the dark gate into the promised land was burst open. The curse had become a blessing, then the sun rose upon him."[3]

[1] G.S. III, pp. 24–5.
[2] E.B., D.B., pp. 248–9.
[3] G.S. III, p. 284.

CHAPTER IX

ON January 30th 1933 Hitler came to power. The National Socialist party had won a large majority in the general election, and President Hindenburg quite properly called upon their leader to form a Government. It was the last democratic event which was to take place in Germany for twelve years.

The following day Bonhoeffer fulfilled an engagement to broadcast over the Berlin radio network on "The Concept of Leadership". The broadcast was extremely moderate in tone. He posed the question as to whether the popular desire for a leader represented a psychological need of youth or a political need of the nation as a whole. He concluded:

"Or is the demand for a leader the expression not only of our contemporary political situation, but also of a certain vital requirement of youth? That is to say, has it historical and psychological necessity? And in that case ,what are the limits of its significance? To what point is leading and being led healthy and genuine, and when does it become pathological and extreme? It is only when a man has answered these questions clearly in his own mind, that he can grasp something of the essence of 'leadership' and something of the nature of the younger generation. In the leadership of youth today almost everything depends upon a clearcut drawing of the lines at this point, so that one may cut through all that is muddled and fantastic and arrive at clarity. At this point the health and integrity of the young is in jeopardy. Ideals and illusions lie here cheek by jowl."[1]

Before it was ended, the broadcast was cut off. The suppression of free speech had begun.

For the time being, Bonhoeffer made no further attempt to express his views. He quietly continued the pattern of his university life, of which the principal feature of the winter term was a series of lectures which he offered on the subject of "Creation and Fall", and which was exceptionally well attended and later published.

The theology set forth in the lectures is essentially Barthian. Bonhoeffer, like Barth, sees all that is significant in creation as taking place within the soul of man; creation for Bonhoeffer *is* created man, and it

[1] *G.S.* II, pp. 20-1.

can only be understood at all in the light of Christ. "As those who only live and have a history in Christ, our imaginations cannot help us to know about the beginning. We can only know about it from the new middle, from Christ, as those who are freed in faith from the knowledge of good and evil and from death, and who can make Adam's picture their own only in faith."[1]

But, though following Barth, Bonhoeffer approaches the subject with his own particular intensity, pouring into it his rich varieties of thought and style, and as a result the lectures often break out into passages of remarkable power and beauty. Without academic preamble we are swept straight in:

"The Bible begins at a place where our thinking is at its most passionate. Like huge breakers it surges up, is thrown back upon itself and spends its strength. Hardly has the first word of the Bible been visible to us for a moment, when it is as though the waves are racing forward again and submerging it with foaming water.

". . . Man no longer lives in the beginning—he has lost the beginning. Now he finds he is in the middle, knowing neither the end nor the beginning . . . What does it mean that in the beginning is God? Which God? Your God, whom you yourself created out of your need, because you need an idol?

". . . In the beginning out of freedom, out of nothing, God created the heavens and the earth. That is the comfort with which the Bible addresses us who are in the middle, who are anxious before the false void, the beginning without a beginning and the end without an end. It is the gospel, it is the resurrected Christ, of whom we are speaking here. God is the beginning and he will be in the end. He is free regarding the world. The fact that he lets us know—this is mercy, grace, forgiveness and comfort."[2]

What follows is in effect the exploration of three circles. The unfallen creation in which God is the centre and man in orbit round him; the fallen creation in which man is the centre, and the redeemed creation of which the centre is Christ. On the way certain qualities in Bonhoeffer are revealed more clearly than they have been in any previous writing, such as his capacity to receive intuitive insights, which is primitive in the sense that it is a gift of mind very easily submerged by the kind of intensive discursive thinking of which he was also master. An example of this is his understanding of "the day" which God created.

[1] Dietrich Bonhoeffer, *Creation and Temptation*, combined edn. 1966, p. 57.
[2] *C. and T.*, pp. 12–18.

"The day is the first finished work of God. In the beginning God created the day. The day bears all other things, and the world lives among the changes of the day. The day possesses its own being, form and power. It is not the rotation of the earth around the sun—which can be understood physically—or the calculable change of light and darkness; the day is something exceeding all this, something determining the essence of our world and our existence. If it were not such an unsuitable thing to say in this context, we might say that it is what is called a mythological quantity . . .

"For us the creatureliness and miraculousness of the day has completely disappeared. We have deprived the day of its power. We no longer allow ourselves to be determined by the day. We count and compute it, we do not allow the day to give to us. Thus we do not live it."[1]

"We might say that it is what is called a mythological quantity." Many passages in *Creation* illustrate Bonhoeffer's capacity to apprehend spiritual truth through the medium of mythology, a capacity that grows increasingly feeble in the present day, as men fall ever more completely under the spell of the belief that critical and analytical thinking is the only kind worthy of the name. An example of Bonhoeffer's freedom from this bondage is provided by a passage on the second creation story:

"Pictures are not lies: they denote things; they let the things that are meant shine through . . .

"Entirely within the framework of this picture it is related how man was put into this garden in order to live in it and how two trees stood in the middle of the garden: one the tree of life, the other the tree of the knowledge of good and evil. And upon these two trees the destiny of man is to be decided. We remain completely in the world of pictures, in the world of the magical, of magic effects by means of forbidden contacts with sacred objects. We hear of trees of miraculous power, of enchanted animals, of fiery angel forms, the servants of a God who walks in his magic garden, of their mysterious deeds, of the creation of woman from the rib of man—and in the midst of this world is man, the intelligent, who knows the world around him, who names it freely, before whom all the animals appear in order to receive their names. Man is naked and unashamed. Man, too, speaks and walks with God as if they belonged to one another. He speaks with the beasts in the fields and lives in his magic garden magnificently and in peace—and

[1] *C. and T.*, p. 26.

114

then he reaches for the fruit of a magic tree and in that moment loses his paradise. 'A myth, a childlike, fantastic picture of the grey, hidden times of old': thus speaks the world. 'God's Word, even in the beginning of history, before history, beyond history and yet in history; we ourselves are confronted, intended, addressed, accused, sentenced, expelled. God himself is the one who blesses and curses. It is our prehistory, truly our own. It is the beginning, destiny, guilt and end of every one of us': thus speaks the Church of Christ."[1]

"*We ourselves* are confronted." Here we receive a characteristic blow between the eyes, reminding us of a fact which for Bonhoeffer was of absolutely vital importance, that in theology man is not enquiring about God; *he is confronted by him.* This leads on directly to the suggestion, not original in Bonhoeffer, but one which he made intensively his own, that man's temptation represented by the conversation with the serpent in the garden was the temptation to ask the wrong question. The serpent tempted Adam to ask a question *about* God, to treat him as an object, something which might be handled, criticised, speculated upon. But God may only be enquired *from.* "Who are you? What are your commandments? What are you saying to us?"

"The serpent asks, 'Did God say[2] You shall not eat of any tree in the garden?' The serpent does not dispute this word but it enables man to catch sight of a hitherto unknown profundity in which he would be in the position to establish or dispute whether a word is the Word of God or not. The serpent itself in the first place only suggests the possibility that man has perhaps misunderstood here, since God could not possibly have meant it in this way. God, the good Creator, would not impose such a thing upon his creature; this would be a limitation of his love.

"The decisive point is that this question suggests to man that he should go behind the Word of God and establish what it is by himself, out of his understanding of the being of God. Should it contradict this understanding then man has clearly made a mistake. Surely it can only serve God's cause if such false words of God, such misunderstood commands are swept aside before it is too late. The misleading thing about this question is therefore that it obviously wants to be thought to come from God. For the sake of the true God it seems to want to sweep aside the

---

[1] Dietrich Bonhoeffer, *C. and T.*, pp. 48-9.

[2] Luther's translation runs: '*Ja, sollte Gott gesagt haben . . .?* Really, is God supposed to have said . . .?'

given Word of God. Beyond this given Word of God the serpent pretends somehow to know something about the profundity of the true God who is so badly misrepresented in this human word. The serpent claims to know more about God than man, who depends on God's Word alone. The serpent knows of a greater, nobler God who does not need such a prohibition. In some way it wants to be itself the dark root from which the visible tree of God then springs up. And from this position of power the serpent fights against the Word of God. It knows that it only has power where it claims to come from God, to be pleading his cause. It is evil only as the religious serpent.[1] The serpent, which derives its existence only from the power of God in the question it is asking and which can be evil only where it is religious, now claims to be the power that is behind the Word of God, from which God himself in the first place draws his power."[2]

According to Bonhoeffer, this question "Did God say?" ("Is God supposed to have said?") leads straight into the man-made edifice which "religion" represents for him, the tower of Babel built by our pride and self-sufficiency. "The serpent's question was a thoroughly religious one. But with the first religious question in the world, evil has come upon the scene."[3]

This symbolic use of the talking serpent to represent the tempter subtly misguiding man to ask the wrong question was to appear again and again in Bonhoeffer's theological argument, and it may be taken as a key to that attitude of mind in which he could welcome a religionless world as one that might be more open truly to receive Christ than the world of religious convention. Throughout this whole series of vivid lectures Bonhoeffer, making use of the theological insights now of Luther, now of Barth, irradiates them with his personal intensity and places them in an intuitive setting which is peculiarly his own. An understanding of these Creation Lectures can contribute much to an understanding of the man who wrote them.

While these lectures were being delivered, events were not standing still in the Reich. Exactly four weeks after Hitler came to power, the Reichstag was burnt to the ground. Karl Bonhoeffer took an interesting part in the aftermath, for as being the most distinguished psychiatrist in Berlin, he was, together with his colleague Jürg Zuck, entrusted with

[1] The German word is *fromm*, normally the adjective used when the idea of personal religion is intended; *religiös* carries a suggestion more closely connected with religious institutions.

[2] Dietrich Bonhoeffer, *C. and T.*, pp. 66–7.

[3] Dietrich Bonhoeffer, *C. and T.*, p. 67.

the psychological investigation of van der Lubbe, the young Dutchman who was responsible for the fire.

The result of the investigation was published in the *Monatsschrift für Psychiatrie und Neurologie*, vol. 89 no. 4, and is of considerable historical interest. On the strength of this report, the popular conception of van der Lubbe as a half-witted tool of the Nazis has to be abandoned. We are shown clearly the picture of a convinced young Communist of above average intelligence, perfectly well aware of what he had done and of his reasons for doing it. The painstaking and lucid report closes with the following summary:

"Only one conclusion is possible: this young man of twenty-four showed remarkable emotional consistency and indeed stubbornness in maintaining an unwavering attitude until his execution. This represents—especially in view of his youth—an outstanding human achievement. But he was in fact an unusual person: he was violently ambitious, at the same time modest and friendly; a scatterbrain, without any demand for intellectual clarity, but nevertheless capable of unwavering determination, incorrigibly closed to contradictory arguments. He was good-natured and not resentful, but he resisted all authority. This fundamentally rebellious tendency was probably his most questionable characteristic, and the one most likely to set him upon the disastrous road which he took. The early conversion to Communistic ideas certainly contributed to the same effect; but the undisciplined elements in his temperament made it unlikely in any case, that he would follow a quiet and orderly pattern through life. Something which was unusual in one way or another was to be expected from him. But he was not for that reason to be regarded as mentally ill."

The true facts about the Reichstag fire will never be known, but whatever they were, it came like a gift from the gods to Adolf Hitler. The following morning the first of the *Notverordnungen* (Emergency Measures) were announced, measures supposed to be taken by the President "for the protection of nation and state" and established "for the present", a "present" which was to continue until Hitler's death. The measures permitted: "restriction of personal freedom, of the rights of free speech including freedom of the press, of the right to form societies and call together public gatherings, a suspension of privacy for letters, telegrams and telephone calls, and the right to search houses and to commandeer and restrict personal property, beyond the legal limits normally imposed".

It requires a determined effort of the imagination to envisage a national state of mind in which these emergency measures could be not only proposed by the government, but also accepted by a large majority of the people in the referendum hastily organised for the following Sunday. They were accepted, in some quarters with enthusiasm.

As a background to this astonishing reaction stands the fact that Germany had had no continuous history of democratic experience. Accustomed to internal divisions and, in Prussia in particular, to a government which had never, until the downfall of William II, ceased to be authoritarian, the nation's only experience of democratic government had been provided by the Weimar Republic, whose efforts had been consistently sabotaged by the parties of the right, and whose final plunge into chaos had established in many politically confused minds the conviction that nothing better was to be expected from democracy. Hitler appeared to the vast majority of the German people as the hero who had rescued their suffering fatherland from this chaos; the fact that he had been instrumental in creating it was appreciated by few. To a country which had not, as a whole, learnt to value civil liberties, the appalling dangers of their complete withdrawal was not immediately obvious, and the sight of Hitler's political troops, the *Sturm Abteilung* or "S.A.", marching about in their brown shirts, had little power to alarm a nation who had become accustomed to the idea of political violence.

Meanwhile in the early days of Hitler's government, much positive good was being achieved. Fearless and imaginative economic measures were applied to deal with the problem of unemployment, and the whole nation was roused to a sense of social responsibility which banished the despair of the depressed classes and which was, among many less worthy ones, a strong positive factor for the immense upsurge in the national morale. It was these positive elements in particular which kindled the enthusiasm of the rising generation; it was not only melodramatic speeches and the heroics of the brown-shirted S.A. that won their hearts for Hitler, but the fact that he offered them a movement in which they could at last find an outlet for their desire for sacrifice and service. When the "National Bishop", Ludwig Müller, said later, "Faith, trust, loyalty and obedience are also spiritual words, which Christ desires to bring to creative power in people," he was at that moment speaking the truth. It is a tragic irony of National Socialism that the stones of its evil edifice were cemented by these very virtues, and Bonhoeffer spoke with a fearful clarity when he wrote eight years later in the *Ethics*:

"If evil appears in the form of light, benefit, loyalty and renewal, if it conforms with historical necessity and social justice, then this, if it is understood straightforwardly, is a clear additional proof of its abysmal wickedness."[1]

The Bonhoeffer family were better equipped than most to retain their independence of judgement in face of the national intoxication. Trained by their father in rigorous intellectual objectivity, the younger members of the family had never fallen victim to the political passions which for the last fifteen years had been boiling around them. All were unanimous now in deploring the direction which events had taken. Karl Bonhoeffer records in his memoir:

"The victory of National Socialism in the year 1933, and the nomination of Hitler to the post of Chancellor, all members of our family, without exception, regarded as a misfortune. My own distaste and suspicion of Hitler arose from his demagogic methods of propaganda, his congratulatory telegram on the occasion of the Potemba murder, his motor drives through the country with the riding whip in his hand, his choice of confederates, details about whom were perhaps better known to us here in Berlin than to those in other parts of the country, and finally from the rumours of his psychopathic symptoms which were going the rounds in our department."

While the psychiatrists were discussing Hitler with clinical detachment, the Bonhoeffers watched with anxiety and distaste as one repressive measure followed another. When, on April 1st, a command to boycott Jewish shops was obeyed amid many scenes of disgusting inhumanity, most of those who did not like them stayed safely out of the way. But Dietrich's ninety-year-old grandmother was not among their number. On April 1st she walked quietly through the cordon of S.A. men and "Hitler Youth" who were picketing the Jewish shop where she was accustomed to deal, made her purchases and withdrew without comment. The cordon fell back to let her pass. Only her expressive and distinguished face spoke her unmistakable thoughts.

The boycott was followed a week later by an order whose purpose was said to be "the Restoration of the civil service". This was the notorious "Aryan Paragraph" which required that the civil service should be purged of all those who were of Jewish or partly Jewish descent. Dietrich Bonhoeffer was among the first to see the implication of this for christians, and possibly for the Church. A number of factors combined to make him quickly sensitive to the central importance of the

[1] Dietrich Bonhoeffer, *Ethics*, p. 4.

situation with which the christians were now faced. One was the presence of a non-Aryan in his own family, his twin sister's husband, Gerhard Leibholz; another was his friendship with Franz Hildebrandt, whose future would now be in jeopardy, and a third was his intimate knowledge of another suffering minority, the coloured people of America. Thus it was on behalf of the Jewish Christians that his first serious protest was made. It took the form of an address given somewhere in Berlin before the end of April.

After an attempt to define the functions of Church and State, which he based upon Luther's doctrine of the two spheres, the one spiritual and the other temporal, he went on to denounce the theory that membership of a Church can ever be based on race. There is one sentence in this paper which is of interest because of having been written before Hitler's dictatorship was three months old. There might be circumstances in the relation of Church with State, Bonhoeffer said, which could make it necessary for the Church, in the expressive German phrase "to fall between the spokes" of the State's wheel. The words slipped by at the time, but later they would be remembered.

Meanwhile the Church was at first hopeful of the new regime. Politically, christians were not less impressionable than others. It was not only the "German Christians" who welcomed the advent of Hitler and took at its face value his promise "to allow and safeguard for the Christian Confessions in school and education the influence that is their due." The surge of enthusiasm for national unity gave fresh impulse to the hope, dear to the hearts of many, that the patchwork of independent provincial Churches might be replaced by a single national Church. Bonhoeffer too saw this as a hopeful possibility.

The main difference of opinion which existed between those who belonged to the "German Christians" and those who did not was that the "German Christians" wished for a Church which should be subservient to the state, while the aim of the others was to safeguard its independence. The first round went to the independent party. A small committee of three members of moderate views met to devise a constitution for the new National Church. The "German Christians" succeeded in foisting upon them a fourth, Ludwig Müller, whom Hitler had appointed as his deputy for ecclesiastical affairs. But Müller had no very powerful effect upon the deliberations, a workable constitution was devised for the new Church, and the three effective members proposed Fritz von Bodelschwingh, son of the founder of the famous Community of Bethel, to be the first "National Bishop". The German

Christians, at the instigation of the Government, made the counter-proposal of Ludwig Müller, but when representatives of the various provincial synods met at Eisenach on May 26th, Bodelschwingh was chosen. The Government and the German Christians were enraged, refused recognition to the proposed new Church and a few weeks after the election suspended the Central Council of the Church of Prussia, dismissed the head of the Council and the general Superintendents, and imposed a government of their own, under the control of the notorious Hossenfelder, whose definition of the German Christian "Faith Movement" as "*S.A. Jesu Christi*" provided a sufficient comment upon his mentality and attitude.

Now public opinion within the Church was roused. A storm of protest arose, and a movement of opposition which had earlier begun to form was consolidated under the name of "the Young Reformers". It was by no means a revolutionary movement. Its members protested their loyalty to the new political regime, clinging to Luther's doctrine of the two spheres, the spiritual sphere, in which the Church commanded, and the temporal sphere which was the legitimate preserve of the state. They searched hopefully for points of contact with the German Christians, but they did at least insist that the Church must remain independent in her own realm, and they repudiated the Aryan Paragraph in its application to the Church. Since the Young Reformers represented the only group which dared to offer some organised criticism, Bonhoeffer worked with them as far as he was able to. But he would never be permanently content with half-measures, and he repudiated entirely their political attitude. A sermon on Gideon, preached a short time after Hitler's rise to power, defines the theological basis of his rejection of the "Führer Principle".

"God's victory means our defeat, means our humiliation; it means God's mocking anger at all human arrogance, being puffed up, trying to be important in our own right. It means reducing the world and its clamour to silence; it means the crossing through of all our ideas and plans, it means the Cross. The Cross above the World. It means that man, even the noblest, must, whether he likes it or not, fall in the dust and with him all gods and idols and lords of this world. The Cross of Jesus Christ, that means the bitter scorn of God for all human heights, bitter suffering of God in all human depths, the rule of God over the whole world.

"The people came to victorious Gideon; it is the final clamour and the final temptation: 'rule thou over us!' But Gideon does not forget his history or the history of his nation . . . 'God shall rule over you, and you shall have no other Lord.' At these words the altars of the gods and the idols are cast down, all worship of man is cast down, all apotheosis of man by himself, they are judged, condemned, crossed out, they are all crucified and flung down into the dust by him who alone is Lord. And beside us kneels Gideon, the man who has been brought to faith out of the midst of fears and doubts, kneels before the altar of the one God, and with us Gideon prays: 'Lord on the Cross, be thou alone our Lord. Amen.' "[1]

The unpopularity of this sermon may well be imagined, but others followed it which were equally grave and uncompromising. In these critical days, when the new National Church was falling both politically and spiritually more and more under the dominion of the government, Bonhoeffer began to see the true and the false elements within the Church in ever deeper contrast. In a daring sermon on the subject of the golden calf, he branded the false prophets in glaring colours. With his friend Franz Hildebrandt he began to consider the possible formation of a new Free Church, whose form and constitution might be considered at an Oecumenical Council of all the Protestant Churches. At the same time he was considering what his own right course might be. Could he accept a pastorate when his friend Franz Hildebrandt might be forbidden to minister because of his Jewish blood? At this time the possibility of a pastorate in England arose. He wrote in July to Erwin Sutz:

"My personal future may take a decisive turn very soon. It has been proposed to me that I might go to London as a German pastor with a special commission for oecumenical work. I think it over a great deal, and it does seem to me that just now, with all the possible developments that have to be considered for the Church here, to be in close touch with the English Churches might in the circumstances be of great value."[2]

Meanwhile Hitler pursued his course. His hope was evidently to use the German Protestant Church as a specialised propaganda agency, but his intentions for the Catholic Church in Germany were different. He seems to have regarded the Roman Catholic Church as something more nearly analogous to a rival state, whose neutrality must be secured if he was to pursue his political policy unmolested. It was with this in mind that he made overtures to the Vatican to secure a Concordat, which guaranteed the independence of the Catholics in religious matters, in

[1] *G.S.* IV, p. 117.
[2] *G.S.* I, p. 39.

exchange for non-interference in national affairs. The Vatican, adhering to its nineteenth-century policy of taking all available measures to make the world safe for Catholicism, fell headlong into the trap. The Concordat was signed. But it was not destined to be honoured, and as in years to come resistance mounted in both Churches, Catholics and Protestants, with the barriers between them broken down, were to meet in the same concentration camps and would often discover a deep spiritual unity revealed in the harsh light of their common suffering.

On July 23rd, three days after the signing of the Concordat, a Referendum was held among the members of all the Protestant Churches which showed an overwhelming majority in favour of the German Christians. Hitler must have believed that he now held the Churches in the hollow of his hand. But he had reckoned without that imponderable element, the thin and often almost invisible line on which the living faith is carried.

While these disturbing developments within the Church went forward, Bonhoeffer for the time being continued his work at the university, and it was in the summer term of 1933 that his last and most outstanding series of lectures was delivered. They were the lectures upon Christology, his own notes for which have been lost, but which have been carefully reconstructed by Eberhard Bethge from notes taken by his students.

Once more the creative power of the work rests in Bonhoeffer's intense concern for his subject. The young man stood up at the desk not to deliver a series of impersonal academic lectures, but to speak to his students about Jesus Christ. For him Christology meant an encounter with the living Christ or it meant nothing. In this course of lectures, the theme already prominent in the creation course reappears. It is of central importance that man shall ask the right question. Just as, in the creation story, Adam's temptation is to ask the wrong question of God the Father, so the same temptation reappears now in man's search for the right question to be asked of Christ. If man asks the wrong question here, his hope of a personal encounter is lost. If we ask "how?" we reduce Jesus to a mere subject for enquiry, an object of discussion. "*How* was he possible? *How* was he God and man? *How* can he be present in the sacrament?" Out of this kind of asking the true answers can never emerge. The question "what?" is also rejected, as being one particular aspect of the how question. We must ask "Who" is Jesus Christ? Who is the Lord, that I might believe in him? It is only when we have asked in humility the personal question, in which we are ourselves involved, in heart as well as in mind, that we may venture to try to formulate a few answers.

First, Christ is Lord. He is the Lord in whom and by whom the truth is spoken. But it is not a general, abstract truth, it is the truth for me, truth spoken within the framework of concrete reality. "Truth is not something which rests in itself and for itself, but something which takes place between two persons. Truth happens only in community. Only here does the concept of the Word acquire its full significance. Christ as Word in the sense of address is thus not timeless truth. He is truth spoken in the concrete moment, the address which puts a man in the truth before God. He is not a universally accessible idea, but the Word perceived only where he allows himself to be perceived."[1]

Secondly, Christ is Sacrament, "embodied Word". This provides an endless labyrinth of possible inconclusive answers to the question "how?". But we must resist the insidious and recurrent temptation to ask it. "*Who* is present in the Sacrament? This is the only form in which the question may be asked. The answer runs: the whole person of the God-man is present in his exaltation and his humiliation; Christ exists in such a way that his is existentially present in the sacrament."[2]

Finally, Christ is community. The Christian community does not simply represent the body of Christ, it actually is that body, where Christ is present in his exaltation and humiliation.

This leads us on to a second legitimate question, "Where" is Christ present? He is present as the centre of my existence, as the centre of history and as the centre of nature. But he is present "incognito", unrecognised by the world, not because of his incarnation but because of his humiliation—poverty, failure, disgrace. But Christ incarnate is both, and both at once, humiliated and exalted, crucified and risen. He is present like this now, he is present *pro me*, for my sake, and his presence is in the Church; in a real sense it *is* the Church.

"The concept of the body, applied to the Church, is not merely a functional concept, relevant only to the members of this body; but in its comprehensiveness and centrality it is a concept of him who is present, exalted and humbled."[3]

With the Christology lectures completed and the summer term at an end, Bonhoeffer had more leisure to devote to the struggle within the Church, and at the same time, Karl Barth entered the fray. A few days before the "German Christian" victory in the referendum, the first of a

[1] Dietrich Bonhoeffer, *Christology*, edited by Eberhard Bethge, translated by John Bowden, p. 51.
[2] *Christology*, p. 58.
[3] *The Place of Bonhoeffer*, edited Martin E. Marty, p. 151.

series of brochures which he was to write under the title *Theological Existence today* appeared as a supplement to the theological journal *Zwischen den Zeiten*.

Like a two-edged sword Barth's limpid and individual mind cut through the mass of rhetorical confusion which was blinding so many Christians to the real issue. "For this is the powerful temptation of the present time," he wrote, "which appears in innumerable guises: that because of the strength of other demands we cease to understand the intensity and exclusiveness of the demand of the divine Word, and so we at once cease to understand this Word at all. That in our anxiety about all kinds of dangers we no longer quite trust the power of God's Word, so that we believe we must come to its assistance with all kinds of devices, and so we entirely cast away our faith in its victory . . . That our hearts are divided between the Word of God and all sorts of other things, which we expressly or tacitly clothe with the majesty of the divine, and by this we show that our heart is not centred in the Word of God."[1]

In the same article Barth made a penetrating analysis of the varied motives which impelled Church members to join the ranks of the "German Christians", and which he described as a psychosis to which "some fall victim in the honest belief that they have heard a messianic message, others on the strength of some very deep theological justification, which people are in the habit of finding with particular certainty just when they have allowed themselves to be most completely over-overtaken by 'actuality', a third group on the simple-minded assumption that whatever is right in the political field is bound to be appropriate in the ecclesiastical field also, a fourth in the timid wisdom which is afraid of getting out of line or of getting its valuable power wasted, since this is the direction in which all is flowing, the fifth with the wise reservation that they only accept what is 'good' in the movement, the sixth with the slightly underhand intention that they will join and then constitute the 'necessary opposition' to overcome the 'one-sidedness' of the movement 'from within'."[2]

With the appearance of *Theologische Existenz* the growing opposition within the Protestant Church had secured for its intellectual leader the most distinguished theologian at that time in Germany, who could cut a clear path through the theological jungle, and view the political developments in the country with the detachment of one whose only

[1] Karl Barth, *Theologische Existenz, Heute*, I, pp. 5-6.
[2] *Theologische Existenz, Heute*, I, pp. 26-7.

nation was, and was truly, the Church of Christ. Meanwhile in the hand-to-hand mêlée, no distinct leader had yet arisen; but now the Council of Young Reformers acted on Barth's theological call to arms by commissioning Bonhoeffer and his colleague Herrmann Sasse to write a confession of faith for the growing movement which would place the "German Christians" in the dock and present them with a theological challenge. For this purpose the two withdrew to the remarkable Community of Bethel, to which the Principal, Fritz von Bodelschwingh, having resigned from his wholly untenable position of National Bishop, had now returned.

Bethel, built up by Friedrich von Bodelschwingh, father of Fritz, began as a hospital for epileptics. It has now grown into a Christian town, with its own churches and schools, its own farms, industries, and shops; but at the heart of the town the great hospitals for the epileptics still form its *raison d'être*. Bonhoeffer was visiting Bethel for the first time and, sensitive to atmosphere as he always was, he described in a letter to his grandmother his first experience of a service in Bethel Church:

"The time here in Bethel has made a great impression on me. Here there is simply a part of the Church, which understands what can be of importance for a Church and what cannot. I am just returned from a service. It is remarkable to see the crowds of epileptics and other sick filling the whole church, among them the male and female nurses, who must help if one falls, and then besides old tramps off the roads, the theology students, the children and pastors with their families; but nevertheless the scene is dominated by the sick, who listen with great devotion. Indeed for these people there must be an experience of life which is quite unusual, since they cannot be master of themselves and must be prepared every moment for their illness to seize them. At such moments I caught a glimpse of this for the first time. For this condition of being actually defenceless may perhaps reveal to these people certain actualities of our human existence, in which we are in fact basically defenceless, more clearly than can ever be possible for us who are healthy."

The letter ends with a comment upon his undertaking:

"Our work here gives us both trouble and pleasure. We want to attempt to extract from the German Christians some answer about their intentions. Whether we shall succeed is certainly very doubtful. For even if they nominally give some ground in their formulations, they are under such powerful pressure that sooner or later all promises must be overborne. It is becoming ever more evident to me that we are to be given a great popular national Church, whose nature cannot be reconciled with Christianity, and that we must prepare our minds for the entirely new paths which we shall then have to follow. The question is really: Christianity or Germanism? and the sooner the conflict is revealed in the clear light of day the better."[1]

The *Confession of Bethel* was completed in about three weeks, and it expressed the theological basis of the Church's struggle in clear and uncompromising terms. But when completed it was circulated for comment among some twenty theologians and, by the time they had prudently whittled away at it, it had lost its character of a battle cry. Bonhoeffer refused to append his signature to this emasculated version. Martin Niemöller, who was beginning to take a lead in the Church resistance, sent it out "in the name of a group of Protestant theologians", but with most of its teeth drawn, it soon became a dead letter. This was a bitter disappointment to Bonhoeffer, and contributed to his final decision to accept the appointment offered him at the Lutheran Church at Sydenham, on the outskirts of London, where he hoped he might gain a period for reflection and an opportunity to see his way ahead more clearly. By the time that the notorious "Brown Synod" had taken place, his decision to go to England had become definite. The "Brown Synod" was held on September 4th; it has been called "the Party Day of the Faith". It was a bitter day for the Church in Prussia. Amid scenes of popular enthusiasm the general superintendents responsible for local administration were deposed and replaced by ten German Christian "Bishops". All members of the Church administration not wholly sympathetic to the regime were removed. It was resolved to apply the Aryan Paragraph to the Church. Hitler's victory seemed complete.

As soon as the results of the Synod were known, a group of the Young Reformers, led by Niemöller, Bonhoeffer and Hildebrandt, met at the house of a young pastor, Gerhard Jacobi. Niemöller, Bonhoeffer and Hildebrandt pressed for a mass resignation of pastors and the setting up of a Free Church. This idea was not supported, but instead there was born the first organ of the Confessing Church, which was to fight for its freedom without creating a schism; this was the *Pfarrernotbund*, the Emergency League of Pastors. In its first form it was pledged to four points:

1 To renew allegiance to the Scriptures and the Creed.

2 to resist any attack upon them.

[1] *G.S.* II, pp. 77 *et seq.*

3 to give material and financial help to those who suffered through repressive laws or violence.

4 to repudiate the Aryan Paragraph.

On September 12th Niemöller sent out copies of this resolution to all sympathetic Prussian Pastors, together with a Protest drafted by himself and Bonhoeffer to be laid before the Prussian Synod. The response was overwhelming. To the twenty-two signatures with which the Protest went out, over two thousand more were added. The resistance within the Church was gathering form and content. But nevertheless, Bonhoeffer was beginning to feel within this movement a sense of the personal isolation which was by now familiar to him. Even Karl Barth, deeply involved though he now was in the theological struggle, failed to see the vital implications of the Aryan Paragraph, which Bonhoeffer alone understood as central. The Young Reformers, struggling with day-to-day problems, argued and hesitated, arriving at last under pressure from Niemöller and a few determined men at *ad hoc* decisions which might carry the struggle one step further, but without any clear sense of the immensity of the issues involved. Bonhoeffer saw the issues as absolute and immediate, and the Church as moving swiftly towards a future of appalling moral danger and almost limitless heroic opportunity. It was a vision which, in its comprehensive intensity, none could wholly share.

Meanwhile the many anxieties and practical demands of this restless year had prevented Bonhoeffer's attendance at a number of oecumenical conferences at which his presence would have been of great value. The German representatives who had attended had generally been concerned to show the upheaval within the German church in a favourable light. Bonhoeffer saw the need to attend one before the year ended, in order to make a more accurate statement of the facts. Accordingly he had put off the removal to his English pastorate long enough to enable him to attend the meeting of the World Alliance in Sofia in the second half of September. Here he described the true position with uncompromising clarity, and he himself, so indifferent heretofore to resolutions, was now instrumental in eliciting one. In response to his information the Conference put on record that: "We especially deplore the fact that the state measures against Jews in Germany have had such an effect on public opinion that in some circles the Jewish race is considered a race of inferior status. We protest against the resolution of the Prussian General Synod and of other Synods which apply the Aryan Paragraph of the state to the Church, putting serious disabilities on Ministers and Church Officers who by chance of birth are non-Aryan, which we believe to be a denial of the explicit teaching and spirit of the Gospel of Jesus Christ."[1]

Bonhoeffer returned in time to put up an ineffectual struggle with Hildebrandt at the overwhelmingly German-Christian election to the National Synod. Amid scenes of considerable emotion, Ludwig Müller was elected National Bishop. Three weeks later, Bonhoeffer was in England. Not till then could he bring himself to write to Karl Barth:

"Dear Herr Professor!

"Now I am writing you the letter, which I wanted to write six weeks ago, and which might have resulted in an entirely different course for my personal life. Why I did not write it then is now almost incomprehensible to me. I only know that two factors contributed. I knew that you were occupied with a thousand other things, and it seemed to me in those distracted weeks that the exterior fate of a single person was of such small concern, that I simply could not feel it important enough to write to you about it. But secondly I feel certain that there was some fear connected with it; I knew that I should have had to do whatever you said, and I wanted to remain free, so I simply withdrew myself. I know today that that was wrong, and that I should ask your pardon. For now I have made my decision 'freely', without being truly free in relation to you. I wanted to ask you whether or not I should go as a Pastor to London. I should simply have believed that you would give me the right answer, you and only you, with the exception of one other person[2] who was however so much concerned with my personal fate, that he was drawn into my own uncertainties . . .

"I cannot now write you the long list of all that was for and against, although I have not nearly finished wrestling with it yet, perhaps I never shall. I hope I did not leave simply out of irritation about conditions in the Church, and particularly about the attitude of our particular group. It would probably not have been long before I had had to make a formal break with my friends—but I really believe that that was a stronger argument against London than for it. If for such a decision one searches afterwards for definite reasons, I believe one of the strongest was that I simply no longer felt able to cope with all the problems and demands which faced me. I felt that unaccountably I stood in radical opposition to all my friends, I became ever more isolated in my view of the situation, although I remained personally in

[1] *Record of the Sofia Conference of the Council for Life and Work*, pp. 12–13.
[2] Hildebrandt.

a close relationship with these people—and all this made me anxious, I feared that self-justification might drive me off the rails—and at the same time I saw no reason to suppose that I should see these things clearer and better than many hard-working pastors whom I genuinely revere—and so I thought it was time to retire for a while into the desert and simply do pastoral work, as simply and humbly as possible. The danger of making, at this particular moment, an empty gesture, seemed greater than that of retiring into silence. And so it has come about. Besides this it seemed to me symptomatic that almost no understanding was shown for the Confession of Bethel, upon which I had co-operated with passion. I think I can truly say, that it did not upset me personally, there was no occasion at all for that. I simply felt spiritually uncertain of myself . . .

"It feels to me, in addition, as though by going away I had been personally unfaithful to you. You may not even be able to understand this. But for me it is a quite serious reality. And in the midst of all this I am infinitely happy to be in a parish, and quite tucked away. And then I also hope that here I shall really gain some light upon oecumenical problems. For I want to continue that work here. Perhaps by this means it will be possible really to stand by the German Church . . .

"Would you write me quite honestly your impression about all this? I think I could even accept a sharp rebuke readily and gratefully . . ."[1]

Bonhoeffer posted the letter, and waited in some trepidation for the reply.

Meanwhile in Berlin National Bishop Müller prepared for a spectacular enthronement.

"Old things are coming to an end," he announced to his exultant followers, "new things are beginning. The political battle for the Church has ended. The battle for the soul of the people begins."

Once more, he spoke more truly than he knew.

---

[1] *G.S.* II, pp. 130 *et seq.*

CHAPTER X

THE "sharp rebuke" came back promptly. It presented with characteristic intensity and passion all the arguments which might have persuaded Bonhoeffer to remain in Germany, and should now, in the view of Karl Barth, persuade him to return, if not by the next ship, then certainly "by the next ship but one". The letter came as no surprise to Bonhoeffer; his decision to withdraw for a time "into the wilderness" had been made in the teeth of the considerations which Barth presented, and the only unexpected factor consisted in the discovery that the withdrawal to England was not destined to provide the period for reflection which he had hoped to gain. During the next year he was to live simultaneously in two countries: in Germany with every problem, failure and achievement of the religious opposition, in England with all that was involved in interpreting the struggle and securing the strongest possible support for the resisting Church leaders. With the overflow of his energies he cared for the two small parishes which had become his charge, and it was typical of his capacity to live several lives at once and each of them completely, that in spite of his intense preoccupations they were not impoverished but enriched during the fifteen months of his pastorate.

His home during the period of this *intermezzo* was an uncomfortable Victorian house in Forest Hill. The main rooms of the house were occupied by a German school; Bonhoeffer lived on the second floor in a flat made habitable for him by a grand piano and some solid rocks of furniture from his home in Berlin. Around the house a large intractable garden was reverting to wilderness. Here Bonhoeffer perched like a bird of passage. Visitors from Germany came and went, forgetting physical discomfort in the delights of music, for which there was always, miraculously, time to spare, and in the intensities of conversation which always returned to the urgent central theme: the condition of the Church in Germany. A month after Bonhoeffer was established Franz Hildebrandt arrived and remained to share the rigours of this bachelor existence until in January he was recalled to Germany.

A less welcome visitor to England in the month of Bonhoeffer's arrival was the notorious "German Christian" Hossenfelder, now a leader in the official Church Government, who had contrived to secure an invitation through Frank Buchman's Oxford Group. He received a markedly cool reception from most of the leaders in the English Church, while Bonhoeffer's and Hildebrandt's outspoken criticisms contributed to his failure to impress his own countrymen. A few weeks after this fiasco in England, Hossenfelder was to take his part in a major event staged by the "German Christians", which came to be known later as "the Sport Palace Scandal". The Sport Palace was the great open-air stadium in Berlin where gymnastic and other displays took place. Here on November 13th the "German Christians" held a mass meeting of 20,000 of their followers, which has been vividly described by Dietmar Schmidt:

"Against the background of a rousing and highly unecclesiastical stage set of swastika-banners, placards, marches of the S.A., brass bands and community singing, a Berlin schoolmaster called Krause, having the rank of *gauobmann*[1] among the 'German Christians', pours forth invective against the Old Testament, which he defines as one of the most questionable books in world literature, on account of what he describes as its 'stories of horsedealing and bullying'. In the same spirit he denounces the 'scapegoat and guilt theology of the Rabbi Paul', which gives him a welcome opportunity to reject as heretical 'dialectic theology from Paul to Karl Barth' which he neither appreciates nor understands, describing it as an intellectual game. The radical would-be reformer of the German Church recommends as an alternative: 'return to the heroic Jesus' whom one may discover if one selects from the gospels 'all that speaks to our German heart' and which, 'and of this we may be proud, is entirely consistent with the demands of National Socialism!' "[2]

But this time the "German Christians" had overreached themselves, and there arose a spontaneous cry of protest throughout the whole of Protestant Germany. National Bishop Müller immediately drew in his horns. He withdrew his personal protection from the "German Christians" and disbanded the Ecclesiastical Ministry which Hossenfelder had led, replacing it with one which was anxious to achieve a compromise with the Church opposition. Meanwhile Hitler recognised the fact that he had lost the first round. He abandoned his original hope of forging the German Protestant Church into a powerful propaganda weapon, and quietly replaced it with the decision to undermine the

---

[1] This word represents a typical linguistic invention of the National Socialist regime, translatable roughly as "regional top man".

[2] Dietmar Schmidt, Martin Niemöller, p. *104*.

Church by any means that offered. Publicly he expressed himself as disappointed, and declared his intention of taking no further interest in the struggle.

For a time the ecclesiastical opposition in Germany were jubilant, but Bonhoeffer was not blind to the dangers of this apparent success. Long and intensive telephone conversations with Niemöller, adjuring him to stand firm, alternated with letters and telegrams, signed by Bonhoeffer and Hildebrandt together.

"Dear Brother Niemöller," ran a letter written on November 30th, the day when the fall of Hossenfelder's Ministry was announced, "We[1] should have liked to pick up the telephone again in order to fling ourselves upon you in a brotherly way with all the power of our youth, to implore you, in this decisive moment, not to hand over the navigation of the ship to people who will certainly revert to an indecisive course and only return the wheel to you when it is too late . . ."[2]

Four days later, when news of an argument within the ranks of the opposition had been relayed to Sydenham, a telegram followed the letter:

"Staggered to hear of split in Brothers' Council stop exclusion of Jacobi from discussions would force us resign immediately and invalidate imminent accession German pastors in England Jacobi as wisest should be promoted stop away with futile compromise why flight from responsibility with brotherly greetings the Londoners."[3]

More letters followed the telegram and a legend exists in Sydenham that Bonhoeffer's telephone bill was so high at the end of the first quarter that the Post Office reduced it on compassionate grounds. The effort to live in two countries at once would have told heavily upon a weaker spirit, but Bonhoeffer's thoughts were never so intensely preoccupied with Germany that he failed to be effective in England.

At a meeting of the German Protestant Ministers held at Bradford-on-Avon from November 27th to 30th, this young man who could still at times look no older than an undergraduate early established his ascendency over the sedate, unimpressionable gathering of middle-aged pastors. He secured unanimous agreement to a letter which was sent to National Bishop Müller in the name of all the Pastors assembled at Bradford, expressing anxiety as to his policy and hinting that it might lead to a loosening of the ties which bound the overseas Churches to the Church of their homeland. To have secured unanimous support for

[1] Bonhoeffer and Hildebrandt.
[2] *G.S.* II, p. 149.
[3] *G.S.* II, p. 150.

even so moderate a protest represents a real *tour de force* on the part of the young newcomer. To say that the majority of the pastors in England were without his political insight is a considerable understatement of the facts. An extract from one pastor's letter represents quite fairly the attitude which then prevailed:

"I spent two years in the front line, I fought and bled for my Fatherland. Many of my best friends, fighting at my side, gave their lives in the service of the Fatherland . . . In my youthful enthusiasm I accepted their death as a sacred charge to us . . . to go on fighting, so that their death for Germany might not be in vain and forgotten. But what did Germany become? A land of injustice and corruption, at the mercy of her black and her red rulers.[1] As a pastor it was not my duty to take part in party political activities. . . . Then the National Socialist Party came to the helm, which did not wish to be a party, which offered a programme that possessed a moral and religious basis. And so I became a member of the movement. Also for another reason. It became evident to me that the lower orders within the movement could not be filled with the deep morality and religious sense of the Führer or permeated with his ideas, that many simply wanted to exchange a red heart for a brown one, that unconscientious hustlers wanted to make use of the upsurge of the movement for their own purposes in order to secure positions of influence— I see the movement of the 'German Christians' as nothing less than this —the result might be, that the proclamation of the gospel was hindered and that thereby the only possible basis for the rebuilding of the Fatherland was withdrawn . . . so it seems to me a necessity for the sake of the Church of Christ and of the community of the nation to co-operate with this in view. That one can do this better if one is a member of the party, is manifest . . ."[2]

It was with men many of whom were in this state of confused political emotion that Bonhoeffer had to deal. It is the more remarkable that he succeeded in leading the majority of them step by step into increasingly outspoken opposition to the policy of the National Church. It was as a direct result of Bonhoeffer's concern to convey a true picture of the internal struggle of the German Church to the Oecumenical Movement that his acquaintance with Bishop Bell, Chairman of the Council for Life and Work, now began to ripen into a friendship. Before he had

---

[1] The "black" rulers would represent the members of the Centrum, the Catholic party and therefore assumed to be priest-ridden, the "red" rulers would be the Socialists.

[2] E.B., *D.B.*, pp. 386–7.

been in England three weeks, Bonhoeffer had been invited to visit Bell in Chichester.

The visit was the first of many, which were always made primarily for the purpose of keeping the Bishop informed on the current situation in Germany. Bonhoeffer soon gained a filial affection for this great-hearted statesman of the Church, and Bell for his part valued the integrity and acuteness of mind of this passionate young German, who saw the struggle as a struggle for the purity of the Christian faith itself, transcending national boundaries. With the humility of a great man, Bell allowed himself to be informed and even instructed, gaining an insight into the issues involved which was second to that of no other man outside Germany. Temperamentally the two men were naturally drawn to one another, and the aspects of English life which the Bishop re-vealed made a natural appeal to the young visitor. The unselfconscious dignity of the Athenaeum and of the palace at Chichester, the casual good manners, the respect for privacy and the built-in emotional restraint of English society, echoed the tastes with which Bonhoeffer had grown up. But he had only intermittent opportunity to abandon himself to the graces of England; Germany continued to command his attention. On January 4th the telephone line from Berlin again carried disturbing news, and two days later it appeared in *The Times* for all to read:

"The *Deutsche Allegemeine Zeitung* states that tomorrow's issue of the *Church Gazette*, which will reach all pastors in the course of the day, contains an order of the Primate forbidding all public discussions of Church policies ... All holders of Church office are forbidden to attack the Church Government or its measures in public, by leaflet, or in any other way. Infringement of these orders will be punished by suspension, and disciplinary proceedings with a view to removal from office will be started immediately against the offender ..."[1]

Bonhoeffer was in action at once. Rallying the German pastors of London he instigated a telegram to the Church government in Berlin:

"Following today's article in Times extremely anxious as to connec-tion of local congregations with home Church request clarification of position German Pastors London."[2]

The same day came a copy of a memorandum circulated by the Emergency League intended to be read aloud from the pulpit, in which hearers were encouraged not to obey the new regulations, and a loss of

[1] *The Times*, January 6th 1934.
[2] *G.S.* II, p. 396.

135

confidence in the National Bishop was clearly expressed. Another telegram was soon on its way to the Church Government:

"For the sake of Gospel and our conscience associate ourselves with protest of Emergency League and withdraw confidence from National Bishop Müller German Pastors London."[1]

A letter followed to President Hindenburg with copies to Hitler, the National Bishop and three leading Ministers. The protests from England seem to have caused some concern to the National Church, and Heckel, an old acquaintance of Bonhoeffer's who was now in charge of the Ecclesiastical Foreign Ministry, began to consider a visit to England to silence the opposition. Meanwhile however a peculiar event was to take place in Berlin, characteristic of Hitler's curious political methods.

A group of pastors and church leaders were invited to meet him personally at the Chancellory, ostensibly with a view to restoring peace and friendship in the Church. A proportion of the members of the Emergency League were invited, with Niemöller as their spokesman. The date was finally fixed for January 25th.

Bonhoeffer, in his exile in England, waited with little except anxiety. His intense critical insight and capacity to see further than any of his comrades in arms increased his sense of isolation. The pain and loneliness of the prophets of Israel was a reality which he understood vividly from his own experience. On January 21st he preached from the text in Jeremiah 20:7, "Oh Lord, thou hast deceived me and I was deceived, thou art stronger than I and hast prevailed." In Luther's version the Hebrew word translated in the Authorised Version as "deceived" is given as "*überredet*" "persuaded against my will." "Oh Lord, thou hast persuaded me against my will, thou art stronger than I." Bonhoeffer was entering a phase of his life when again and again this sense of being under divine pressure would overwhelm him.

"God," cries Jeremiah and Bonhoeffer with him, "You have made a beginning in me. You have lain in wait for me and have not let me escape, have suddenly stood before me in this place or that, have lured and enchanted me, have made my heart pliable and willing, have spoken to me of your longing and your eternal love, of your faithfulness and power; when I sought strength, you strengthened me, when I needed support you upheld me, when I sought forgiveness you forgave my sin. I did not want it, but you overcame my will, my resistance and my heart, you seduced me irresistibly so that I gave myself up to you. Lord, you have

[1] *G.S.* II, p. 158.

persuaded me against my will, and I have been persuaded. You took hold of me all unsuspecting, and now I cannot get away from you . . ."[1]

The day after this sermon was delivered, Hildebrandt returned to Berlin to act as curate to Niemöller at Berlin-Dahlem, and to help him in prosecuting the Church struggle. Bonhoeffer was left alone to hold the fort in England.

And now the fateful day arrived in Berlin. There had been a good deal of plotting and planning and manoeuvring for position among the rival Church leaders, and some injudicious telephone calls had been exchanged. But when the delegation entered the Presence, the atmosphere appeared favourable. The Chancellor received all the members affably and spoke with disarming moderation of his hopes that peace might be restored in the Church. Then, at a moment which one can only assume to have been prearranged, Göring hurried in and asked to speak to the Chancellor. A telephone conversation had been intercepted, between Pastor Niemöller and another leader of the opposition in which Niemöller had said: "We have laid our mines well, the Ministry of the Interior is in a favourable state, the President will receive the Chancellor beforehand and give him the final anointing. But if we still achieve nothing, we may yet dive off into a free Church."

Accounts of what followed vary. But it seems that Hitler reacted with restraint, assuming the character of an upright father of his country, betrayed by the underhand methods of men whom he was only anxious to help. It seems that the members of the opposition, caught at a disadvantage, confused and embarrassed, and mesmerised by the uncanny fascination which Hitler's immediate presence notoriously exercised, did little more throughout the remainder of the interview than assure him of their personal loyalty. All the bishops present, including those who had hitherto supported the opposition, swung in behind the Church government and the National Bishop, making a declaration of loyalty, "under the impression," as they added, "of that great hour, in which the leaders of the German Protestant Church were assembled with the Chancellor." Müller seized the opportunity to tighten his hold upon the Church; a shower of new regulations poured out from his ministry, and a large number of opposition pastors were suspended from office, Niemöller among them.

Then, in the second week of February, Heckel's projected visit to London took place. Himself an able, persuasive and moderate man, he

[1] Sermon delivered to congregation at Sydenham, January 21st 1934, unpublished.

made a long report to the assembled pastors in which the Müller regime was shown in as favourable a light as possible. He painted for their benefit his own vivid picture of what had happened on January 25th. He warned the assembled pastors against succumbing to the influence of the foreign press, and indicated that opposition to Müller was now equivalent to opposition to the state. The pastors remained unimpressed, and headed by Bonhoeffer they pressed him to comment upon Krause's rejection of the Old Testament, the withdrawal of the freedom of the religious press and the vacillating policy of Müller, who after once annulling the Aryan Paragraph in the Church had now reinstated it. Heckel was unable to satisfy them on any of these points, and after a day of unsatisfactory debating, when he endeavoured to secure their promise that they would not interfere with the interior affairs of their home Church, he produced a declaration of loyalty to the National Bishop and approached the subject of their signing it. With a single exception, none was willing to do so.

An interview with Bishop Bell was no more successful. Heckel was soon on the defensive against an uncompromising and well-informed opponent. Heckel pressed on with his commission, representing the Bishop's concern for the Church in Germany as an unwarrantable interference in the internal affairs of another country. Bell refused to be drawn by this and categorically rejected the suggestion that he should observe at least a six months' truce. Heckel returned to Germany without having accomplished anything, and his statement in the press that his visit to Bishop Bell had led to mutual understanding and had been a valuable oecumenical occasion was politely but firmly refuted by the Bishop in a letter to *The Times* on February 10th. For the complete failure of his visit to England, Heckel rightly believed he had Bonhoeffer chiefly to thank. He was aware, not only of the young man's influence over the German pastors, but also of his growing intimacy with Bishop Bell, and finally, before Bonhoeffer himself knew of it, he had received information that the Archbishop of Canterbury wished to question Bonhoeffer about conditions in the German Church.

He accordingly summoned the recalcitrant pastor to appear before him at the offices of the Ecclesiastic Foreign Office in Berlin. The Foreign Office had received orders "to bring the care of the Protestant diaspora and the contacts between the German Protestant Church and friendly Churches abroad into an organisational unity". On this account he asked Bonhoeffer to sign an undertaking to abstain from oecumenical activities which were not authorised from Berlin, indicating that failure to do so might be regarded as "involvement with foreign intervention in the internal affairs of Germany", and might therefore be dangerous to himself.

Bonhoeffer agreed to consider it, and meanwhile he seized the opportunity to take part in a "Free Synod" of his own Church of Berlin Brandenburg in which the decision was made to call a further Free Synod of all Protestant Germany to consider the theological foundations of the opposition movement. This was to be the famous Synod of Barmen. A few days later Bonhoeffer wrote to Heckel from England saying that he could not sign the undertaking and, far from withdrawing, he now plunged more deeply than ever into oecumenical activities.

In August the biennial meeting of the Universal Christian Council for Life and Work was to take place at Fanø in Denmark, and Bonhoeffer, as one of the three secretaries of the Youth Commission, would receive an invitation. He had also been asked before the Church struggle began in Germany to prepare a paper to read before the whole Council on "The Church and the World of Nations". Now his mind turned firmly in the direction of securing oecumenical intervention in support of the German Church opposition, and in a manner not at all in keeping with his normal polite reserve, he set himself to pursue Bishop Bell. In English which staggered a little under the weight of his emotions, he now wrote:

"My Lord Bishop, May I just let you know, that I was called last week again to Berlin—this time by the Church government. The subject was the oecumenic situation. I also saw Niemöller, Jacobi, and some friends from the Rhineland. The Free Synod in Berlin was a real progress and success. We hope to get ready for a Free National Synod until 18th of April in Barmen. One of the most important things is that the Christian Churches of the other countries do not lose their interest in the conflict by the length of time. I know that my friends are looking to you and your further actions with great hope. There is really a moment now as perhaps never before in Germany in which our faith into the oecumenic task of the Churches can be shakened and destroyed completely or strengthened and renewed in a surprisingly new way. And it is you, My Lord Bishop, on whom it depends whether this moment shall be used. The question at stake in the German Church is no longer an internal issue but is the question of existence of Christianity in Europe; therefore a definite attitude of the oecumenic Movement has nothing to do with 'intervention'—but it is just a demonstration to the whole world that Church and Christianity as such are at stake. Even if the information of the newspaper is becoming of less interest, the real situation is as tense, as acute, as responsible as ever before. I shall only wish you would see one of the meetings of the Emergency League now—it is always in spite of all gravity of the present moments a real uplift to one's own faith and courage—Please, do not be silent now!"[1]

As the opposition pastors in Germany prepared for the Barmen Synod, letters passed swiftly to and fro between Bell and Bonhoeffer. At last, on May 10th, a message went out from the Bishop to the representatives of all the Churches on the Council for Life and Work, which had a considerable effect upon oecumenical opinion, and became widely known as the Ascensiontide message. It was Bell's carefully considered response to Bonhoeffer's appeals, and to the requests of many of the participants for guidance on this perplexing issue.

"I have been urged from many quarters," so the letter ran, "to issue some statement to my fellow members of the Universal Christian Council for Life and Work upon the present position in the German Evangelical Church, especially as it affects other Churches represented on the Universal Christian Council for Life and Work.

"The situation is, beyond doubt, full of anxiety. To estimate it aright, we have to remember the fact that a revolution has taken place in the German State, and that as a necessary result the German Evangelical Church was bound to be faced with new tasks and many new problems requiring time for their full solution. It is none the less true that the present position is being watched by members of the Christian Churches abroad not only with great interest, but with a deepening concern. The chief cause of anxiety is the assumption by the Reichsbishop in the name of the principle of leadership of autocratic powers unqualified by constitutional or traditional restraints which are without precedent in the history of the Church. The exercise of these autocratic powers by the Church government appears incompatible with the Christian principle of seeking in brotherly fellowship to receive the guidance of the Holy Spirit. It has had disastrous results on the internal unity of the Church; and the disciplinary measures which have been taken by the Church government against Ministers of the Gospel on account of their loyalty to the fundamental principles of Christian truth have made a painful impression on Christian opinion abroad, already disturbed by the introduction of racial distinctions in the universal fellowship of the Christian Church. No wonder that voices

[1] *G.S.* I, p. 184.

should be raised in Germany itself making a solemn pronouncement before the whole Christian world on the dangers to which the spiritual life of the Evangelical Church is exposed.

"There are indeed other problems which the German Evangelical Church is facing, which are the common concern of the whole of Christendom. These are such fundamental questions as those respecting the nature of the Church, its witness, its freedom and its relation to the secular power. At the end of August the Universal Council will be meeting in Denmark. The Agenda of the Council will inevitably include a consideration of the religious issues raised by the present situation in the German Evangelical Church. It will also have to consider the wider questions which affect the life of all the Churches in Christendom. A Committee met last month in Paris to prepare for its work, and its report will shortly be published entitled, *The Church, the State, and the World Order*. I hope that this meeting will assist the Churches in their friendship with each other, and in their task of reaching a common mind on the implications of their faith in relation to the dominant tendencies in modern thought and society, and in particular to the growing demands of the modern State.

"The times are critical. Something beyond conferences and consultations is required. We need as never before to turn our thoughts and spirits to God. More earnest efforts must be made in our theological study. Above all more humble and fervent prayer must be offered to our Father in Heaven. May He, Who alone can lighten our darkness, give us grace! May He, Who knows our weakness and our blindness, through a new outpouring of the Spirit enable the whole Church to bear its witness to its Lord with courage and faith!

"(Signed) George Cicestr   "Ascensiontide 1934
                              "(10 May 1934)"[1]

Three weeks later opposition pastors from all northern and central Germany met at the Synod of Barmen in Prussia. They firmly took their stand upon the Constitution of the original Federation of the Protestant Churches in Germany recognised by the Reich Government in 1933. They boldly claimed that they represented the true Protestant Church of Germany continuous since the Reformation, and made a confession of their faith which had been drawn up by Karl Barth. Of this great document Bishop Bell wrote: "It burst like a thunderbolt in the very middle of the National Socialist campaign to unify the

[1] *G.S.* I, pp. 192–3.

Church by means of force, corruption and insincere practices."[1]

The Declaration consists of six lucid statements, of which the first and the last contain the essence of the whole:

"Jesus Christ, as He is testified to us in Holy Scripture, is the one Word of God which we have to hear, and which we have to trust and obey in life and death . . .

"The Church's commission, on which freedom is founded, is this: in Christ's stead, and so in the service of His Word and work, to deliver, by means of preaching and sacrament, to all men, the message of the Free Grace of God."

And with this claim and this declaration of faith, the Confessing Church of Germany was born.

Bonhoeffer saw it as his immediate task to secure oecumenical recognition for this Church as the true Protestant Church of Germany, and wrote to Hans Schönfeld, German representative at the Secretariat for the Council for Life and Work at Geneva, asking that it should be invited to send representatives. H. L. Henriod, secretary to the Council, answered that the delegates were already chosen, and pointed out the legal and political difficulties in the way of inviting representatives from a Church which had not offered itself for official recognition. Bonhoeffer turned to Bishop Bell, and Bell, after consultation with his colleagues, invited Präces Koch, the leader of the Confessing Church in Westphalia, to come as an individual adviser, bringing a second representative. Bonhoeffer, who had at first resigned his place in the Conference in protest against the inclusion of the official German delegation, was now persuaded to remain on the list of representatives. In the event Koch did not venture to accept the invitation, and Bonhoeffer was left to represent the Confessing Church alone.

While these letters were being exchanged, political events were racing forward in Germany.

On July 2nd, Bonhoeffer opened his *Times* to be confronted with the astonishing headlines:

Herr Hitler's Coup
A Midnight Descent on Munich
General von Schleicher and his wife shot dead
Arrest and Execution of S.A. Leaders

The Roehm massacre was under way. On July 3rd *The Times* leading article commented:

[1] Significance of the Barmen Declaration for the Oecumenical Church. Foreword to *Theology, Occasional Papers*, New Series No. 5.

"An official announcement issued yesterday in Berlin proclaims that: 'law and order prevail throughout the Reich. The whole nation stands with unprecedented enthusiasm behind the Leader' . . .

"In Berlin and Munich the grim events of the weekend appear to have been followed with intense curiosity, but also with a certain cynical detachment which is deeply significant. Economic distress and long-term political unrest have weakened the moral fibre of the nation. The prolonged sporadic warfare between Nazi and Communist which preceded the Hitler regime, with its almost daily tale of violent collision and cold-blooded murder had the effect of dulling all normal sensitiveness, and since then there has been little to restore respect for the old standards of civilised life . . .

"The brutal persecution of all who were suspected of disaffection, or who for any reason were regarded as outside the pale; the suppression of all freedom of speech and even, so far as possible, of all freedom of thought; the plague of spies and informers who infested the land and made every man suspicious of his neighbour, the waves of intense propaganda by speech and wireless and cinema to keep people in a state of almost hysterical emotion; the preaching of eccentric pagan doctrines and the constant glorification of force and violence—all these things have helped to widen the gulf which separates Germany today from other western nations . . ."

The majority of the Lutheran pastors in England, impervious to these comments from a foreign press, responded with the required amount of "unprecedented enthusiasm". But, on the following Sunday, while paeans of praise and thanksgiving for another deliverance of the Fatherland were ascending from many pulpits, Bonhoeffer was reacting characteristically and in depth. In a disjointed but powerful sermon, he was calling his flock to repentance. He took for his texts St. Luke's story of the Galileans, whose blood Pilate mingled with their sacrifices, and the reference to the men on whom the town of Siloam fell, and then he lauched forth:

"Think ye? . . . No! But except ye repent ye shall all likewise perish . . . Siloam . . . What is going on here? Jesus does, on the strength of this judgement, what he has done throughout his life, he calls to repentance. God is here—therefore repent. For Jesus this shattering 'newspaper report' of the terrible event in the temple is nothing else than a fresh and inescapable call from God to repent, and that all who hear it should return to Him. For Him it is nothing less than a concrete and living illustration of His message: that man must humble himself before the mystery and power of God, and repent and admit that God is just.

"Now the situation grows dangerous. Now we are no longer spectators, observers, judges of this event. Now we ourselves are addressed, it concerns us. For us this has happened, it is we who are meant, God is speaking to us."[1]

Upon the fearful events of June 30th and July 1st, more was to follow. A few weeks later came the murder of Dollfuss, and on August 2nd the death of Hindenburg was followed by the decision, made by Hitler and applauded by the nation, to combine in himself the functions of Chancellor and President, under the official title of "*Der Führer*". While the fateful plebiscite was being held, the meetings of the Council for Life and Work and of the World Alliance were taking place in Fanø. Bonhoeffer alone, and unofficially, represented the Confessing Church at the meetings of the Council. But in the Youth Commission a group of young men was gathered round him, many of whom would later fight by his side in the Church struggle. One of these, Otto Dudzus, has written:

"Bonhoeffer's contribution both to the theme [of the Conference] and also to the direction taken, can hardly be estimated highly enough. He effectively saw to it that it did not turn into an ineffectual academic discussion."[2]

There is no doubt that the Conference represented a landmark in the development of oecumenical co-operation. The meeting of the Council at Fanø "stands out as perhaps the most critical and decisive meeting of its history. Here the Council solemnly resolved to throw its weight on the side of the Confessing Church in Germany against the so-called 'German Christians', and by implication against the Nazi regime."[3]

The clear and unequivocal nature of this decision seems to have been achieved through the clearcut statesmanlike leadership of the Chairman, Bishop Bell, and the tireless work of Bonhoeffer in all discussions and behind the scenes. At the final session of the Council a determined resolution on the subject of the German Church was carried in a combined session of the Council for Life and Work and the World Alliance. The core of the Resolution ran as follows:

"The Council declares its conviction that autocratic Church rule, especially when imposed upon the conscience in solemn oath, the use of

[1] Sermon on Luke 13: 1–5 preached at Sydenham, July 8th 1934: unpublished.
[2] *Begegnungen*, p. 71.
[3] Rouse and Neill, *History of the Oecumenical Movement*, p. 583.

methods of force, and the suppression of free discussion, are incompatible with the true nature of the Christian Church, and asks in the name of the Gospel for its fellow Christians in the German Church:

"Freedom to preach the Gospel of our Lord Jesus Christ and to live according to His teaching;

"Freedom of the printed word and of Assembly in the service of the Christian Community;

"Freedom for the Church to instruct its youth in the principles of Christianity and immunity from the compulsory imposition of a philosophy of life antagonistic to the Christian religion."[1]

Explanations, protestations and requests that the Council would refrain from interference in Germany's internal affairs had been delivered at intervals throughout the week by Bishop Heckel, as spokesman for the official German delegation. They had failed to evoke a response from the delegates, but now he succeeded in securing a small amendment to the resolution which went almost unnoticed at the time, but which kept a wedge in the door for the official German Church, so that till the outbreak of the war they could never be excluded from participation, with the result that Fanø was the last full-scale conference in which Bonhoeffer was willing to take part.

Of the paper on "The Church and the World of Nations" which he delivered to a joint session of the Christian Council and the World Alliance, no copy remains, but it seems from the preliminary notes which he sent to Schönfeld at Geneva that he confined himself to a consideration of the Church's attitude to war. An address given at one of the daily gatherings for morning prayers has been preserved. It was a passionate call to the Christian Churches to be daring in the cause of peace. He spoke in the same vein to an informal gathering which met daily for prayer during the Conference:

"There is no way to peace along the way of safety. For peace must be dared. It is the great venture. It can never be made safe. Peace is the opposite of security. To demand guarantees is to distrust, and this distrust in turn brings further war. To look for guarantees is to want to protect oneself. Peace means to give oneself altogether to the law of God, wanting no security, but in faith and obedience laying the destiny of the nations in the hand of Almighty God, not trying to direct it for selfish purposes. Battles are won not with weapons, but with God. They are won where the way leads to the cross. Which of us can claim

[1] *Universal Christian Council for Life and Work, Minutes of the Meeting at Fanø,* August 24th-30th 1934, p. 51.

to know what it might not mean for the world if one nation should meet the aggressor, not with weapons in hand, but praying, defenceless, and for that very reason protected by 'a bulwark never failing'?"[1]

In spite of Bonhoeffer's strenuous participation in the conference, he still, characteristically, found plenty of time for recreation with the friends and university students who had gathered round him at the meetings of the youth Commission. Nor did the seriousness of the occasion blind him to its lighter aspects. Otto Dudzus treasures a scrap of paper which Bonhoeffer slid along the table to him during one extensive speech by a corpulent father of the Eastern Church. Upon it is written a couplet by Christian Morgenstern:

> *"Ein dickes Kreuz auf dickem Bauch,*
> *Wer spürte nicht der Gottheit Hauch?"*[2]

In the autumn which followed the Fanø Conference, the situation in the German Church continued to develop. On October 6th Bishop Wurm of Würtemberg was placed under house arrest for refusing to take the required measures to bring his diocese into line with the National Church. A week later, the same fate befell Bishop Meiser of Bavaria. This accelerated the calling of a second national synod at Dahlem. The synod took place on 19th and 20th, and the outcome was an explicit rejection of the wholly irregular government of the new National Church, and the setting up of an independent government for the Confessing Church. Henceforth the Confessing Church was to be governed by a *Reichsbruderrat*, a National Council of Brothers, with a local council, the local *Bruderrat*, in each area; they were to work entirely without reference to the official Church. The resolution which brought them into existence concluded:

"We urge the Christian Congregations, together with their Pastors and Presbyters, not to accept any directions from the existing Church Government or its agencies and to withold co-operation from those who continue to give obedience to this ecclesiastical regime. We urge you to acknowledge the rule of the Confessing Church and its institutions."

The opposition had now, under the pressure of events, achieved two acts of great courage. At the Synod of Barmen it had laid fairly and squarely the theological foundations of its struggle, and come into being as the Confessing Church, now at Dahlem, it fearlessly repudiated the authority of the official Church government, and openly asserted its own, setting up the machinery which should make it effective. From hence-

[1] *G.S.* I, p. 448.
[2] "A portly cross on portly breast, Here surely must the Spirit rest?"

forth these two achievements were to represent the principles by its adherence or non-adherence to which, the Confessing Church would have to be judged.

The resolutions of the Synod of Dahlem caused a considerable flutter even in government circles. The two Bishops were released, the Protestant Churches of Bavaria and Württemberg were no further molested. Only in the North German Churches did the battle continue. But now some elements in the Church resistance were weakened by its very success. The hope that the new government of the Confessing Church might be officially recognised began to bedevil the issue. With this in mind, the new executive body to be known as the V.K.L.[1] was carefully composed of mild men who were willing to compromise, and this once more strengthened the resolve of the Nazi government. They had been impressed in spite of themselves by the original act of courage; they were not impressed by this gesture of compromise.

But the hopes for an easy solution were not universal. The new *Bruderrat* of the Old Prussian Union continued to act with independence, and it now resolved to set up a number of seminaries for the training of confessing pastors, and a letter was sent to Bonhoeffer to ask whether he would return to Germany to take over the direction of one of these in Pomerania. He replied that he would consider returning in the spring. In the meantime he set to work to bring the German congregations in England into line with the latest development. On November 5th representatives from almost all the German congregations in England met at Christchurch, Sydenham, and resolved to take their stand with the Confessing Church, and a letter to that effect went to the Church Government, couched in terms which safeguarded the still prevailing loyalty to Hitler, but which nevertheless stated the pastors' adherence to the Confessing Church in no uncertain terms. Heckel, well aware that Bonhoeffer was behind this determined move, tried to divide the ranks by insisting that each congregation must express its determination independently. Even so, few wavered. Their almost complete unanimity was Bonhoeffer's last achievement in England for the Confessing Church; for now his thoughts were turning in other directions.

At the end of this year he made one last attempt to prosecute his plan of visiting India. Through Bishop Bell he had received a personal invitation from Gandhi to spend some time with him in his *ashram*. At last India seemed almost within his reach. But then the pressures to

[1] *Vorläufige Kirchenleitung*, Provisional Church Government.

147

return to Germany became too urgent. Bonhoeffer accepted the invitation to become the first Director of the new seminery to be set up in Pomerania, only asking for enough time to visit one or two religious communities in England before he left, and with a colleague, Julius Rieger, he visited the communities at Mirfield and Kelham. He took back from this brief visit to the monasteries impressions which went deep and would considerably influence his handling of the new task which awaited him in Germany.

The visits to the monasteries could be only brief, but for Bonhoeffer they provided the first glimpse of a country for which he had been seeking. His search for spiritual concentration and Christian discipleship had prepared him to appreciate the power of life lived in community; what he had hoped to find in Gandhi's *ashram* he now began to find within the framework of his own faith. Not only the life of fellowship lived in mutual charity, but also some elements in its outward pattern, made an immediate appeal to him. The sacrosanct hours of offices, the meditative singing of the psalms and the unfailing observance of the hours of corporate silence impressed their value upon him. Here too he beheld for the first time since his months in Rome a life in which the observance of every day was centred round the Mass. With his capacity to receive deep impressions quickly, he gathered all that he saw into his heart and mind, and added these practical lessons to the spiritual lessons which he had been learning through those profound meditations on the Sermon on the Mount which he had begun during his first year of disillusionment in pre-Nazi Berlin, and which he had continued into his London years.

He wrote to his friend Sutz asking him how he preached upon the subject, confessing that he often attempted it himself, very plainly and simply, and expressing his conviction that it was only in the light of the Sermon on the Mount that the struggle within the Church would be resolved. Meanwhile these demands of Christ, at once gentle and stringent, revolutionary and simple, were becoming for Bonhoeffer himself the increasingly solid basis for his thought and action. This steady attempt to follow Jesus was supported by the inspiration of the daily reading and prayer which was now a discipline never omitted, and whose power was penetrating ever deeper into the hidden roots of his life, to issue more and more frequently as the years went by in the direct and powerful insights which so often set him apart from those who were not capable of this kind of perception. These insights, often criticised and rejected in his own day, often misunderstood and misappropriated in our own, were like the overflow from an underground river, that deep secret flow of his soul's development which would roll forward strongly and steadily to the end, beneath all the exterior chaos and destruction of hopes and achievements which now lay in wait for him only a few years ahead. Now, after his eighteen months in England, he was returning into a world of tyranny and intrigue to which his exterior life would fall victim again and again, until at last, in death, it went down to total defeat. But within this dark and violent setting the victory of his spirit would shine the brighter, blazing forth at last as the fruit of this very tragedy.

CHAPTER XI

IN January 1935, Bonhoeffer wrote to his brother Karl Friedrich: "The restoration of the Church must surely come from a new kind of monasticism, which will have only one thing in common with the old, a life lived without compromise according to the Sermon on the Mount in the following of Jesus. I believe the time has come to gather people together for this."[1] Six months later, in the country manor house of Finkenwalde, he had begun upon this task.

When the Confessing Church gave Bonhoeffer the commission to create and direct one of the handful of seminaries for the training of young pastors which they had resolved to set up, they doubtless wished for a normal, conventional establishment which differed from those officially provided only in the purity of the theology taught there. If this was what they hoped for, they were to be disappointed.

They were, however, not wholly unaware that the appointment of Dietrich Bonhoeffer to his new post carried, from the point of view of conformity, certain indefinable risks. In particular, his theological convictions could never quite be contained within an established framework. He was a Barthian—or was he? He was as passionately concerned to guard the understanding of God's absolute supremacy as any Barthian could be, and yet he seemed in unexpected ways to break out of the mould; sometimes he would seem to be using a language which came out of an altogether different world and which was rooted in insights remote from any experience common to the members of the *Bruderrat*.

To counteract these unpredictable tendencies, the *Bruderrat* took care with their second appointment. The director of a German seminary has for his second-in-command an "Inspector of Studies", who is not left without opportunities of inspecting the director himself. This post was given to a young pastor named Wilhelm Rott. Rott was an orthodox Barthian, firm, reliable and not wholly free from prejudice. It says much for the character of these two men, and for the power of their mutual charity, that they worked admirably together, Rott never losing his independence of mind, Bonhoeffer never hampered by Rott's critical attention.

[1] *G.S.* III, p. 25.

Having received their instructions, the two young men set out to find a home for the proposed seminary. It was to fall under the jurisdiction of the Confessing Church in Pomerania, and the aim was to find a home for it in some inconspicuous country village not too remote from Stettin, the headquarters of the Pomeranian *Bruderrat*.

The first weeks were spent at Zingst, on the shores of the Baltic Sea, where an institution known as the "Bible Circles of the Rhineland" had a somewhat ramshackle conference centre. Some of the first classes and discussion groups took place among the dunes, with the wind whistling through the coarse grass, and the sea beating in the background its continuous refrain. In June, however, a more permanent home was found in a rambling country house outside the small village of Finkenwalde, first stop on the line going East from Stettin. It had last been a school, but now it stood empty and half-derelict, waiting for occupation. Its condition might have daunted a less ardent pair than Bonhoeffer and Rott, but they were of a calibre to make light of practical problems; they took the house, and the group of young men who had begun their life together at Zingst transferred it to this more substantial establishment.

The spirit which the moment created must have been an exceptionally fertile one. These young men all knew what it was to suffer—frustration, repression, enmity, even personal danger. Four had been turned out of a theological college in Wittenberg because of their refusal to compromise with the official line. All were ready to sacrifice themselves in order to guard the purity of the faith; at the same time they were young, healthy and boisterous. So that these first weeks at Finkenwalde must have uniquely combined the atmosphere of a deeply serious enterprise with that of a glorious lark.

The young men arrived to find very little in the house and little money to spend on it. A contingent was deployed to dig the garden and plant vegetables, another to paint and scrub the rooms, a third to tour the surrounding district on begging expeditions. Amid laughter, repartee and musical impromptu singing, the work went forward. Cartloads of produce trundled in from neighbouring estates. Loads of large solid country furniture arrived to fill the rooms. By some magic means, two grand pianos appeared. Some of the students had brought their instruments. In a few days an orchestra had formed. Bonhoeffer went to Berlin and fetched his entire library for the students' use. The first course was ready to begin.

And now the young men received a considerable shock. For they found themselves precipitated without ceremony into Bonhoeffer's "new kind of monasticism".

First of all a rule was established. The day began with half an hour of common prayer: antiphonal repetition of the psalms, lessons from the Old and New Testaments, two chorals, one Gregorian chant and finally an extempore prayer. Breakfast followed, and after breakfast, most alarming surprise of all, the students found that they were to meditate for half an hour in silence upon a passage of scripture, which was set for the whole week. Then followed a morning of study; homiletics, exegesis and the groundwork of dogmatics, then lunch, recreation, further study and after supper an evening of relaxation, music, reading aloud or games. The day ended with a further half-hour of common prayer, after which complete silence was required until breakfast time, the next morning.

The loudest outcry was against the period for meditation. What, the young men asked, were they to *do* with this silent half-hour? Might they smoke? Might they get on with their reading? Might they clean their shoes? No, Bonhoeffer replied, they were to meditate, and then he did his best to explain to them how the heart and mind may learn to listen. They remained for some time sceptical, but the example of their director's stillness and concentration, and the evident and intense reality of this silent prayer as he knew it, began to have its effect.

Not only into the silent meditation, but also into the common worship, Bonhoeffer was able to infuse the intense and vital reality that it had for him. In particular he had learnt to value the antiphonal singing of the psalms at Mirfield and Kelham, and now he spoke of the psalms as "the prayer book of the Bible". He saw them as the prayers of mankind in which we all may share, and also as the prayers of Christ who would have used them during his lifetime and who prays them with us now. After his experience in Finkenwalde he was to write:

"The Psalter is the prayer book of Jesus Christ in the truest sense of the word. He prayed the Psalter and now it has become his prayer for all time. Now do we understand how the Psalter can be prayer to God and yet God's own word, precisely because here we encounter the praying Christ? Jesus Christ prays through the Psalter in his congregation. His congregation prays too, the individual prays. But here he prays, in so far as Christ prays within him, not in his own name but in the name of Jesus Christ . . .

"In the Psalter we learn to pray on the basis of Christ's prayer. The Psalter is the great school of prayer."[1]

[1] Bonhoeffer, *Life Together*, pp. 36–7.

This sense of intense and vital significance also gave point and power to the courses in theology. Through them all ran three strands of enquiry: Who is Christ? What is the nature of the Church? What is discipleship? The answers to these questions were sought not only in study and discussion, but above all in life, in endeavouring to make Finkenwalde a living cell of the Church, where Christ might be truly encountered, "existing as community". For this to begin to be true, the brothers must learn to live together in love, not simply in a mild tolerance but truly in that charity which is the gift of God's grace, and which must be understood as different in kind from human love. Bonhoeffer has defined his sense of this fundamental difference:

"Within the spiritual community there is never, nor in any way, any 'immediate' relationship of one to another, whereas human community expresses a profound, elemental human desire for community, for immediate contact with other human souls . . .

"Human love is directed to the other person for his own sake, spiritual love loves him for Christ's sake. Therefore human love seeks direct contact with the other person; it loves him not as a free person, but as one whom it binds to itself . . . Because Christ stands between me and others, I dare not desire direct fellowship with them. As only Christ can speak to me in such a way that I can be saved, so others too can be saved only by Christ himself. This means that I must release the other person from every attempt of mine to coerce and dominate him with my love."[1]

Now, what are the demands of this kind of love? "It is the fellowship of the Cross to experience the burden of the other. If one does not experience it, the fellowship he belongs to is not Christian. If any member refuses to bear that burden, he denies the law of Christ. It is first of all the *freedom* of the other person, of which we spoke earlier, that is a burden to the Christian. The other's freedom collides with his own autonomy, yet he must recognise it . . . to bear the burden of the other person means involvement with the created reality of the other, to accept and affirm it, and in bearing with it, to break through to the point where we take joy in it."[2]

None of these words represented idle theorising. At Finkenwalde their truth was wrought out daily in struggle and sacrifice and daily experienced in victory and joy.

Bonhoeffer himself practised this selfless charity with inspired

[1] *Life Together*, pp. 22-3.
[2] *Life Together*, p. 91.

153

warmth and unremitting self-discipline, and he expected the same discipline and emotional control in his students. He understood and conveyed to them both by precept and example that like the life of prayer, the life of love in Christ must be learnt. Perhaps it was his uncompromising insight into the true nature of Christian relationships that preserved his next experiment from the dangers which might otherwise have been attendant upon it.

It was the practice at Finkenwalde that once in the month all students took part in a Communion service. One Saturday evening before the service, Bonhoeffer spoke to them about the practice of confession between brethren, which Luther had believed should take the place of sacramental confession to a priest. One of Bonhoeffer's students, Wolf Dieter Zimmermann, has given us an impression of an introductory talk of the same kind which he made to the third course of students.

"He approached us with great seriousness, and made clear to us the depth of his concern, even though he left everyone free to make his own decision. If a man wished to be free, he must be willing to confess anything that he had been harbouring in his heart against another. For a long time on this evening, we went to and fro to each other, and all the resentments which had been gathering in the last weeks were confessed. We found much with which to reproach one another. What surprised us most was the extent to which we had wounded one another. Almost all of it had happened unintentionally, by chance, incidentally. We discovered what it meant to be considerate for one another. The atmosphere was clear again. We could go together to the Holy Communion without any resentment between us. We never made this new beginning again, but its effect continued in many pastoral conversations, sometimes it was a confession, sometimes only a seeking for advice. Finally Bonhoeffer suggested to us that each should seek out a brother who should accompany him with continuous intercession. It served as a visible sign that even in the worst predicament one was never left alone."[1]

As the practice of mutual confession became established, among the members of the community, many students made their confession to Bonhoeffer himself, and one of them vividly recalls this experience:

"In listening he practised a conscious self-effacement the effect of which was to communicate strength, to stimulate, to compel and at the same time to liberate and release; I realised that this strong-willed individual who seemed so strange to me understood me nevertheless, and there would have been no sense in concealing anything or in any

[1] *Begegnungen*, p. 93.

internal withdrawal."[1] But now the problem arose: to whom should Bonhoeffer confess? He chose one of the students from Saxony, a young man from a small country manse. The student was shy and unpretentious, but there was a largeness of heart and mind and a spiritual dignity which showed through the diffidence, and probably convinced Bonhoeffer that here was one who could bear the weight of another's confession.

The assaults of the particular temptation which he privately called his *acedia* were an experience which till now he had confessed to no one. Those to whom he described it in theological discussion little knew how intensely personal his acquaintance with this particular demon was:

"Satan robs the believer of all joy in the Word of God, all experience of the good God; in place of which he fills the heart with the terrors of the past, of the present and of the future. Old long-forgotten guilt suddenly rears up its head before me, as if it had happened today. Opposition to the Word of God and unwillingness to obey assume huge proportions, and complete despair of my future before God overwhelms my heart. God was never with me, God is not with me, God will never forgive me; for my sin is so great that it cannot be forgiven."[2]

It was the old battle with the self that usurped the place of God, that crept back and back into the centre of the universe, the self that battened upon success, that hugged its own righteousness, that secretly despised others, and that then, having crept up unobserved almost to the crowning pinnacle, would be suddenly revealed and fall headlong to the brink of despair. These were the particular onslaughts of *acedia* or *tristitia* which Bonhoeffer now revealed to Bethge, and with them came a destructive question. Already in his mind there were growing the thoughts and insights which he would later embody in his book *Life Together*. "In the community of the Spirit," he wrote, "the Word of God alone rules; in human community there rules, along with the Word, the man who is furnished with exceptional powers, experience, and magical, suggestive capacities. There God's Word alone is binding; here, besides the Word, men bind others to themselves."[3] Was he such a man? And was all that he did to be poisoned by this creeping back of the self-righteous ego into the centre of the stage? It was a question which only his life and the fruits of his life could answer;

[1] *Begegnungen*, pp. 107–8.
[2] *Creation and Temptation*, p. 124.
[3] *Life Together*, p. 22.

155

but now, when the confession was made, the sense of guilt seemed lifted, and looking into the steady eyes of this other man, who had borne the impact of the revelation with gentle composure, and who possessed the treasure of humility as a native gift, Bonhoeffer will not have been tortured by any sense of superiority. This was the beginning of a friendship which was to become the most fruitful single ingredient of both their lives. As the relationship ripened, Bethge became sensitive to every nuance of his friend's thought, and enriched by every contact with Bonhoeffer's great gifts, he was himself able to bring to the work which they were soon sharing certain qualities of mind which the other lacked.

Meanwhile Bonhoeffer was approaching the realisation of a plan which he offered to the *Bruderrat* of the Old Prussian Union with some trepidation. On September 6th 1935 he wrote to them:

"With a number of students, whose names are listed below, I have proposed the plan upon which I have been ruminating for some years, of setting up a Protestant Community of Brothers, in which we will, as pastors, attempt for some years to live a common Christian life."[1]

The brothers would be willing, the report continued, to renounce all financial and other privileges of their status as pastors and to hold themselves in readiness to go wherever their services were required. They would consider the House of Brothers to be their home and would go out from it and return to it when any particular tour of duty was finished. "Not monastic seclusion, but intensive concentration for outgoing service is their intention".[2]

"Concentration for outgoing service", this phrase epitomised the particular character of the proposed community, There was to be a concentration of thought and aim, but above all a concentration on living under God's inspiration a Christian life. For "a message that comes out of a practical knowledge of Christian brotherhood lived and experienced will be able to be more factual and fearless and less in danger of sinking into the sand".[3]

The *Bruderrat* were sceptical. It smelt a little like something that Bonhoeffer had picked up outside, among the insufficiently Protestant Anglicans perhaps. There was no lack of old and wise heads ready to dismiss the whole idea as *Schwärmerei*, a particlar form of empty, fanatical enthusiasm for which Germans have the word because they

[1] *G.S.* II, p. 448.
[2] *G.S.* II, p. 449.
[3] *G.S.* II, p. 449.

so well know the condition. However, it was difficult simply to forbid an enterprise which was willing to be self-supporting and which might certainly have some practical advantages, so rather grudgingly the *Bruderrat* gave its consent.

By the end of September the *Bruderhaus*, the House of Brothers, was in existence. The lives of the brothers differed from the lives of the other members of the seminary, who were also in fact spoken of as Brothers, in two ways only; first, they were to remain permanently on the strength of Finkenwalde, and secondly they met for half an hour before lunch for prayer, reading and consultation when it was needed. The leader of the House of Brothers was Eberhard Bethge.

Meanwhile in the now firmly established seminary, life quietly blazed up. Bonhoeffer not only refused to tolerate spiritual mediocrity, he was also almost incapable of seeing that it existed, and under the infectious power of this fruitful blindness, his students discovered in themselves capacities and dimensions of which they had before been unaware. Even those who were in opposition, for there was an opposition, were enriched rather than impoverished through their critical reservations, for Bonhoeffer, always sensitive to the unspoken attitudes of his students, elicited their opinions, and where they seemed to him useful, he acted upon them. Many continued to complain of the half-hour of meditation, and accordingly the director agreed that once or twice a week the meditation should be made in common and aloud and, insofar as teaching was possible, he set himself to teach it. His not always uncritical Inspector of Studies, Wilhelm Rott, remembers with warmth his achievement here: "Although unfortunately I kept my distance from the *Bruderhaus* in Finkenwalde, because I suspected it of fanaticism, at least I learnt the practice of meditation on the Bible, to my lasting profit. Here I must take off my hat to our director with admiring respect for his gift of teaching and his singular success. What Dietrich Bonhoeffer managed to teach to the mixed bag of candidates in the few short months of a seminary course, was truly astounding."[1]

It will hardly seem remarkable, that one of those who learnt most quickly and deeply from Bonhoeffer was his friend Eberhard Bethge, and when in July 1936, the *Bruderrat* of Saxony wrote to ask for some explanation of the mysterious practice of meditation at Finkenwalde, it was Bethge who wrote a lucid reply:

"Why do I meditate? Because I am a Christian, and because therefore every day is a day lost

[1] *Begegnungen*, p. 115.

for me in which I have not penetrated deeper into the understanding of the word of God in scripture . . . Because I need a firm discipline of prayer. We like to pray according to our mood, short, long or not at all. That is self-will. Prayer is not a free offering to God, but a service which it is our duty to render, and which he requires . . . How do I meditate? There is free meditation, and meditation on the Scriptures. For the firm establishment of our prayer, we recommend meditation on Scripture. And also for the discipline of our thoughts. Also the knowledge of being united with others, who are meditating on the same text, will endear to us the Scriptural meditation.

"As the word of a loved person may follow you the whole day, so the word of Scripture should go on echoing in your mind and working in you. Just as you do not take to pieces the words of a loved person . . . (here follows a paraphrase of Bonhoeffer's passage in the letter to Rüdiger Schleicher).

"We begin our meditation with a prayer for the Holy Spirit, and with a prayer for recollection for ourselves and for all those whom we know to be also meditating. Then we turn to the text. By the end of our meditation we should like to be at the point at which we can give thanks out of a full heart. What text, and for how long the same text? It has proved fruitful to meditate for a week on a single text of from ten to fifteen verses. It is not a good plan to meditate on a new text every day, as we are not always equally receptive, and the texts are generally much too large . . .

"The time for meditation is in the morning before the beginning of work. Half an hour will be the shortest time which a meditation requires. Complete outward quiet and the resolution not to be distracted by anything, however important, are necessary foundations . . .

"How do we overcome difficulties in meditation?

"Whoever seriously subjects himself to the daily discipline of meditation, will soon find himself faced with difficulties. Prayer and meditation must be practised long and earnestly. For this the first rule is: Do not become impatient with yourself. Don't give up in despair over your distractions. Sit down again every day and wait very patiently. If your thoughts keep on straying, do not strain to hold them fast. There is no harm in allowing them to go on and reach their destination; but then take the place or the person to which they have strayed into your prayer. In that way you will find the way back to your text, and the moments spent in this distraction have not been lost and will no longer torment you . . .

"Behind all difficulties and perplexities remains the basic fact of our poverty in prayer. Many of us have remained far too long without any help or guidance. The only remedy for this is to begin again from the beginning, faithfully and patiently, the very first exercises in prayer and meditation. We shall also draw courage from the fact that other brethren are meditating with us, and that at all times the whole Church in Heaven and on earth prays with us. This is a comfort in the weakness of our prayer. When we really do not know what we should pray for, and are in despondency, then we may remember that the Holy Spirit speaks for us with groanings which cannot be uttered . . . From the Theological Seminary at Finkenwalde, May 22nd 1936."[1]

But not all who read this exposition were convinced of the value of the practice it described. Karl Barth, after reading it, wrote to Bonhoeffer:

"I read it with care, but I cannot honestly say that I felt very happy about this thing. I cannot quite accept the difference you claim both in this note and in your own letter between theological work and edifying contemplation. And again in this paper I am disturbed by an indefinable odour of the eros and pathos of the cloister . . ."[2]

Karl Barth, seldom at a loss, found some difficulty now in defining his criticism. In fact what Barth suspected, in company with many others in the Confessing Church, was that Bonhoeffer was open to Catholic influence to an extent which seemed to him dangerous. The extent to which he was in fact so influenced, and the manner of it, is not easily defined.

In the field of Dogmatic Theology there seems to be very little evidence of it. After his early theological formation in which the inspiration of Karl Barth had acted as a kind of catalyst to transfigure the rich cultural training received in the liberal school of Berlin, Bonhoeffer had begun to make his own theological explorations, but always well within the Calvinist-Lutheran framework. The Reformation's insistence upon extreme formulations appealed to his own intense and single-hearted nature, and now for the embattled Confessing Church of Germany, unsupported by any ultimate ecclesiastical authority to which it might appeal, concentration upon the rigorous theological demands of the Reformation was essential if their strength was to be maintained. In this conviction Bonhoeffer and Barth were united.

But into the formative years of Bonhoeffer's early life a third stream of influence had entered; and this was in fact Catholic. During the

[1] *G.S.* II, pp. 478 *et seq.*
[2] *G.S.* II, p. 290.

three months spent in Rome in 1924, he had seen and entered into the rich fecundity of Catholic life, as it poured through the Churches of Rome at the great festival of Easter. Here, for the first time, he saw the Church as the true supra-national nation of God's people, "Christ existing as community". The tremendous impact of this experience seems to have touched some deep springs in his intuitive faculty, so that he began from this time on to feel about in the dark for some of the Christian insights which Lutheranism had abandoned, and was able to make a quick response when he found them. So it had come about that, with a minimum of exterior stimulus, he had early begun to train himself in mental prayer, and had brought it to the point at which he could now teach it to his students. His sense of the uniting power of prayer in the Christian community had led him to an early concern for the visible demonstration of this unity, and from this perhaps arose his interest in the actual possibilities of life in community. When the opportunity arose for experimenting with such a life, he was not afraid to cast it in a disciplinary framework in which liturgy, meditation, regular periods of silence and confession of a kind bore their part. These were in fact Catholic insights in the sense that they belonged to the treasury of the Christian tradition, and had proved their value through some fifteen hundred years of religious history. In his own Church, where so much of the tradition had been abandoned, and where the witchhunt for "works" was always liable to break out, these practices remained suspect.

Bonhoeffer himself made no attempt to defend Catholic insights as such. He made use of them without prejudice and built them into his own conception of the possibilities of Christian life, but in the oecumenical field he was not in this sense a pioneer, and he quite willingly fell in with the current attitude, by which the movement felt able to regard itself as oecumenical, even though the greatest Church in the world was at that time self-excluded from it.

His main concern now with the Oecumenical Movement was to induce it to recognise the Confessing Church as the only true Protestant Church of Germany. But this was an increasingly unlikely prospect. Towards the end of his period in England, Bonhoeffer had written to Erwin Sutz:

"You know as well as I do what is going on in the Church in Germany. National Socialism has brought with it the end of the Church in Germany and effectively carried it through. For that we may be grateful to him, as the Jews had to be grateful to Sennacherib.

"There seems to me no doubt that we are faced with this evident fact. Naive and imaginative characters like Niemöller still believe themselves to be the true National Socialists—and it may be a kindly providence that preserves them in this illusion, and it may perhaps be in the interests of the Church struggle—assuming that one is still at all interested in this struggle. The point at issue is no longer in the least what it appears to be there; the lines of battle lie in wholly other fields.

"And although I am throwing all my energies into the ecclesiastical opposition; it is quite clear to me that this opposition represents no more than a provisional stage in transition to an entirely different opposition, and that the men concerned with this first rattling of sabres are only to a very minor extent the same as those who will be concerned with that second battle. And I believe that the whole of Christendom has need to pray with us that the resistance shall become 'resistance to the point of blood', and that men shall be found who are ready to endure it. Simply to endure it—that will be the need then—not to fight, stab and lay about them—that may be possible and permissible for the preliminary skirmish; but the real battle, what it may come to later, must be simply believing endurance, and then, then perhaps God will again recognise his Word in the Church, but until that time there must be very much faith and prayer and endurance. You know, I believe—perhaps you are surprised—that the whole thing will be resolved through the Sermon on the Mount."[1]

Looking back at these words over the intervening years, one is caught for an instant by a vision of what the German Church struggle might have meant for the whole Christian world if it could have been fought out at this depth, and in the single-hearted simplicity which could actually welcome martyrdom for the truth clearly seen. A Church which could have understood the struggle as its own punishment and redemption—the Cross—was the Church for which Bonhoeffer prayed. But it was a vision which only rare individuals would be able to see. Years later he was to write:

"A man can hold his own here only if he combine simplicity with wisdom. But what is simplicity? What is wisdom? And how are the two to be combined? To be simple is to fix one's eye solely on the simple truth of God, at a time when all concepts are being confused, distorted and turned upside down."[2]

It was a period of confusion and distortion that the Confessing Church

[1] *G.S.* I, pp. 39-40.
[2] Dietrich Bonhoeffer, *Ethics*, p. 7.

was now entering. The good effects of the Church's victory through the bold decisions made at the Synod of Dahlem were now being subtly inverted. The government, impressed by the determination shown at Dahlem, had abandoned the policy of trying to force the whole Protestant Church into the National Socialist framework, and now decided upon compromise. The Protestant Churches of Bavaria and Würtemberg were no further molested and settled down to enjoy their immunity. They came to be known as the "intact" Churches, and took no further part in the struggle. From henceforth the battle was largely confined to the Churches of the Old Prussian Union, and even they began to be weakened in their resistance by the hope of peace. In some cases their leaders' vision of the true issues involved began to be clouded. And at this juncture, when in fact they sorely needed him, they were to lose the theologian who, on the subject of the Church struggle, had most reliably combined simplicity with wisdom. Karl Barth lost his Chair at Bonn.

Since early in 1934, university Professors had been required to make the oath of personal loyalty to Hitler. Until the end of 1935, the oath was not enforced upon Barth. But at last the authorities decided on firmness. Barth refused to sign the oath without an explicit reservation, in which he stated that he owed his first allegiance to God. The reservation was not permitted and he was removed from his post. Now the Confessing Church might have acted. Barth was heart and soul in the struggle. He, like Bonhoeffer, saw it as one whose importance spread far beyond the boundaries of Germany. If the National *Bruderrat* had offered him the opportunity of founding a Theological High School in which students could have followed courses at university level, it is believed that he would have taken it. But Barth's uncomfortable lucidity did not suit the mood of the majority during this unheroic period, when it looked as though only a very little blurring of the confessional outlines could lead to peace with what they blindly hoped might be honour. So the Confessing Church did not offer Barth a post. He accepted a call to the University of Basle and was lost to the Church struggle.

And now the combination of simplicity with wisdom became daily more difficult. The Lutherans were weakened in the resolve to resist by their adherence to a distortion of Luther's doctrine of the two spheres, which taught them that obedience to the authority of the state was a part of their religious duty; and most remained at this time politically faithful to Hitler. In the theological field they were not at one with the Calvinists. Excursions into Luther's teaching on the divine order in nature seem to have suggested to some that the claim of the "German Christians" for a mystical significance attached to blood and soil might possibly be justified and made a basis for racial discrimination and nationalism. The Calvinists, few and without their leader, had little answer to make to these hopeful speculations, and many of those Evangelicals who combined Lutheran with Calvinist doctrines became frankly uncertain. More and more, yearning for unity in what seemed to them a single Church divided, began to long for compromise.

To the leaders of the Oecumenical Movement the position had now become understandably obscure. The months after the Fanø Conference, when it might have been possible for the Movement to recognise the Confessing Church as the only true Protestant Church in Germany, were quickly left behind, and now the *de facto* position seemed to have altered drastically. Bonhoeffer, invited in July 1935 to take part in a Conference of Faith and Order, and refusing on the grounds that the National Church was to be represented, was soon involved in a correspondence with Leonard Hodgson, in which both stated with precision their divergent attitudes. Hodgson spoke for the Oecumenical Movement when he wrote: "I think you will understand our position when I say that we cannot, as a Movement, exclude the representatives of any Church which 'accepts our Lord Jesus Christ as God and Saviour'. Right from the start there has been a general invitation to all such Churches, and we cannot arrogate to ourselves the right to discriminate between them."[1] Bonhoeffer spoke for the hard core of uncompromising resistance in the Confessing Church when he answered: ". . . We have to fight for the true Church against the false Church of Anti-Christ. Fighting in this faith we derive no small power from considering the fact that we are fighting for Christianity not only with regard to the Church in Germany but in the whole world. For everywhere on the earth are to be found those pagan and antichristian powers which appeared openly in our field. All Churches may be attacked by the very same power one day or another."[2]

This correspondence occasioned an essay, written in the following month, which was in fact Bonhoeffer's last contribution to oecumenical thought, "The Confessing Church and Oecumenism". In this essay he asked the question whether the Oecumenical Movement should not cease to think of itself as a movement and understand itself as being itself The Church, divided but seeking unity. This was the only

[1] *G.S.* I, p. 231.
[2] *G.S.* I, p. 234.

means, he suggested, by which it could speak with authority. But since it was the Oecumenical Church, it was absolutely required to make a Confession of Faith. If the truth is only to be found in unity, it is equally true that unity can only be found in truth. Here oecumenism could learn from the experience of the Confessing Church,

". . . that a Church without a Confession is a Church lost and defenceless, and that it is in its Confession of Faith that a Church has the only weapon which will not break."[1]

But the Church's Confession of Faith is at the same time a confession of sin, a confession of having had her part in the division of Christendom and failed to preach the gospel with power. "The Confessing Church is the Church which lives not in her purity but in her impurity, the Church of sinners, the Church of penitence and mercy, the Church which through Christ alone, through grace alone, through faith alone, finds her way to life . . . She has discovered that this truth is her only weapon in a battle of life and death."[2] For the few men who stood humble, uncompromising and fearless at the heart of the Confessing Church, Bonhoeffer's words blazed with truth. For the waverers round the edge, they were no more than an embarrassment.

We shall never know what might have been the effect within the Oecumenical Movement if the Confessing Church had retained its power to speak with such a humble and yet decisive voice. But in fact, during the years which followed, it ceased to speak at all in the Oecumenical field.

A month before the correspondence with Faith and Order began, Bonhoeffer had been involved in the third National Synod of the Confessing Church, which took place at Augsburg. The Synod passed without incident, and in the eyes of many it was a satisfactory occasion. Bonhoeffer was among the few who protested against its ignoring of the real issues. He pointed out that no word had been spoken in defence of the Church's freedom to teach and preach biblical truth, no criticism had been made of the false doctrine of "Positive Christianity" still proclaimed by the National Church; there had been no protest against the requirement of the oath to Hitler and no word had been spoken on behalf of the Jews.

Few followed Bonhoeffer's lead in criticising the Synod, but at the end of July an uncompromising circular drafted by Niemöller went out to all Confessing pastors in Prussia, calling upon them to stand

[1] G.S. I, p. 252.
[2] G.S. I, pp. 259–60.

firm. The forty-nine signatures to the document, among which was Dietrich Bonhoeffer's, represented the small number who were clear-sighted enough not to balk the issues. The letter quoted I Peter 1 : 13: "Wherefore gird up the loins of your mind, and hope to the end for the grace that is to be brought unto you at the revelation of Jesus Christ". The letter continued:

"It is our failure at this point which hangs like a curse over our Confessing Church; because of this the spirit of doubt and anxiety is filtering in among our ranks; this is the reason for the absence of clear direction; it is why our young theologians are, for the most part, un-certain whether they are right to put themselves at the disposal of the Confessing Church, without considering the effect on their future in training, examination requirements and service.

"This curse we have brought upon ourselves, for we have denied that with which God entrusted us at Barmen and Dahlem. Both Synods called the Church to submit to the sole rule of the Lord Jesus Christ; Barmen called her to depend solely upon the Word of God's revelation for witness and teaching, Dahlem for order and organisation. This should have closed the door for us upon every thought of compro-mise. Let us return and accept once more the binding character of these decisions. Then we shall once more be clearly led. Let us not be oppressed by the fact that the Church's future appears to rest in what, to our eyes, seems to be impenetrable darkness; let it be enough for us to know what we are commanded to do.

"We are commanded to make a clear, uncompromising answer of No in face of every temptation to solve the Church's problem in a way which contradicts the decisions of Barmen and Dahlem. May God help us—if it comes to the point—to be able to speak this No, gladly and in unity."[1]

The letter met, in many quarters, only a tepid response, and the government, encouraged by the generally more accommodating attitude, pressed on with their efforts to placate the vacillating majority, and with this in view a new Ministry for Ecclesiastical Affairs was created, and a colourless character, Hans Kerrl, was put in charge of it.

In October Kerrl called on Bishop Mahrarens, Chairman of the V.K.L., and told him that he was proposing to disband the *Bruderrat*. Did the Bishop think he asked hopefully, that they might be persuaded to retire gracefully of their own accord? Mahrarens temporised, but when Fritz Müller-Dahlem, representative of the *Bruderrat*, was

[1] *G.S.* II, pp. 206–7.

approached, he replied with an uncompromising refusal. Kerrl's next venture, however, was more successful. He prevailed upon Wilhelm Zoellner, the much respected Lutheran General Superintendent, now retired, to accept an assignment which was destined to do more than any persecution to disrupt the Confessing Church; for he was put in charge of a National Church Committee, on which both the official Church and the Confessing Church were to be represented, and which was to explore every avenue of compromise. Upon the National Committee there followed a crop of Provincial Committees, assembled for the same purpose. Now the Confessing Church was rocked. Was it right to co-operate with these committees or not? Many, after agonising searching of conscience, decided that it was. Meanwhile the Bishops of Bavaria and Würtemberg spoke favourably of the undertaking, and Mahrarens declared his intention of sending representatives to the National Committee from the V.K.L. But Niemöller and the Old Prussian *Bruderrat* stood out, and Dietrich Bonhoeffer's immediate reaction was characteristic: "Between Church and pseudo-Church there can be no co-operation!"

But the Pomeranian *Bruderrat* was shaken. On January 10th 1936, a meeting of the Confessing pastors of the province took place in Stettin-Bredow to consider the burning question of the attitude to their local Church Committee. Bonhoeffer spoke, and a large contingent of passionately concerned students supporting him from Finkenwalde contained their emotions with difficulty. To a letter complaining afterwards that they had to some extent failed to do so, Bonhoeffer replied:

". . . If at a moment when it is a case of the right or the wrong road for the Church, of truth or falsehood, a moment at which at every second the Church is in danger of being led fearfully astray, if at such a moment there are mild emotional outbursts, I cannot really feel all that much upset about it. Something very much more serious is at stake, namely the necessity that God's word alone shall have authority. Improprieties in speech and behaviour are not irreparable. I know that every one of the brothers here (at Finkenwalde) is ready to apologise for any failure of which they believe themselves guilty, and in this case I think that is the important thing. But it is very much more difficult to repair the situation when the Church, in her witness to Christ, abandons the road of faithfulness and truth."[1]

But to many meeting at Bredow, this road was far from clear. In all

[1] *G.S.* II, pp. 210–11.

good faith many believed that they should follow the way of compromise. Even the students at Finkenwalde were unsettled. Intense discussions went on among them till far into the night, and at this time a blow fell which shook the nerve of the whole community. One of the ablest and most serious-minded of the students defected to the supporters of the Church Committees. We have a record of this disaster in the same letter:

"I must say that, in my opinion, anyone who subjects himself to the Church Committees in any way cannot remain a member of our Church. But here the valid word is not that of a single individual, but the word of the Synod or of the *Bruderrat*, for which many are waiting. The prevailing uncertainty on this point seemed to me both symptomatic and disastrous. Brother W. was one of the most thoughtful and responsible of our brothers. I had a real affection and respect for Brother W. What his defection means to us we ourselves know better than anyone else. And we told him this ourselves. I believe, if you could have been present during the last two hours that Brother W. spent at the Seminary, you would understand that there was no question of any one of us having reproached him with 'faithlessness, cowardice and treachery'. It was after earnest, personal and pastoral discussion, after a meeting in which I spoke once more to all the brothers of the seriousness of the occasion, after honest prayer together, that we finally parted. To say anything about the interior emotion by which we were all shaken, would not I think be right."[1]

With this blow for the Seminary and intense personal disappointment for Bonhoeffer, the year of 1936 began.

<hr />

[1] *G.S.* II, pp. 212–3.

CHAPTER XII

'IN his capacity to return from agonising questions to the cheerful discipleship of Jesus Christ lies the secret of Dietrich Bonhoeffer as a man.'[1]

Though Bonhoeffer remained passionately involved in the trials and tribulations of the Confessing Church, he could still give himself up to the life of Finkenwalde with interest undimmed and vitality unimpaired. In June 1936 he wrote a letter to Staemler, the Chairman of the *Bruderrat* in Saxony, which described simply and exactly the stage of achievement which the Seminary and *Bruderhaus* had now reached:

"The brothers who quickly succeed one another in the seminary here learn two things: first to live a common life in shared obedience to the will of Jesus Christ, and in practising all the services, small or great, which Christian brothers can perform for one another; they are to learn to recognise the power and release of energy which lies in brotherly service and in the shared life of a Christian community, for they will need it. Secondly, they are to learn to serve the truth alone in their study of the Scriptures and in expounding it in preaching and teaching. I take this second requirement as my personal responsibility. But the first I cannot achieve by myself. There has to be a group of brothers who, without talking about it, by means of their own common life, draw the others in. That is the purpose of the *Bruderhaus*. These brothers, a number of whom are already ordained, have made the serious decision that they will live solely for the service of the Church, making no demands and renouncing many of the rights of a pastor, and giving their service from within the centre of a life lived in common with other brothers. It is, therefore, a society of young theologians always ready to take a hand, who, without any binding commitment as to time, are nevertheless prepared to remain together for the present. The spirit of the seminary is supported by this society, in the clear recognition that no law may be made about this, and that our mandate is to serve. Each of the brothers now has a field of service which extends far beyond the confines of the seminary, and for most of them the seminary is only the house in which he spends his morning and evening times of common prayer and meditation, and when possible shares the

[1] Franz Hildebrandt, address at the Bonhoeffer Memorial Service held in London, 1945.

communal meals. The reason for this is that each one has his steady parish work outside the community, and that in addition he must take his part in fulfilling every task that is required of us, and this is often almost too much to cope with. So our activities reach out in many directions, but the strength and the joy for the task comes from within. We have also from the centre of the *Bruderhaus* made various experiments in the direction of a popular mission, and recently, under the direction of the *Bruderhaus* the whole seminary spent a week in the villages. I hope that the opportunity for new and exceedingly important work may arise for us here, but it can only be carried forward through the *Bruderhaus*. A most essential task, which appears of quite minor importance, but which is perhaps still more vital than the five months' work at the seminary, is the regular keeping in touch, through letters and visits, with the brothers who have left the community. The short time in the seminary can only bear fruit if the work is faithfully followed up. In the first months of independent work after leaving the seminary, such numerous professional and personal problems arise that we daily receive letters which need to be carefully answered . . . Shall I add to this that we have to take care of the Confessing Congregation at Stettin almost without help? That we are constantly required to lecture? That here in Finkenwalde we look after the parish? I could add much more to the list. It is unfortunately the case that 'the quiet and godly life' here in the seminary is often drawn into the struggle. And yet all of us who are involved in this work and this fellowship are thankful that it is so."[1]

The task which appeared of minor importance, that of keeping in touch with the old students, was rendered doubly significant by the fact that the prospect which confronted these young men when they left the Seminary to begin their service in the Confessing Church was extremely bleak. None could hope for a normal post which offered a fixed salary and a home. A young pastor might find an opening as "assistant preacher" under a fearless Superintendent, with free accommodation offered by a generous layman; a determined "Confessing" congregation might fight to secure him when a post became vacant, or he might be given an opportunity under the *Bruderratce* to lead an emergency group in a private house. But he must give up all hope of normal prospects and privileges, and be ready to bear ridicule and hostility from the majority of his neighbours wherever he went. So the work of the *Bruderhaus* in keeping in touch with these young men and

[1] *Bonhoeffer Auswahl*, edited by Richard Grunow, pp. 258–9.

in giving them the sense that they still belonged to a Christian community that cared for them, could mean everything to them in their isolation. Each one knew that he was welcome to return to Finkenwalde when he had any time free, as he would to his own home. Whenever possible, a member of the *Bruderhaus* or a fellow Finkenwaldian would visit him at his lonely post, and each month a circular letter went out to every old student. The letters adjured the young pastors to stand firm, to have no truck with the Church Committees, and to recognise no authority but the *Bruderrat*, while preaching nothing but what they knew to be the truth. The letters assured them of the steady support of their old seminary, and of the intense reality of their communion through prayer. One such letter ran:

"Dear Brothers, in times such as those that lie ahead of us we cannot arm ourselves otherwise than by strong and persistent prayer, and now we shall see whether our life and prayer have really been a preparation for this hour when we must confess our faith. If we persevere in prayer, then we can have confidence that the Holy Spirit will give us the right words at the time when we need them, and that we shall be found faithful. It is a great favour when we are permitted to strive in the company of other brethren, but far or near, we are united every day in the prayer for one another, that in the day of Jesus Christ we may stand before him united in joy. In this each one of us stands or falls by his Lord. Christ leads us home—that is Advent—'blessed are those servants whom the Lord when he cometh shall find watching'.

"With the affectionate greetings of

"Your faithful brothers at Finkenwalde."[1]

The young pastors, upheld by prayer, and faithful to the spirit of Finkenwalde, boldly stood their ground in the lonely outposts. And now a new factor was added. In the little village of Seelow, outside Frankfurt am Oder, a young pastor, Johannes Pecina, was arrested and imprisoned. At once a *vikar*, Willi Brandenburg, was sent in his place. He too was arrested. The third to go, Adolf Preuss, had been a member of the first course at Finkenwalde, and so the Finkenwalde students became involved with the parish and concerned themselves with the fate of Preuss' predecessors. The constant prayer for these two pastors deepened the special colour of the second course. The thought that these two men, young as themselves, were suffering imprisonment for their faith, intensified for the students their own sense of dedication, and made their daily lives more serious and at the same time more vivid than

[1] *G.S.* II, p. 460.

lives lived in normal conditions of safety commonly are. A letter which Willi Brandenburg was able to write to one of them in June was read and reread many times:

"My dear R.,

"To you, brother Bonhoeffer and all the brothers, grateful thanks for everything, visible and invisible. We feel aware that you think of us and pray for us. We trust with all our hearts and with full conviction, in the Grace of our Lord Jesus. That is often so hard, when day and night one sees nothing but the cheerless prison walls, and has the sense of being forsaken by God and man. But nevertheless! Psalm 73 is a great source of strength to me. You cannot imagine what a blessing such a time as this is for us! One lives as a wretched little broken mortal so completely through God, and one becomes so strong in all one's weakness. One has so much time to think over many things. It is amazing with how few things a man can survive. I beg and pray for this, that all that I am perceiving now may not be lost again later on.

"But I must not let myself remember that outside all is in blossom. One's love for all the living creation is never so strong as when one is shut away from it. But still we see a patch of blue sky, a little sunshine and a few stars, and the Lord who created it will still hold us in his way . . ."[1]

Bonhoeffer, enclosing a copy of this letter in the monthly circular to the ex-students, added a pregnant comment:

"Dear Brothers!

"Alas, I can never manage more than a short greeting. The longer we stay here, the wider grows the field of our activities. I thank all who have written most warmly for their letters. It is the greatest joy for me to hear from you and to think of you. The half-hour every morning still continues.

"I believe we should all prepare for the day on which our trial will come, by physical and mental discipline. My thoughts are now constantly with our imprisoned brothers. They have much to teach us. Everything depends now upon our daily obedience. If we now become careless and frivolous, how can we face our imprisoned brothers, and still more the Son of God, who suffered for our sake to the point of death? Now it is a case of standing firm. That is a trial. But it carries a great promise with it, for us and for our community.

"In the community of faith and prayer greetings,

"Yours, Dietrich Bonhoeffer."[2]

[1] *G.S.* II, p. 485.
[2] *G.S.* II, pp. 485–6.

It was in this year, 1936, that the Bonhoeffer parents sold the large house in the Wangenheimstrasse and moved into one which they had had built for them in the Marienburgerallee. In this time of uncertainty and frustration and the first rumblings of danger, the family drew together. Ursula and her husband, Rüdiger Schleicher, moved into the house next door to her parents. Nearby lived the Dohnanyis. The Leibholzes were in Göttingen, Gerhard Leibholz without occupation because of his Jewish ancestery.

In January the indomitable Tafel grandmother had died at ninety-four. Dietrich, at her funeral service, gave the address, which for the Bonhoeffers rang like an elegy for the world into which they had been born:

"With her a world is buried, which we all in some way bear within us, and wish so to bear. The unbending authority of the right, the free vow of a free man, the binding power of a promise once made, clarity and moderation in speech, honour and simplicity in public and private life—this she cared for with all her heart. In this she lived. She had discovered in the course of her life that it costs trouble and effort to achieve these aims in one's own life. She did not flinch from this trouble and effort. She could not bear to see these aims despised, or to see human rights denied. Therefore her last years were darkened by the distress she felt over the fate of the Jews in our country, for this she herself grieved and suffered. She belonged to a different age, to a different spiritual world—and this world shall not be buried with her. This inheritance, for which we must thank her, puts us under obligation."[1]

But how different from these were the standards of the Third Reich! Violence, bombast, racial oppression and shameless bravado held the field. This had its effect upon all Europe, and the German people were intoxicated by what they took to be successes: the occupation of the Rhineland, the unopposed repudiation of the Locarno Pact, the anti-Comintern pact with Japan, support from Franco's Spain, the Rome-Berlin Axis; and in 1936 all this was crowned when the world flocked to Berlin for the Olympic Games.

Against the background of these political triumphs, the Confessing Church staggered on into a state of ever increasing confusion. After Mahrarens went over to the Church Committees, a new V.K.L. was formed. The Lutherans answered this by forming a "Lutheran Council" of their own, which intended to work with the Committees.

[1] *G.S.* IV, pp. 458-9.

Now a tug of war began between the Prussian *Bruderrat*, the Lutheran Council, the Church Committees and the reconstituted V.K.L., while the official Church looked on with satisfaction. The Pomeranian *Bruderrat* was drawn into the struggle, and two of its members went over to the Church Committees. Meanwhile the Theological Faculty at Greifswald, the Provincial University, with whom Finkenwalde had necessary contacts, decided upon compromise and strongly criticised the attitude of Finkenwalde, which remained an island stronghold of uncompromising resistance, becoming increasingly isolated and unpopular. But the courses pressed on with unbated energy, invigorated by their sense of being involved in a gallant adventure for the cause of truth.

Meanwhile their existence had been rendered precarious through an Act passed by the Government in September 1935 "For the Settlement of the German Evangelical Church". By a series of "Emergency Measures" the new Minister, Kerrl, had put its provisions into effect. The first Order set up the Central Church Committee and the Ecclesiastical Finance Department, the fourth made provision for the establishment of the Provincial Committees and the last, announced in December 1935, dealt a direct blow at the whole organisation of the Confessing Church. By the Orders set down in this notorious "Fifth Emergency Measure", unauthorised groups or Assemblies were forbidden to fulfil any ecclesiastical functions in six vital fields: appointments of clergy, ordination, announcements of policy, the disposal of money received in collections, the calling of Synods and the training and examination of theologians. Thus, at a single stroke, all the Seminaries set up by the Confessing Church became illegal, and Finkenwalde lost its right to exist.

When the news broke, Bonhoeffer called together the students and earnestly set before them the seriousness of the situation, opening the way for anyone of them to leave the course. Not a single student turned tail, and indeed the particular combination of seriousness with high spirits which was the special climate of the second course may be not unconnected with this liberating decision, a decision by which they abandoned all conventional hopes for their future, the uncertain safety and the uneasy possibilities of peace in their time, which had beclouded the issue while there were still some reasons to hope for recognition. Now they were outlaws and knew where they stood.

On Dietrich's birthday, February 4th, the high spirits broke in a particular wave of daring. In the midst of hilarious celebrations, the students turned on their director and asked for a birthday present from *him*. "Take us abroad!" they cried. Dietrich had often fired their hearts with glimpses of the oecumenical world, kindling in their minds the thought of that greater Church, for the sake of whose total integrity they were now standing firm in their own national struggle. "Let us see it!" they cried, "Let us see this greater Church!" In 1936 this would already have seemed to most people in Germany like reaching for the moon. Foreign travel was tightly controlled, and for a whole group of young theology students which technically did not even exist to leave Germany in a body for a foreign tour would have seemed to others an unheard-of idea.

But the suggestion had no sooner been made than Bonhoeffer was in action. He wrote letters in various directions, and answers came back promptly. The Churches of Denmark and Sweden, through the local Oecumenical Councils, were ready to invite the director and students of Finkenwalde as their guests. Preparations went forward swiftly and secretly. Less than a month later the whole seminary slipped out of Germany, under the nose of the authorities, and for ten crowded days they travelled through Denmark and Sweden, welcomed and fêted by the Churches wherever they went.

When the fact of this illicit journey was made known, there was some angry banging of stable doors by the hoodwinked authorities: letters flew between Hans Kerrl and the Minister for External Affairs. The luckless Heckel was heavily involved, and wrote tactfully reprimanding the Archbishop of Sweden for this interference in Germany's internal affairs. But a rather cool and nominal apology was the most he could extract. The direct result of the journey for Bonhoeffer was the withdrawal by the Ministry of Culture of his right to lecture at Berlin University. He let it go with the comment: "I have long ceased to believe in the University." Now his energies were more than ever concentrated upon the training of his students, for upon the clear heads and steadfast hearts of the young pastors who were now being "illegally" trained by the Confessing Church the continuance of the struggle would more and more depend.

In April, soon after the second course had broken up, the students of the first course assembled at Finkenwalde for their first reunion. It was for these young men, who had now had six months' experience of the realities of service in a suppressed and despised Church, that Bonhoeffer's Bible study on the books of Nehemiah and Ezra was written. It is a study characteristic of his highly individual method of exposition.

The stories, christologically interpreted, are used as an analogy for the struggle in which the uncompromising central core of the Confessing Church was engaged. But the Bible study is more than this. Coming as the fruit of earnest prayer and profound meditation, it represents a glimpse of the pattern, repeated in many forms, and many situations, of God's means of dealing with his people. What Bonhoeffer illustrates through these two stories is a truth which will be true in all generations; that it was being demonstrated with concrete immediacy at the time when the paper was delivered, made its impact more intense, but did not for Bonhoeffer make its truth less universal. The two first paragraphs epitomise the content of the whole discourse.

"Only God himself can turn away his own judgements upon his people. For ruined Jerusalem nothing remains but to trust him. God will return to his people according to his promise, otherwise there is no hope. If a man set to work, without any special call or commission, to build the ruined Church up again, it would be a defiance of God's judgement. And this would be so however virtuous the intention, however pure the teaching, however deep the pastoral concern for the people. This is the way that impertinent 'carnal piety' would act, but not the faith of God's community. Faith waits and bows before the judgement, till God himself returns; it waits and prays for the awakening. From the awakening through God's spirit comes the renewal of the Church. Never through a restoration, never through a self-willed setting aside of the judgement of God. God returns to his community only by passing through his judgements, never by circumventing them. The awakening leads through judgement to mercy. Therefore prayer and awakening are the beginning of true renewal of the Church.

"Jerusalem is in ruins, the Holy Temple of God has been desecrated, the priests taken prisoner or exiled from the city, the walls torn down, so that there is no more protection from any sort of enemy. The city is helplessly exposed to any attack. Foreign powers, foreign lords, foreign gods have entered Jerusalem. The community of God's people, struck by his judgement and his anger, have been carried away captive by foreign tyrants. The people of Israel must live as strangers among the godless. And who has any right to be surprised or indignant if, during ten years of foreign rule under heathen power, many have grown tired and acquiescent, and if many, in spite of all the shame and oppression, now prefer to vegetate weakly in comparative safety under the protection of the foreign king, rather than return to the desolate, restless city of God where only one thing remains: his promise? It is true that, through all the years of captivity, there were those who sang songs of longing for Jerusalem and of anger against the godless tyrants. It is true that they awaited the day when God's judgement would fall upon Babylon, and Jerusalem would be free, with joy and trembling. But it was only a proportion of the exiles who remained faithful to God's promise. A rising in their own strength could never have led to the goal. It was a situation in which they had to wait in obedience for God's call." Now there follows an exploration of the stories and a vivid exposition of their relationship to the Christian Church in similar situations, with the final assertion: "But all this is written for the Church of Christ, as a reminder and a warning, right to the present day."[1]

The paper was published in the periodical *Junge Kirche*, and critically received, especially at the University of Greifswald, where a Professor wrote a pamphlet against it, seeing, or affecting to see in it, a menace to scholarship and a dangerous tendency to press the Bible into the service of Church politics. The exigencies of the last years had created in Germany a new adjective with strongly pejorative overtones, *Kirchenpolitisch*, "Church-political", freely used against Bonhoeffer both now and later. Only a few months after this a much more violent outcry was to be raised against his article "On the Question of the Boundaries of the Church", published in the periodical *Evangelische Theologie* in June of the same year.

The function of the Church, he wrote in this hotly debated article, is not to draw her own boundaries; but in times of crisis she must make a clear confession of her faith, and her boundaries will then be determined for her by those who reject it. The Protestant Church in Germany had made this confession at the Synods of Barmen and Dahlem, and had thus drawn a clear line between herself and the pseudo-Church of the Reich. But now her adherence to the very truths she had confessed seemed to be in doubt.

There followed an outpouring of burning questions. The Confessing Church was the Church of Jesus Christ, what did this mean? The National Church was heretical. Did this mean that all who served it fell under the same condemnation? Was every "German Christian" pastor separated from the Church? Further, was every "German Christian" in a confessing congregation, was every confessing congregation that accepted a "German Christian" pastor to be regarded as outside the Church? To these and to many other questions it was the duty of the Confessing Church to give a definite answer. Above all, the Church

[1] *G.S.* IV, pp. 321 *et seq.*

176

must make a clearcut decision with regard to the Church Committees. The National Church Government had shown itself heretical, and in co-operating with it the Church Committees made themselves a party to the heresy. Neutrality was not possible. The Church which was responsible for proclaiming the true faith must proclaim it. And then came the passage which cost Bonhoeffer what remained of his reputation with the theologians of the Third Reich:

" '*Extra Ecclesiam nulla salus*'. The question of belonging to the Church is the question of salvation. The boundaries of the Church are the boundaries of salvation. He who knowingly separates himself from the Confessing Church in Germany, separates himself from salvation. This is what the true Church has been forced to recognise from the beginning."[1]

"*Extra Ecclesiam nulla salus*"! The words were seized upon by enemies and "neutrals" alike. The rest of the passionate and closely-reasoned article was thrown to the winds, the "*nulla salus*" passage was blazoned everywhere. This, cried the enemies and neutrals, put Bonhoeffer right outside the pale of reasonable theologians. But Bonhoeffer knew for whom he was speaking. He was voicing the cry from the heart of a generation of Christians demoralised by compromise and confusion, of whom the bravest were seeking passionately a faith that was clear, that asked for everything, and for which a man might live and die. It is a miracle of the years that followed that in fact the Christian faith did break through the enfeebling tangle, simple, powerful and demanding, and that there was no lack of men and women, both in the Catholic and in the Protestant Churches of Germany, who were ready for the sake of that faith to risk all that they had, not excluding their lives, when individual acts of splendid courage showed that the Church of the Apostles and Martyrs was not dead.

Bonhoeffer, for whom the demands of this faith were abolute, took little notice of the outcry against him. He did not much value the opinions of men, who, however meticulous their scholarship might be, seemed to him to have sold the pass at a deeper level. His concern was with the clear-headed and single-hearted following of Christ by the Church, but as he struggled for clarification of the issues he was not always free from the onslaughts of the demon *tristitia*. " 'What a proud and despondent thing the heart is!' " he wrote to Bethge, "pride and despondency, all this is only overcome by prayer."[2]

[1] *G.S.* II, p. 238.
[2] *G.S.* II, p. 277.

For Bonhoeffer the summer of 1936 began with the publication of his controversial article, and ended with the Olympiad. Somewhat reluctantly he agreed to give an address in the Church of Paul the Apostle, where its confessing pastor von Rabenan had arranged for a series of addresses which might give foreign visitors some understanding of the struggle in which the German Church was involved. The Church was thronged throughout the whole series, and Bonhoeffer's sermon was so heavily attended that it had to be repeated in another church. Meanwhile addresses given by theologians from the University were only feebly supported, much to their chagrin; and at other levels too, animosity smouldered. In the window of a shop near St. Paul's Church a placard was prominently displayed:

> "*Nach der Olympiade*
> *Hauen wir die BK zu Marmelade;*
> *Dann schmeissen wir die Juden raus,*
> *Dann ist die BK aus.*"[1]

It is possible that this lampoon was partly occasioned by an event that had taken place a few weeks before. Earlier in the summer the most courageous members of the Prussian *Bruderrat* had drafted an outspoken memorandum to Hitler, which dared to criticise the oppressive measures against the Church and the treatment of Jewish Christians.

This memorandum had been handed in at the Chancellory on June 4th. But that was not all. When its contents appeared to have been ignored, Werner Koch, a student at Finkenwalde, and Ernst Tillich, nephew of the theologian, had sent the *Baseler Nachrichten* a verbatim copy which appeared on July 23rd, causing a considerable stir in the European press. The *Bruderrat* expressed regret at the leakage, but a modified version was nevertheless read aloud from the pulpit by eighty per cent of confessing pastors on August 23rd.

Bonhoeffer was by this time at a meeting of the Oecumenical Council for Life and Work in Chamby, having accompanied a delegation which the Confessing Church had finally decided to send under Präces Koch, and he was witness of the profound impression which the report of this act of courage made upon the delegates from other European countries. The delegation sent by the National Church under the leadership of Zoellner, Chairman of the Central Church Committee,

[1] After the Olympiad
We'll beat the Confessing Church to pulp;
Then we'll throw out the Jews,
And that will be the end of the Confessing Church.

was put in an embarrassing position by the manifest enthusiasm, but no official reference was made to the event, and the presence of the two opposing delegations from Germany somewhat stultified the effect of the Conference. For Bonhoeffer the whole occasion had only a negative significance, confirming his personal conviction that it was no longer possible for the Confessing and National Churches both to be represented, and it was in fact the last Oecumenical Conference at which a delegation from the Confessing Church was able to be present.

Bonhoeffer took the opportunity to spend a few weeks after the Conference in the freshness and freedom of Switzerland with Eberhard Bethge, from whom he was now seldom parted. They returned in September to find the effects of the publication of the memorandum to Hitler still continuing. The Lutheran Council had disclaimed any responsibility for it, and the breach between the Lutheran Council and the Government of the Confessing Church was now almost complete. At the same time the Gestapo was pursuing an intensive investigation to discover who had been responsible for the leakage, and finally in November Werner Koch and Ernst Tillich were arrested and sent to a concentration camp together with Friedrich Weisler, an employee of the *Bruderrat*, who, because he was Jewish, was beaten and tortured to death.

Finkenwalde supported the two survivors in every way. Koch and Tillich took the place in their intercessions of Pecina and Brandenburg, who had been released from prison at last and were now recuperating at the seminary. From now on there was never to be a time when some of its members or ex-members were not in prison. And indeed, now that Finkenwalde was proscribed by the government, the whole enterprise was in hourly danger. One learnt to live on friendly terms with total insecurity. Dietrich said simply, "We accept every day as a gift from God," and this was the spirit which gave to each day as it came its particular quality of light-hearted intensity. Each day was lived through in faith and cheerful acceptance of danger, in the peculiar freedom of heart which the abandonment of all human hopes can give. The moment had something in common with the precarious and triumphant period of first-century Christianity, when the life of truth in the world mattered to the Christian incomparably more than his own.

For Bonhoeffer it was a year of adventure and joy inextricably bound up with bitter disappointment as he watched his heroic vision for the Church buried under the mountain of a much more pedestrian reality, and to overcome the bitterness was no easy matter. " 'What a proud and despondent thing the heart is!' Pride and despondency, all this is only overcome through prayer." Bonhoeffer overcame them again and again, and in the peace of these victories he could write to the scattered brothers at the end of the year:

" 'He hath done all things well.' Let this be the word we speak about every week, about every hour that has passed. Let us take these words with us into our prayer until there is not a single hour left about which we are not ready to say, 'He hath done all things well.' And just the days that were hard for us, that tormented and frightened us, days that have left a trace of bitterness in us, are the ones that we will not leave behind until we can also say of them, humbly and thankfully, 'He hath done all things well'. We are not to forget, but to overcome. And that is done through gratitude. We are not to try to solve the unsolved riddles of the past and fall to brooding, but leave behind what we cannot understand and give it back peacefully into the hands of God. That is done through humility. 'He hath done all things well.' "[1]

In spite of all that had happened and not happened, the year had been good. Good for Bonhoeffer, and good for the young men whose lives had blazed up in the light of his. Wilhelm Rott, in a reminiscent essay, gives us two glimpses of his friend which are significantly simple and vivid. The first is a wholly personal recollection:

"Brother Dietrich practised his love for the brothers in many small services around the seminary. The Director liked to play the part of orderly. On our small budget the food was simple, and became monotonous in the long run. Once, during a short illness, the Inspector[2] felt this too, though of course without saying so. But the warm-hearted medical orderly was aware of the depressing situation, disappeared into the kitchen and returned after a short time with a luxurious breakfast in the best English tradition. 'No rule without its exception,' he remarked, laid the little table, and disappeared again to prepare a strong brew of tea. Over the shared meal all discomforts were forgotten."[3]

The second recollection he shares with a few others:

"And so during these two years 'Brother Dietrich'—who always had time for his brothers—used sometimes to sit down on a little staircase which led to the Inspector's room, generally after lunch and before he made his tour of the 'classrooms' of the seminary. It is an unforgettable picture: the small wooden staircase, and the man sitting with his legs

[1] *G.S.* II, p. 506.
[2] Wilhelm Rott.
[3] *Begegnungen*, p. 118.

crossed, taking a cigarette and a cup of coffee willingly spared from the establishment's single coffee machine. Dietrich talks. Yesterday he was in Berlin. Late in the evening he had given all who were awaiting his return a vivid account of the aberrations and entanglements of that period of the Church Committees. He had talked of spiritual and temporal, of ecclesiastical and political matters, of those who stood firm, of those who wavered and those who fell. But there are still telling details which have not escaped his keen observation, and which are not suitable for sharing with the wider circle."[1]

Werner Koch, one of the students later imprisoned, offers us an impression of a different order. He records the impact of his first sight of Bonhoeffer in a Berlin café, before he was aware of his identity.

"Perhaps a Catholic Christian would have said: 'I had the sense of being in the presence of a saint.' Today I myself would rather say that I had a distinct impression: This is he! A man with the mark of God upon him, set apart, singled out for his future martyrdom."[2]

These words, sincere as they are, can hardly be quite free from an element of hindsight. But undoubtedly the special quality was there. One may call it the stuff of which sanctity is made, one may call it the mark of God, the distinction seems irrelevant. It was a reality in the face of which language tends in any case to fall out of gear, lacking the necessary dimension.

"A man can hold his own here only if he can combine simplicity with wisdom . . . because the simple man knows God."

It was such a man that Werner Koch had seen.

---

[1] *Begegnungen*, p. 116.
[2] *Begegnungen*, p. 97.

CHAPTER XIII

THE year 1937 opened with a dramatic breach between Kerrl, the Minister for Church Affairs, and Superintendent Zoellner, Chairman of the National Church Committee. In addressing a meeting of the Chairmen of the Church Committees, Kerrl had complained of Zoellner:

". . . that he, like the Catholic Bishop Graf von Galen, spoke always of belief in Christ as the Son of God. This was laughable. For that was a dogma of the past; true Christianity was represented by National Socialism; National Socialism was the fulfilment of God's will; it was not the Church which had exhibited the faith which moves mountains, it was the Führer, and he was therefore the herald of a new revelation."[1]

Now even Zoellner was forced to confess what Bonhoeffer had declared at the very outset of the Church Committee experiment: "that between Church and pseudo-Church there could be no compromise". He resigned his post, and the Church Committees melted away. With this decisive turn of events, the Church struggle went into its final phase. Abandoning its attempts at compromise, the government once more changed its policy. Since the Church could be neither united behind the government and used as an instrument of propaganda, nor yet silenced by means of the Church Committees, it should simply be suppressed, and as far as possible Rosenberg's nationalistic paganism should be made to take the place of Christianity for the rising generation.

To take charge of the suppression policy, two men were appointed, Dr. Friedrich Werner and Dr. Muhs, and under their direction the new policy quickly began to operate. The measures of the Fifth Emergency Decree began to be rigorously enforced. The Church collections, upon which the Confessing Churches had hitherto largely depended, were sequestered and handed over to the Ecclesiastical Finance Department. A close watch was kept for announcements from the pulpit, public buildings were watched, duplicated circulars were confiscated. The illegal nature of the unofficial seminaries was emphasised, and pastors ordained through the organs of the Confessing Church were repeatedly declared to be without status. In support of these suppressive measures, large numbers of arrests were made.

[1] Karl Kupish, *Zwischen Idealismus und Massendemocratie*, p. 262.

Bonhoeffer made one last effort to press the true facts of the situation in the German Church upon the leaders of the Oecumenical Movement. In February, a week after the resignation of Zoellner, he took part for the last time in a meeting of the Youth Commission in London, to prepare for the full-scale meeting to be held in Oxford later in the year. Only Bishop Bell, whom he visited before he left England, clearly understood the direction in which ecclesiastical affairs in Germany were moving. The Secretary of the World Council clung firmly to the official line that all elements in the German Protestant Church should be represented, and the general view seems to have been that Bonhoeffer, in voicing the Confessing Church's unwillingness to take part together with the National Church, was making demands upon the Movement which it could not be expected to fulfil. After this meeting Bonhoeffer resigned his position as Joint Secretary of the Youth Commission, and henceforth his contacts with the Oecumenical Movement were to be of an altogether different nature.

Meanwhile the last year at Finkenwalde was beginning. Bonhoeffer's devotion and vigour as its director were never impaired by his disappointments in the Oecumenical Movement or his anxieties for the Confessing Church. Life at the seminary continued in its characteristic pattern of concentration and richness. The *Bruderhaus* was still its nerve centre, leading the community in its life of prayer, taking responsibility for the missions to surrounding parishes and holding together the students of the earlier courses through letters, visits and organised reunions.

To this work of supporting and befriending the students of earlier courses, Bonhoeffer and the *Bruderhaus* devoted immense resources of time and energy. The students of Finkenwalde past and present were welded into a community of Christian brothers who found in their unity a source of strength and a shared treasury of spiritual riches. It was an experience which to this day shows its profound effect upon those who survive, and what Finkenwalde might have meant for the Christian life of Germany if it could have continued into the present may still be conjectured. Its achievement in the less than three years of its existence was prodigious, and its influence was extended not only through the young pastors who went out from it, but also by means of those missions in surrounding parishes which were a special concern to the *Bruderhaus*.

Bonhoeffer himself radiated a particular influence among the Junker families who helped to support the seminary, and they in turn took him warmly to their hearts. His aristocratic dignity and unconstrained air of authority appealed to men who possessed the same qualities; and for Bonhoeffer, hours spent with these families in their graceful homes, where deep and simple piety and leisured culture spoke directly to a large area of his many-layered being, were among the most precious of his joys during the period at Finkenwalde. Of all the friendships made with these Pomeranian families, that with the Kleists and the Kleist-Retzows was to prove the most significant. From the first weeks of the seminary's life, the widowed head of the family, Frau Ruth von Kleist-Retzow, had supported the establishment with offerings of all kinds from her estate at Klein Krössin, and from her town house in Stettin she often came over herself surrounded by a crowd of grandchildren to take part in a morning service at the seminary. Among these grandchildren was a blue-eyed child, Maria von Wedemeyer, who at that time represented for Bonhoeffer just one member of the large, lovable, undifferentiated group; but five years later, in the last tense and dangerous months before his arrest, he was to see her again, a tall girl just flowering into womanhood, and her beauty and her particular quality were to dawn upon him. For the old lady, Frau von Kleist-Retzow, the coming of the seminary to Finkenwalde was the great event of her last years. It seemed to bring with it a Christian Renaissance for which she had long been waiting and praying. At the end of 1936, when Werner Koch was in prison, she wrote to his wife:

"It is extraordinary that now of all times people are speaking of the 'emptied' Word of God; I mean religious people, for whom the intensity and the rigour of this 'Word' is too great, and who would prefer it mild, edifying and reassuring. While I, an old woman, am making the discovery that it has never been so 'filled' as it is now."[1]

"This year I enjoyed most wonderful Easter days in my little country house, because Bonhoeffer and Bethge were with me for twelve days. The former wanted a quiet place in which he could work at a book on Christian Discipleship. What riches it was for me can hardly be expressed in words . . ."[2]

In the quiet backlands of rural Pomerania, it was still possible to celebrate Easter peacefully. But as the summer approached, the pressure upon the Confessing Church intensified. Five of the leading men in the reconstituted V.K.L. were arrested and sent for trial on charges of disobeying measures laid down in the Fifth Emergency Decree. Paul

[1] *Begegnungen*, p. 100.
[2] *Begegnungen*, p. 101.

Schneider, who two years later was to die a martyr's death in Buchenwald concentration camp, was arrested in his parish of Dickenschied for having imposed the discipline of the Church upon some party members, while on June 23rd the Gestapo entered a meeting of the Prussian *Bruderrat* in the Friedrich Werner Church and arrested eight of its members, including Bonhoeffer's friend, Friedrich Justus Perels, and on July 1st the offices of the new V.K.L. were searched and then closed and sealed off.

On this fateful day Bonhoeffer and Bethge arrived in Berlin in order to discuss the recent arrests with Martin Niemöller. They reached his house soon after breakfast, to be greeted with the news that he himself had just been arrested by the secret police. While they were discussing the situation with Frau Niemöller and Franz Hildebrandt they caught sight through the window of an unmistakable cortege of black Mercedes cars. The men attempted to escape through the back door, but walked straight into the arms of a Gestapo official and were herded back into the sitting room. Now began a long, strange day. For seven hours the Gestapo officials searched the house. They went through Niemöller's meticulously orderly papers page by page. They discovered 30,000 Reichsmark in a safe hidden behind a picture, vital resources of the V.K.L., and took possession of it. They were cold, impersonal and reasonably polite. As the hours dragged on from morning into afternoon, the news of what was happening by some means found its way to the Marienburgerallee, and Bonhoeffer, venturing an occasional glance out of the window, now saw his family's dark limousine cruising slowly up and down the street, with his mother's anxious face pressed against the window. At last the search was ended, and for the present the men who had spent seven hours in the sitting room were free to go. Anxiously they dispersed to their homes, and Frau Niemöller was left alone. She was to be alone for seven years, for her husband's long imprisonment had begun. But as she sat with her heart pounding, the rich harmonies of a choral stole upon her ear. The music came nearer. The women's choir of her husband's church had heard of his arrest. Under her window they were singing to her. That lovely characteristic gesture typified the spirit of the Dahlem Congregation. The imprisonment of their pastor had no power to intimidate them. Services continued under the ministry of Franz Hildebrandt, who continued to read from the pulpit all notices circulated by the *Bruderrat* and to make use of the collection in support of the church. Soon after Niemöller's arrest a service of intercession for their imprisoned pastor

185

was announced to the congregation for August 8th. Punctually on the morning of the day, members of the Dahlem church began to pour into the square on which it was situated. But they found their church cordoned off by the police. The crowd refused to disperse, and a march of protest began, one of the very few spontaneous demonstrations against the regime which ever took place in Nazi Germany. The police made some 250 arrests, among them Franz Hildebrandt, and this put an end to his career in Germany. Because of his half-Jewish extraction he was now in great danger, and the Bonhoeffers did not rest until they had secured his release. But it was no longer possible for him to live and work in Germany. Though his possessions had been searched the police, by a signal mercy, had not found his passport, so he was able to escape to England, where for many years he was active among German congregations. He has not returned to Germany.

Meanwhile the net was closing in around the illegal seminaries. Many of the Finkenwalde-trained pastors were in prison; a letter of August 26th gives an impression of the situation:

"Dear Brothers,

"The first word must be about our brothers in prison. After Brother Danicke and Brother Schrader, Brother Mickley and for the second time Brother Giese have also been arrested . . . on the famous Sunday at Dahlem Brother Grosch was also arrested. In the letters of these brothers one can hear the undertone: 'Certainly not everything is easy to bear, but . . . "be silent bow your head a little, our King will soon turn away our fear".'[1] Add to this a word from another letter: 'You must know that we are well aware of protection here. One cannot always tell, where one finds the patience. Only remain faithful in intercession for us, then we will not fear the battle. Ex. 17:11 . . .' "[2]

And so the last course came to an end. The brothers spent a few days together on the shores of the North Sea in the little conference centre at Zingst. They were hilarious days full of singing and uproarious laughter. The young men were light-hearted as only those can be who have abandoned their future to God, and accept every day of freedom as a gift from His hand. They parted on September 8th. Twenty days later, returning from a holiday with Bethge, Bonhoeffer heard that on orders from the Government, Finkenwalde had been closed.

A few weeks after this, his friend Helmuth Gollwitzer looked in upon

[1] From the words of a hymn: *Schweige, beuge Dich ein wenig, unser Konig wird behende machen, dass die Angst sich wende.*

[2] *G.S.* II, p. 520.

the Bonhoeffer family in their country house at Friedrichsbrunn. "I can still see us," he recalls in a memorial essay, "sitting on the terrace in a friendly circle and gazing out over the sunlit meadows, conversing with the light-hearted gaiety which was a particular feature of those years."[1]

Four hundred years ago, when a friend asked St. Ignatius Loyola how he would feel if the Pope dissolved the Society of Jesus, he is said to have answered, "A quarter of an hour's prayer, and I should think no more about it."

In Gollwitzer's slight vignette of Bonhoeffer, quietly radiant after Finkenwalde had been trampled under, we catch a glimpse of Loyola's own quality, that freedom of the spirit which has been one of the mysteries of sanctity through all the Christian ages. In the hard years that lay behind him, when he had been learning through prayer and discipline, and through a more and more total gift of his life to God and men, what it meant to be a disciple of Jesus, he had been gaining this freedom. And now the book that had been growing out of these struggles and that had been written in fleeting moments of leisure in Friedrichsbrunn and Finkenwalde and Klein Krössin, his great book, *The Cost of Discipleship*, was soon to appear.

This book is hard-lived, hard-prayed-for stuff. Throughout the book, much of which is cast in the form of an exposition of St. Matthew's version of the Sermon on the Mount, Bonhoeffer explores what it means to be a disciple. What is God demanding of us? What does it mean to follow Christ?

What it does not mean is adding a little more righteousness to an already passably righteous life. We are offered the example of the rich young man, who, like Adam tempted by the serpent, exposes himself by asking the wrong question, "What can I add to my life to make it perfect?" But the call of Christ is not a call to add something to what is already there, a little more morality, a little more discipline or a little more justice. It is an absolute demand: "Sell that thou hast, and give to the poor, and thou shalt have treasure in heaven, and come and follow me."

"The answer to the young man's problem is—Jesus Christ. He had hoped to hear the word of the good master, but he now perceives that this word is the Man to whom he had addressed his question. He stands face to face with Jesus, the Son of God; it is the ultimate encounter."[2]

---

[1] *Begegnungen*, p. 111.
[2] Dietrich Bonhoeffer, *The Cost of Discipleship*, 1964 edn., p. 66.

This is the situation for the disciple. He is face to face with a reality that makes absolute demands. The reality of Christ. Now Bonhoeffer begins to explore what that means:

"We must face the truth that the call of Christ does set up a barrier between man and his natural life. But this barrier is no surly contempt for life, no legalistic piety, it is the life which is life indeed, the gospel, the person of Jesus Christ. By virtue of his incarnation he has come between man and his natural life. There can be no turning back, for Christ bars the way. By calling us he has cut us off from all immediacy with the things of this world. He wants to be the centre, through him alone all things shall come to pass.

"Now we learn that in the most intimate relationships of life, in our kinship with father and mother, brothers and sisters, in married love, and in our duty to the community, direct relationships are impossible. Since the coming of Christ, his followers have no more immediate realities of their own, not in their family relationships nor in the ties with their nation nor in the relationships formed in the process of living. Between father and son, husband and wife, the individual and the nation, stands Christ the Mediator, whether they are able to recognise him or not. We cannot establish direct contact outside ourselves except through him, through his word, and through our following of him. To think otherwise is to deceive ourselves."[1]

And so the disciple sets out.

"It is not for us to choose which way we shall follow. That depends on the will of Christ. But this at least is certain: in one way or the other we shall have to leave the immediacy of the world and become individuals, whether secretly or openly.

"But the same Mediator who makes us individuals is also the founder of a new fellowship. He stands in the centre between my neighbour and myself. He divides, but he also unites. Thus although the direct way to our neighbour is barred, we now find the new and only real way to him —the way which passes through the Mediator."[2]

What then is the nature of this new life with our neighbour?

"What does it really mean to be a Christian? Here we meet the word which controls the whole chapter, and sums up all we have heard so far. What makes the Christian different from other men is the 'peculiar' the περισσόν, the 'extraordinary', the 'unusual', that which is not 'a matter of course'. What is the precise nature of the περισσόν. It is

[1] C. of D., pp. 85–6.
[2] C. of D., p. 90.

the life described in the beatitudes, the life of the followers of Jesus, the light which lights the world, the city set on the hill, the way of self-renunciation, of utter love, of absolute purity, truthfulness and meekness. It is unreserved love for our enemies, for the unloving and the unloved, love for our religious, political and personal adversaries. In every case it is the love which was fulfilled in the cross of Christ. What is the περισσόν? It is the love of Jesus Christ himself, who went patiently and obediently to the cross—it is in fact the cross itself. The cross is the differential of the Christian religion, the power which enables the Christian to transcend the world and to win the victory. The *passio* in the love of the Crucified is the supreme expression of the 'extra-ordinary' quality of the Christian life."[1]

This difference then, seems to be a difference in the very nature of our love. This love must issue in an unconditional gift of our lives to other people:

"We come to them with an unconditional offer of fellowship, with the single-mindedness of the love of Jesus.

"When we judge other people we confront them in a spirit of detachment, observing and reflecting as it were from the outside. But love has neither time nor opportunity for this. If we love, we can never observe the other person with detachment, for he is always and at every moment a living claim to our love and service. But does not the evil in the other person make me condemn him just for his own good, for the sake of love? Here we see the depth of the dividing line. Any misguided love for the sinner is ominously close to the love of sin. But the love of Christ for the sinner in itself is the condemnation of sin, is his expression of extreme hatred of sin. The disciples of Christ are to love unconditionally. Thus they may effect what their own divided and judiciously and conditionally offered love never could achieve, namely the radical condemnation of sin."[2]

It is such a love as this which is the pre-condition for the entirely unnatural love of our enemy:

"To the natural man, the very notion of loving his enemies is an intolerable offence, and quite beyond his capacity: it cuts right across his ideas of good and evil. More important still, to man under the law, the idea of loving his enemies is clean contrary to the law of God, which requires men to sever all connection with their enemies and to pass judgement on them. Jesus however takes the law of God in his own

[1] *C. of D.*, pp. 136–7.
[2] *C. of D.*, pp. 163–4.

hands and expounds its true meaning. The will of God, to which the law gives expression, is that men should defeat their enemies by loving them."

Such love as this can only be the fruit of grace, that grace which must be sought for and which costs us everything.

"Costly grace is the gospel which must be sought again and again, the gift which must be asked for, the door at which a man must knock.

"Such grace is costly because it calls us to follow, and it is grace because it calls us to follow Jesus Christ. It is costly because it costs a man his life, and it is grace because it gives a man the only true life."[1]

This is the life in God, whose love demands all that we have to give, and gives infinite riches in return:

"God's love for man is altogether different from the love of men for their own flesh and blood. God's love for man means the Cross and the way of discipleship. But that Cross and that way are both life and resurrection. 'He that loseth his life for my sake shall find it.' In this promise we hear the voice of him who holds the keys of death, the Son of God, who goes to the Cross and the Resurrection, and with him takes his own."[2]

It is only by accepting this love, and by giving ourselves wholly in reponse to it, that we can enable God's purpose for us to be fulfilled.

"To be conformed to the image of Christ is not an ideal to be striven after. It is not as though we had to imitate him as well as we could. We cannot transform ourselves into his image; it is rather the form of Christ which seeks to be formed in us (Gal. 4:19), and to be manifested in us. Christ's work in us is not finished until he has perfected his own form in us. We must be assimilated to the form of Christ in its entirety, the form of Christ incarnate, crucified and glorified."[3]

Just as this formation is the will of God for the individual Christian, so it is his will for the Christian community which is the Church:

"The form of Christ incarnate makes the Church into the Body of Christ. All the sorrows of mankind fall upon that form, and only through that form can they be borne.

"The earthly form of Christ is the form that died on the Cross. The image of God is the image of Christ crucified. It is to this image that the life of the disciples must be conformed: in other words, they must be conformed to his death (Phil. 3:10; Rom. 6:4f.). The Christian life is a

[1] C. of D., p. 37.
[2] C. of D., p. 196.
[3] C. of D., p. 272.

190

life of crucifixion (Gal. 2:19). In baptism the form of Christ's death is impressed upon his own. They are dead to the flesh and to sin, they are dead to the world, and the world is dead to them (Gal. 6:14). Anybody living in the strength of Christ's baptism lives in the strength of Christ's death. Their life is marked by a daily dying in the war between the flesh and the spirit, and in the mortal agony the devil inflicts upon them day by day. This is the suffering of Christ which all his disciples on earth must undergo. A few, but only a few, of his followers are accounted worthy of the closest fellowship with his sufferings—the blessed martyrs. No other Christian is so closely identified with the form of Christ crucified. When Christians are exposed to public insult, when they suffer and die for his sake, Christ takes on visible form in his Church. Here we see the divine image created anew through the power of Christ crucified. But throughout the Christian life, from baptism to martyrdom, it is the same suffering and the same death.

"If we are conformed to his image in his incarnation and crucifixion, we shall also share the glory of his resurrection. 'We shall also bear the image of the heavenly' (I Cor. 15:49). 'We shall be like him, for we shall see him even as he is' (I John 3:2). If we contemplate the image of the glorified Christ, we shall be made like unto it, just as by contemplating the image of Christ crucified we are conformed to his death. We shall be drawn into his image, and identified with his form, and become a reflection of him. That reflection of his glory will shine forth in us even in this life, even as we share his agony and bear his cross. Our life will then be a progress from knowledge to knowledge, from glory to glory, to an even closer conformity with the image of the Son of God. 'But we all, with unveiled face, reflecting as a mirror the glory of the Lord, are transformed into the same image from glory to glory' (II Cor. 3:18)."[1]

In this great book, the most active period of Bonhoeffer's Christian life had flowered. In the more obscure years which followed it the seed would begin to form which at last, before it could bear fruit, was to fall into the ground and die.

[1] C. of D., pp. 272–3.

CHAPTER XIV

". . . IN deep gratitude for all that God has given us in two and a half years of work at the seminary, we have taken leave of Finkenwalde, ready to take up the new tasks which are prepared for us. What we have learnt remains to us, what was of no value will fall away. And we can already tell you today that the new ways by which we are being led give us great cause for thankfulness."[1]

So ran the first part of Bonhoeffer's Christmas letter for 1937 to the scattered Finkenwalde brothers. It was not safe to say more about the "new ways" into which he was being led. But the fact was that the Prussian *Bruderrat* with its illegal seminaries finally closed, had decided upon the plan of *Sammelvikariate*. It is a word unrewarding to translate, for the first half of the term one may make a beginning with "collective" but *vikariat* must be translated "curacy" and by that time we have come a long way from the sense; so there is nothing for it but to keep the German term and discover what it represented.

The invention of the *Sammelvikariate* was based on the observation that the practice of sending a theological student as an apprentice curate to a pastor in a parish, which is a normal procedure in pastoral training in Germany, had not so far been interfered with, even when the pastor was an uncompromising supporter of the Confessing Church. The plan which was accordingly followed, not unknown before among some Protestant minorities, was to attach the students nominally to various obscure parishes, but in fact keep them all together in small groups and go on teaching them as though they were in a normal seminary.

Bonhoeffer was assigned to one such *Sammelvikariat*, which had two centres. One was in Kösslin, under the control of Superintendent Onnasch, the father of Fritz Onnasch who had been Bonhoeffer's Director of Studies at Finkenwalde in succession to Wilhelm Rott. Onnasch, a staunch supporter of the Confessing Church, had no difficulty in persuading ten of the pastors under his jurisdiction each to accept the "help" in his parish of a young man whom he rarely, if ever, saw. The ten young men were accommodated in the Superintendent's own capacious house, and his son Fritz became their Director of Studies.

[1] *G.S.* II, pp. 524–5.

A companion to this secret theological college was established in the country parsonage of Gross Schlönwitz, a few miles east of the country town of Schlawe, in the eastern wilds of Pomerania. Eberhard Bethge became Director of Studies to this group, and Bonhoeffer divided his time between the two, teaching half the week in Kösslin and the other half at Gross Schlönwitz. In order to escape the observation of the authorities as far as possible, he was registered as a curate attached to the parish of Schlawe, under the jurisdiction of Superintendent Block, and made this remote country town his official residence. Superintendent Block lent his support to all the necessary deceptions with imperturbable good humour, expertly covering Bonhoeffer's tracks, while keeping him informed of day-to-day events in a code of his own invention; and Bonhoeffer thankfully relied on this sturdy ally, whose humorous serenity no machinations of the government and no confused heart-searchings of the Confessing Church were able to disturb.

Very soon, under the protection of Onnasch and Block, the two groups of young men were hard at work, and the daily order which had been followed at Finkenwalde was re-established in their two secret centres. The Confessing Church at large knew only that somewhere Bonhoeffer, with Bethge as his lieutenant, was still training young pastors—it was wisest not to ask where. But though so little was known, the legends which surrounded the seminary at Finkenwalde still persisted, and not every student came to take part in the mysteries of the *Sammelvikariat* without misgiving. Early in 1939 one young man wrote to Bethge:

'I did not come to Schlönwitz in a glad or hopeful frame of mind . . . I shuddered at the prospect of this period of mental and physical straitening. It was to my mind a necessary evil . . . which one must endure gracefully and get through as well as possible on grounds of self-discipline . . . but then everything turned out quite different from what I had feared. Instead of entering the stuffy world of theological bigotry, I found myself in one which combined much of what I loved and needed; clear theological work in companionship with others, who never let one be wounded by feeling one's own incompetence, but who made the work a joy; brotherhood under the Word which united us all without respect of persons; and at the same time an appreciation of all that gives charm to the fallen creation: music, literature, sport and the beauty of the earth; a magnanimous way of living . . . when I look back I can see a clear picture . . . The brothers sitting in the afternoon over coffee and bread and jam. The chief returns after a long absence . . . now we get the latest news, and the world breaks into the quiet and simplicity of our country life in Pomerania . . . does it dull the exactness of your theological vision, if I tell you that it was the peripheral things which enhanced my appreciation of the central one ?"[1]

It is plain from these few lines that much of what had given Finkenwalde its special quality had now been recreated with this new venture.

At the same time Bonhoeffer exerted himself to encourage and hold together the Finkenwalde students. The year 1938 was a hard one for these young pastors. The Confessing Church was still torn by arguments between Lutheran and Reformed and between the compromisers and the non-compromisers. The young pastors were in a frustrating position. Since their ordination by the Confessing Church was illegal, they were without any official status, and meanwhile the Government, failing to gain anything by multiplying arrests, were devoting their energies to preventing the work of the Confessing Church by all manner of less spectacular means, and the young men found more and more doors closed to them. Many of them, who had willingly risked life and liberty in earlier, more spectacular battles, now began to weaken, when it seemed to them that they were wasting their energies in a dying cause. It is easier to give all than to endure the apparent impossibility of giving anything. Bonhoeffer was painfully aware of their dilemma, though never in doubt as to what course they should take. He did everything he could to strengthen their resolve.

In June he and Bethge gathered together as many as they could for a reunion at Zingst, the simple little holiday centre on the shores of the Baltic Sea, where the first weeks of the seminary's life had been spent. Bonhoeffer commented in a circular letter to those who could not be present that it was "a time of such riches as I have seldom experienced"[2] and another brother described the setting of the memorable days:

"The eldest brothers will be able to picture at least the exterior framework, the swimming, the games on the beach and the discussions among the sand-dunes, and all the rest of what has made this place so intimate in our memory . . . The day began of course with our common prayer in the form you remember and the meditation after breakfast, which was followed at once by singing. Before supper too, we sang for half an hour. In the morning Brother Bonhoeffer led a Bible study on temptation . . ."

This Bible study has survived, and the context in which it was delivered lends it a special intensity. All temptation is seen as the

[1] E.B., *D.B.*, p. 669.
[2] *G.S.* II, p. 533.

temptation to abandon the Word, the Word spoken by God through the Bible and in the person of Jesus Christ. This is the heart of the matter, and it is a temptation to which they are now exposed with especial force and directness, for if a brother grew weary of suffering for the integrity of the Word, he had only to capitulate to the Konsistorium[1] and allow himself to be ordained into the official Church in order to pursue his religious calling unmolested.

In this series of studies Bonhoeffer makes a passionate plea to his hearers to understand the true nature of temptation and to strip off its disguises. They will hardly have been surprised to meet the serpent, their old familiar, with his question: "Really, did God indeed say?" bringing in its train all the self-centred moral entanglements which followed upon his godless argument. But in fact, said Bonhoeffer, all temptation is ultimately the temptation to abandon Christ, for when the Christian is tempted it is Christ himself who is tempted in him.

"All temptation is temptation of Jesus Christ and all victory is victory of Jesus Christ. All temptation leads the believer into the deepest solitude, into abandonment by men and by God. But in this solitude he finds Jesus Christ, man and God. The blood of Christ and the example of Christ and the prayer of Christ are his help and strength. The book of Revelation says of the redeemed: 'they overcame . . . because of the blood of the lamb' (Reb. 12:11). Not by the spirit, but by the blood of Christ is the devil overcome."[2]

It was strong Lutheran theology, uncompromising and tough, and to these young men whose integrity was at stake, it spoke with compelling urgency. Meanwhile to those of the brothers whom he could not meet personally, Bonhoeffer wrote again and again, adjuring them to stand firm. At the end of the year he sent to all a strong and compelling letter on the necessity and power of patience:

". . . Here we have recently worked and thought together a great deal about the New Testament concept of patience. And by this means it has become quite evident to me that today, all along the line, we have reached a point at which everything depends fundamentally upon the question of whether we are willing to learn from the gospel what patience means. The various questions under whose heading impatience nowadays repeatedly creeps in, do not, it seems to me, need to be taken so seriously as they would like to be. But what is serious is the evil tricks that our impatience plays upon us, when by giving itself out to

---

[1] The official body by whom his ordination could be legalised.
[2] C. and T., p. 127.

be some quite particular form of obedience, it seduces us to faithlessness . . . We think we are acting in a particularly responsible way, when every few weeks we reopen the question as to whether the course that we have begun to follow is really the right one. And in this connection it is particularly noticeable that these 'responsible questions' begin to arise exactly at the moment when serious difficulties confront us. We then persuade ourselves that we no longer feel 'the requisite joy and conviction in following this course' or else, what is still worse, that God is no longer present to us in his Word with the old clarity, and basically all we are trying to achieve by this means, is to avoid what the New Testament means by 'patience' and 'steadfastness'. . . It is noticeable how much significance the New Testament attaches to patience. Only he who is patient receives the promises (Matt. 24:13) only he who is patient truly bears fruit (Luke 8:15). A faith which does not issue in patience is neither genuine nor effective. Faith must be steadfastly maintained. And steadfastness is only proved through suffering. Only through endurance, through remaining faithful will patience have her perfect work (James 1:3). If we consider that the word faith—*pistis*—contains within it the idea of patience, then the close connection between faith and patience will not seem strange to us. Patience can only be in Jesus (Rev. 1:9) for Jesus practised patience when he carried his cross. Hebrews 12:2 describes Christ's way of the cross as remaining faithful, as patience. Remaining faithful means for us having our part in the communion of Christ's suffering (I Cor. 1:6) and so learning confidence. If we share in the patience of Jesus, we shall ourselves grow patient, and at last we shall have our part in his kingdom (2 Tim. 2:12). The road to patience goes by way of discipline (2 Peter 1:6). The more we free ourselves from self-indulgence, indolence and personal demands, the more willing we shall be to have patience."[1]

Many were strengthened and encouraged by these exhortations, but from some, letters came back whose words would have weighed heavily upon a weaker spirit:

"The question I ask myself is what I ought to do if actually, at any rate here in Pomerania, the Confessing Church has got to the end of the road. Should I look round for another profession? Or should I say: against my better judgement and against my ecclesiastical convictions I will go to the Konsistorium,[1] because otherwise it is impossible for me to follow my vocation?"[2]

[1] *G.S.* II, p. 543.
[3] Letter from O. Kistner, quoted in E.B., *D.B.*, p. 688.

"I cannot regard the continuation of the course which we have followed hitherto either as theologically justified or as one for which I can be responsible either in my own case or in that of others."[1]

Such letters grew increasingly numerous, and in addition to the growing tendency to capitulate to the Konsistorium, the vast majority of pastors, even in the Confessing Church, took the oath of loyalty to Hitler without any reservation. When on November 9th, during the notorious "Crystal Night", Jewish Synagogues, shops and houses were burnt to the ground all over the Reich, the Confessing Church was silent. This was the year when the Confessing Church was at its lowest ebb, and the small number who refused all compromise seemed at this time to be an ever dwindling minority. These hard years of the Church's struggle, and of the struggle within the struggle, are a period in which one might have expected Bonhoeffer to be again overtaken by the familiar sense of isolation. Established in the remote provincial backlands of eastern Pomerania, cut off from his fellow theologians who were fighting their own battles at the universities, at loggerheads with the lukewarm party even in his own Confessing Church, he was becoming something of a legend to his contemporaries.

But the very fact of involvement in the struggle warmed and simplified the relationships of those few who, refusing to compromise, were daily risking their liberty together, and while his daily life was enriched by this particular quality of comradeship, his intellectual curiosity spurred him on to the voluntary explorations for which in his swift-moving life there was somehow always time; while, as the sources of inspiration remained limited, he came more and more to rely on the qualities of mind and character which Eberhard Bethge brought to the work that they were sharing. During these days of intellectual privation and spiritual hardship their friendship was developing a character of such stability and richness that a colleague, looking back on it after the war, could say of the relationship between these two outstanding men that he regarded it as one of the great friendships of history. By this time the two had become almost perfectly complementary to each other, and while Bethge's spirit was quickened by Bonhoeffer's fire, he could himself provide, through his own particular quality of quiet steadfastness, that shadow of a great rock in a weary land which met a fundamental need in Bonhoeffer's more dynamic nature. As the years went on, and the strains of living increased to a point which might have weakened and disintegrated the humanity of lesser men, these two grew

[1] Letter from G. Krause, E.B., *D.B.*, p. 688.

in stature together, while their friendship was strengthened and intensified by the stresses of the years through which it passed. Continually enriched by the sharing of multifarious joys, tempered by the challenge of disappointments, difficulties and finally of mortal danger, it was fulfilled at last in separation, and out of it the great last letters were born.

But besides the joys of comradeship, the stimulus of wide reading and the delights of this single deep friendship, there was another element which now entered Bonhoeffer's life and preserved him from the possibility of mental stagnation. Köslin and Schlawe, though further than Finkenwalde from Stettin, were nearer to Klein Krössin, the country house of Frau von Kleist-Retzow, and here Bonhoeffer and any of his students past or present, were free to come and go. Here he met many of the local landowners and others from further afield, among them Ewald von Kleist-Retzow and Fabian von Schlabrendorff, and there was talk of many matters besides theology.

In spite of the distance from Berlin, and the fact that Bonhoeffer was now forbidden by the government to enter the city on any business connected with the Church, he went home as often as he could. The new house in the Marienburgerallee was as lively a centre for old and young as the house in the Wangemheimstrasse had been. The Bonhoeffer parents were not noticeably aged and still took an intense interest in all their children's activities; with foreboding they watched the polluting life of Nazi Germany closing its tentacles round them, while the whispered word "resistance" began to be heard in influencial circles. The most deeply involved at this time in the dangerous business of political criticism was Christine's husband, the lawyer, Hans von Dohnanyi. As personal assistant to Gürtner, the Minister of Justice, he took part in Gürtner's losing battle to keep Germany's legal system free from Government interference. When in 1937 the Commanding Officer of the Reichswehr, Werner von Fritsch, had been court-martialled on a trumped-up charge of homosexuality, Dohnanyi had been entrusted with the assembling of material related to the case, and this had brought him in touch with Admiral Canaris, head of the *Abwehr*, the Government's Counter-Espionage Department, with his second-in-command, Major General Hans Oster and with Dr. Karl Sack, the Judge Advocate General, all important contacts for the future. Von Fritsch was eventually acquitted, but only after months of persecution, and it was at this time that Dohnanyi began to keep his "Chronicle of Scandals" in which he noted with a lawyer's meticulous precision any political injustices of which he had reliable information.

Hans von Dohnanyi was not easy to know. He had a cold, critical intelligence and a manner which could be reserved to the point of rudeness. But inside the shell there lurked a boyish gaiety which on rare occasions could break out and transfigure his whole personality, and with it there slept, half-buried, a deep unreflecting piety which quickened his conscience and made him care deeply for Christian values. In school and university days, Hans had been the particular friend of Klaus Bonhoeffer, but now, when his secret knowledge and his still more secret thoughts pressed heavily upon him, he would often turn to Dietrich for guidance and relief, and in the years immediately before the war they became intimate. Through Dohnanyi Dietrich came to know Hans Oster and Admiral Canaris, and through Klaus he met Dr. Otto John, a colleague of his in the Legal Section of the Luft Hansa. These were to be fateful friendships, and now conversations began to take place in the house in the Marienburgerallee which the Gestapo would have been interested to hear. But the Bonhoeffer family were learning perforce the arts of secrecy. To discretion in all their daily contacts they now added a family code, by means of which they could communicate by letter and telegram without arousing suspicion. As the autumn of 1938 approached, "Onkel Rudi" became the code-sign for Hitler's war preparations, and from Hans von Dohnanyi the family received exact information of many of Hitler's intentions months before they were made public.

To this world of inside knowledge and the first stirrings of conspiracy, Bonhoeffer would return as often as he could out of the political innocence of his rural retreat. And when he returned to Köslin and Gross Schlönwitz, bringing the waiting students "all the news from Berlin", those who knew him best had sometimes the impression that there might be certain news which would have interested them greatly, but which they were not privileged to hear.

It was in the autumn of this year that Helmuth Traub, a hot-headed disciple of Karl Barth, met Bonhoeffer for the first time. He had long been impatient to see this firebrand of the Confessing Church, this admired and notorious character, a beacon light to the faithful few, a thorn in the side of the majority.

Helmuth Traub was profoundly disappointed. Bonhoeffer was lecturing on Romans 13, "Let every soul be subject unto the higher powers". He spoke carefully, almost hesitantly. With scholarly accuracy and meticulous attention to detail, he analysed the chapter, paying attention to every question raised, carefully following out each side issue. Helmuth Traub was like a cat on hot bricks. At last he broke in with his own question: "What should actually be done, what *must* be done, since there was no doubt that resistance must be not only religious but also political?" The question remained unanswered.

But after the lecture Bonhoeffer took Traub aside. He assured him that he understood very well what he was concerned about, but it was necessary to face the facts and not act impulsively or irresponsibly. Then Bonhoeffer spoke of the Christian's responsibility. Traub suggested that he might be taking refuge in "reflection", to which Bonhoeffer replied that patience and reflection were necessary, but that they could only have value if they were combined with a resolute involvement in the life of the world. The Christian must be willing to abandon, not the Church, but the protective enclosure of Churchliness, if his witness was to be of value. Traub's disappointment was evaporating. Yet he was dimly aware of some interior struggle, some unresolved question in Bonhoeffer's own mind. This was indeed a hard period of transition for Dietrich, and even as he talked to the eager and innocent Traub, he bore a weight of dangerous and detailed secret knowledge which could not but foment searching questions within his own conscience.

For in the days of the Fritsch crisis, in which Hans von Dohnanyi had been so heavily involved, a centre of serious resistance to Hitler had begun to form. This centre was at the very heart of the machine, for it was in no other place than the Government's own Counter-Espionage Department the *Abwehr*, and the head and second-in-command of the department, Canaris and Oster, were its central figures. The leader of the movement in the older generation was to be General von Beck, at that time Chief of the General Staff.

At a secret conclave held on November 5th 1937, Hitler had made plain to the leaders of the armed forces his intention of satisfying Germany's territorial demands by force. Beck's reaction to this meeting had been to try to raise his fellow generals in revolt, and when, on May 30th 1938, Hitler made known to the government and the generals his intention of invading Czechoslovakia, Beck redoubled his efforts. With all the energy of a strong character trying to force a determined course of action upon a weak one, Beck urged upon van Brauchitsch, Commander-in-Chief of the Army, his absolute duty to protest to the Führer and to refuse to prepare for the invasion. But his peremptory appeal went unheeded. Under the title "Operation Green" the strategic planning for the invasion of Czechoslovakia went forward. On August 18th General von Beck resigned his post, and he now became the acknowledged leader of the secret forces of resistance within the Reich.

By this time it was the firm conviction of the circles in which the Bonhoeffers moved, that unless the government could be overthrown, a European war was inevitable. At the same time, as a result of the latest anti-Jewish regulations, all Jews would very soon be required to carry the letter J in their passports, which would make it an easy matter to prevent their leaving the country, and since, in any case, in the event of a war the frontiers of the belligerent countries would be closed, many Jewish families made a last-minute dash for freedom. Among these was the family of Bonhoeffer's twin sister Sabine, whose Jewish-born husband would be a victim of the new regulations. Their eldest daughter Marianne remembers with a painful exactness the last months in Göttingen which culminated in their flight:

"In the summer of 1938 I gathered from tiny hints thrown out by my mother that my parents were definitely preparing to leave Germany. I was just eleven. I knew about the Czech crisis and that there might be a war, that the likelihood of war was growing every day, that we did not want to be caught in Germany in a war because then we would no longer be able to leave the country if necessary. I knew that any plans to leave should be kept absolutely secret, and that if my parents told me no more than they did they had their reasons. I watched for hints of anything unusual in our lives, and on days when I got a strong feeling that something ominous would soon be happening put several large or small crosses in my diary, according to the strength of my suspicions.

"On August 23rd my parents went to Berlin for four days and Great-Aunt Elisabeth von Hase came to supervise the household. On August 31st my father went to Hamburg for the day, on September 4th my parents left for Berlin, returning late on September 8th with Uncle Dietrich Bonhoeffer and Pastor Eberhard Bethge. On all these days I put down huge crosses.

"The morning of September 9th was gloriously sunny in Göttingen. As usual our Nanny woke my seven-year-old sister Christiane and me at half past six and began to help us dress for school. Suddenly my mother came into the night nursery in a great hurry and said, 'You're not going to school today, we're going to Wiesbaden,' and to our Nanny, 'We'll be back on Monday. The children are to wear two lots of under-clothes each.'

"I knew at once that something very serious was happening to us. My parents never went to Wiesbaden, this was obviously said to mislead our Nanny, and never before had we had to wear two lots of underclothes. I said to myself: We're leaving; as we can't take more out of the country than goes into the car and we have hardly any money abroad, wearing two lots of underclothes is an inconspicuous way of getting some extra clothes out of the country. I tore downstairs and ran round the whole of our huge garden, saying goodbye to it. I wanted to say goodbye to all the rooms in the house but feared the adults would guess I knew what was up and confined my goodbyes to one floor. I collected two finger-length dolls, their passports and certificates of birth and baptism which I had previously made, crayons, my diary; these would go into my pocket. I realised that any big toys would take up valuable car space. My best friend Sybille came rushing up the stairs; we always walked to school together. 'You aren't ready! We'll be late for school!' 'I'm not coming, we're going to Wiesbaden for three days.' She stared at me, astonished and disappointed. 'Oh, well, goodbye then, I must dash.' I looked after her hard, thinking I must remember forever what she looked like.

"Our car was very full, but packed to look as if we were going on a normal holiday. Christiane and I were embedded in the back. Uncle Dietrich and 'Uncle' Bethge had brought another car, Uncle Dietrich's, and intended to accompany us to the frontier, and during the drive my parents and the uncles sat in the front seats of the two cars, changing places frequently, so that all came to sit with us children in turns.

"We stopped briefly in Göttingen where the men bought a giant torch for the journey. When we were out of the town my mother said, 'We're not going to Wiesbaden, we're trying to get across the Swiss border tonight. They may close the frontier because of the crisis.'

"The roof of our car was open, the sky was deep blue, the country-side looked marvellous in the hot sunshine. I felt there was complete solidarity between the four grown-ups. I knew that unaccustomed things would be asked of us children from now on but felt proud of now being allowed to share the real troubles of the adults. I thought that if I could do nothing against the Nazis myself I must at the very least co-operate with the grown-ups who could. Christiane and I spent most of the time singing in the car, folk songs and rather militant songs about freedom, my mother, Uncle Dietrich and 'Uncle' Bethge singing with us. I enjoyed the various descants. Uncle Dietrich taught me a new round *Über die Wellen gleitet der Kahn*.

"During the drive my uncle seemed to me just as I always remember him: very strong and confident, immensely kind, cheerful and firm.

"We stopped at Giessen and picknicked by the wayside. The grown-ups' mood did not strike me as depressing. Then all of a sudden they said it was getting late and that we must hurry. 'We have to get across the frontier tonight, they may close it at any moment.' We children settled in our car, our parents got in, and I remember Uncle Dietrich and 'Uncle' Bethge waving farewell to us, until they became tiny and were cut off by a hill. The rest of the drive was no longer cheerful. My parents drove as fast as they could, we stopped talking so that they could concentrate. The atmosphere was tense.

"We crossed the Swiss border late at night. Christiane and I pretended to be asleep and very angry at being wakened, to discourage the German frontier guards from doing too much searching of the car. My mother had put on a long, very brown suede jacket, whose brownness was meant to pacify the German officials. They let our car through and the Swiss let us in. My parents were not to cross the German border again till after the war.

"The sense of liberation after leaving German soil and entering a free country was so overwhelming in those days that an echo of that feeling still returns now, twenty-eight years later, whenever I cross the German frontier into Switzerland."[1]

So it was that Bonhoeffer's beloved twin sister left Germany with her family. They were not to return until after his death. Now they moved on from Switzerland and crossed over to England, where after a short time they settled in Oxford which was to be their home until after Hitler's fall.

By this time it had become evident to political observers within the Reich that Hitler was bent upon the destruction of Czechoslovakia as an independent state. As the mobilisation of the German forces got under way, Beck determined upon a *coup d'état*. He was convinced that it would succeed, for two reasons. First, because he believed that France, who had a military alliance with Czechoslovakia, would declare war as soon as her ally was attacked and that Britain would support her, and thus the invasion could be shown to be precipitating a European crisis; and secondly because he believed that the German people were whole-heartedly opposed to war, and that Hitler's stock was lower than it had ever been since his rise to power. Under the imminent threat of a major war, the commanding generals now rallied to his standard, and

[1] From a note written for the author by Marianne Leibholz and quoted with kind permission.

the *Abwehr* prepared to implement the *coup d'état*. The group around the house in the Marienburgerallee were heavily involved. In the last months Dr. Karl Bonhoeffer with a group of psychiatrists from the Charité hospital had been secretly working at a report on Hitler's mental condition, which the lawyers considered to be valid evidence. At the same time Oster and Dohnanyi had been preparing a plan of action. At the moment when Hitler gave the command for "Operation Green" to go into effect, he was to be seized by the conspirators, brought before his own "People's Court", and accused of irresponsibly involving the nation in war. The case would be in the hands of Dr. Karl Sack and Hans von Dohnanyi. It was expected that Hitler could be proved to be insane, or at least criminally irresponsible and unfit to continue in office. After his downfall the country would be temporarily administered by a military government until democratic elections could be arranged. To try to ensure a firm attitude on the part of Britain, several distinguished emissaries, including Bonhoeffer's friend Ewald von Kleist, were sent over to give all relevant information. Britain's reaction appeared indeterminate. The first action of Neville Chamberlain was to recall the British Ambassador for consultation and to concoct the plan of the visit to Hitler. Two more emissaries were sent over by the secret opposition, but without result.

Still the hopes of the plotters ebbed and flowed. The meeting between Chamberlain and Hitler at Berchtesgaden was followed by an apparent deadlock at Godesberg. Then the leaders of the resistance prepared to act. September 27th was an oppressive day. The spectacular parade of a new armoured division through the streets of Berlin was received in stony silence. When Hitler made an appearance on the balcony of the Chancellory there were no cheers. And Operation Green was to begin on September 30th. The conspirators believed that the decisive moment had come. The plan to seize Hitler was set for September 29th. And on September 28th the flight of Mr. Chamberlain to Munich was announced. The plot collapsed.

German historians are virtually unanimous in their conviction that it was Chamberlain's flight to Munich which sabotaged this first carefully-laid plan to overthrow the government. Whether it would have been possible in 1938 to bring Hitler before his own People's Court, and what would have been the effect upon a nation the vast majority of whom, though alarmed at the prospect of war, were still loyal to the Führer, provide somewhat intractable material for conjecture. But that intelligent and responsible leaders in the national life had every hope of success is certain, and the collapse of the plot was a severe blow to the resistance, from which it did not recover until the war had begun.

Upon Dietrich Bonhoeffer the knowledge of this secret story must have weighed heavily. With Dohnanyi and with Bethge he had many heartsearching conversations as to what must be the duty of a Christian in a country where some of its best citizens were involved in such ambiguous proceedings. Bethge records how one evening Dohnanyi asked his brother-in-law in what sense one should understand the passage in the New Testament in which Jesus warns his disciples that they that take the sword shall perish by the sword. Bonhoeffer replied that the words must be taken as they stood and as being valid for the present time. Christians must accept the fact that they came under the power of that judgement, but that the times had need of men who would be willing to take it upon them. It was an uncompromising verdict, and even as Dietrich spoke these words to Hans, he must have heard them spoken in his own heart to him. And with how terrible a truth for them both!

CHAPTER XV

On March 15th 1938 the Occupation of Prague was added to the accumulation of Adolf Hitler's bloodless victories. In Germany the man in the street began really to believe that all Germany's territorial demands would be met in answer to a skilful combination of intimidation with infiltration and propaganda. But in the informed circles to which the Bonhoeffers belonged the firm conviction continued that as a result of Hitler's policies a European war was inevitable, and in all probability imminent.

For Dietrich, this posed a serious personal dilemma. Though firmly opposed on Christian grounds to war, he was not a pacifist who would have refused to fight in any circumstances whatever. But to fight in order to maintain the Nazi state would be for him a moral impossibility. Meanwhile political indications seemed to suggest that in 1939 his age-group would be called up, in which case, unless he was regarded as being in a reserved occupation, the decision as to whether or not to refuse military service was likely to be required at any time. The Confessing Church was aware of this attitude, and feared that their position in Germany would be further weakened if one of their most prominent members made this refusal. Bonhoeffer himself intensely disliked being overtaken by events. It was in order to gain a respite to clarify his ideas that in 1934 he accepted the call to Sydenham and Forest Hill. Towards the end of 1938 a similar idea entered his mind; he put out one or two feelers to explore the possibility of making a lecture tour in the United States, and took the opportunity which a short visit to England provided, to discuss his problem with Bishop Bell.

During this visit to England Bonhoeffer also met Visser 'tHooft who had succeeded Henriod as Secretary to the World Council of Churches. It was the beginning of a friendship which was to continue through the war years. Visser 'tHooft has written his recollections of the occasion:

"My first meeting with Dietrich Bonhoeffer took place in the spring of 1939. It was at Paddington Station in London. We had heard much about one another, but it was still a surprise to find that we could so quickly break through the zone of first contact into the deeper zone of serious conversation, and that indeed he was soon treating me like an old friend. One was aware that in the battles of the recent years he had discovered a freedom which allowed him to approach people quite directly.

"We walked for a long time to and fro in the station. He described the situation of his Church and his country. Remarkably free from illusion, and sometimes almost like a clairvoyant, he spoke of the coming war which would soon break out, probably in the summer . . . But what would that mean in concrete decisions? Was not the hour come to refuse to serve a government which was consciously directing the country towards war, and ignoring every law? But what would be the consequences for the Confessing Church if he adopted this attitude? I remember his sharp questions better than his answers. But I think I learnt more from his questions than he did from my answers. In the obscure world between 'Munich' and 'Warsaw', in which hardly anyone ventured to formulate the actual problems, this questioning voice was like a liberation."[1]

Bonhoeffer's enquiries with regard to the possibility of finding some academic occupation for a time in America soon began to bear fruit. Reinhold Niebuhr and Paul Lehmann constituted themselves a committee to offer him round the American universities, and meanwhile Dr. Henry Smith Leiper, General Secretary of the Federal Council of Churches, hearing that there was some urgency in the matter, secured the offer of a summer appointment for him at Union Theological Seminary and at Columbia University and a more permanent appointment as pastor to German Christian refugees. But for Bonhoeffer the decision to make a second journey to the States seems to have lacked conviction from the outset. He was by no means clear what his real motives and intentions were. The main ingredients of the decision seem to have been his strong desire to live in freedom and pursue his theological calling untrammelled by the increasing political pressures of Nazi Germany, together with a wish to escape the decision about military service, which resolved in one way would have embarrassed the Confessing Church, and in the other was likely to embarrass his own conscience. Added to these considerations was the rather thin justification that the journey might provide openings for service in the oecumenical field. Against the journey was his deep concern for the Confessing Church; his sense of involvement in the life of his country, and the strongest of all perhaps, only half-acknowledged in the depths of his heart, the fact that Bethge was to remain behind. Meanwhile the question of how long he proposed to stay remained open. In the earlier

[1] Visser 'tHooft, *Zeugnis eines Boten*, pp. 6–7.

stages of the plan he may have been not entirely unwilling to stay in America for the duration of the war which he so clearly saw approaching, but soon after arriving he ceased to treat this as though it had ever been a possibility. That he was going to America to escape political danger was never in the forefront of his or his German friends' minds; by later standards his physical danger then was not great. But his American friends believed themselves to be engaged on a rescue operation. In a letter of May 31st Leiper wrote: "I had word from Reinhold Niebuhr in Edinburgh that Dietrich Bonhoeffer was slated to go into a concentration camp unless we could get him out of Germany."[1] It would have shocked and surprised Bonhoeffer if he had known that they saw it in this light. But in the urgency of the arrangements, this divergence between the American assumption and his own had no time to appear. On May 10th a radiogram arrived from Leiper: "Central Bureau Interchurch Aid urgently requests your coming New York immediately at latest by mid June to accept important combination post theological lectureship and Church work at Summer Conferences and Universities."[2]

On June 4th Bonhoeffer left Germany. His post with the *Sammelvikariat* was taken over by Helmuth Traub. On June 8th, accompanied by his brother Karl Friedrich, who was also engaged for a lecture tour in the States, he sailed from Southampton. In the next weeks a hard and far-reaching decision was to be made. Should he remain in the States, as his American friends confidently expected him to do, or should he return home? As the weeks went by it became increasingly plain that if he was to return at all, he must return immediately, since war in Europe was manifestly imminent.

The decision which Bonhoeffer made in the summer of 1939 determined the final course of his development, and in the next decade it was to cost him his life. The story of these vital weeks emerges from Bonhoeffer's journal and from contemporary letters with a vividness that comment could only obscure. The journal begins on the first day of his voyage out, with a quotation from *Losungen*, a series of daily Bible readings published annually by the Moravian Brethren, which Bonhoeffer and Bethge read together for many years:

"Zechariah 9:9: Execute true judgement, and show mercy and compassion every man to his brother.

"Matthew 5:7: Blessed are the merciful, for they shall receive mercy.

[1] *G.S.* I, p. 289.
[2] *G.S.* II, p. 349.

"Yesterday evening, shortly after writing[1] I made the acquaintance of a young American theologian, a one-time member of Union.[2] It was like a cross-examination. We spoke of Christianity in Germany, in American and in Sweden, whence he has just come. What a task there is in America!

" 'Execute true judgement . . .' This I desire first of all from you, my brothers at home. I do not want you to spare me in your thoughts. But how can true judgement before the merciful God, and before the Cross of Jesus Christ be other than merciful? Not a blind mercy; for that would not be merciful, but a seeing and forgiving, brotherly mercy as the just judgement upon us.

" 'Execute true judgement . . .' that is a necessary warning and predication for the task in America. It forbids all arrogance and establishes the greatness of the task. If we recognise in the others brothers who stand in Christ's mercy as we do, and do not go on living and speaking simply out of our own perceptions and experience, then we shall not be censorious but merciful. So long as God will remain merciful to *us*!

9th June 1939

"Isaiah 41:9: Thou art my servant; I have chosen thee and not cast thee away.

"John 12:26: If any man serve me, let him follow me; and where I am, there shall also my servant be.

"God chooses the sinner to be His servant, so that His grace may become perfectly evident. The sinner shall do God's work, and show forth His Grace. When God forgives a man, he gives him work to do. But this work can be sustained only in discipleship. Large programmes only lead to the places where we stand ourselves; but we ought only to be found where God is. We can be no longer anywhere else than where He is. You may work over there and I in America, but each of us are only where He is. He takes us with Him. Or have I left behind me the place where He is? Where He is for me? No, God says: thou art my servant."

"10th June 1939

"Psalm 28:7: The Lord is my strength and my shield; my heart trusted in Him and I am helped; therefore my heart greatly rejoiceth, and with my song will I praise Him.

[1] To Eberhard Bethge.
[2] Theological Seminary.

"Ephesians 4:30: Grieve not the Holy Spirit of God, whereby ye are sealed unto the day of redemption.

"In what can the heart rejoice, except in the certainty that God is our dear Father, and Jesus Christ our Saviour! And how can we grieve the Holy Spirit more than by retaining sad thoughts and not trusting ourselves wholeheartedly to his direction, his language and his comfort? Until the day of redemption arrives, really arrives!"

"11th June 1939
"Psalm 44:21: he knoweth the secrets of the heart.

"I Corinthians 13:12: now I know in part; but then shall I know even as also I am known.

"Today is Sunday. No service. The hours are already so much changed, that I cannot take part in your service at the appropriate time. But I am completely with you, today more than ever. If only I could overcome my doubts about the way for me. The search for the secrets of one's own heart, which are not to be fathomed—'He knoweth the secrets of the heart'—when the tangle of accusations and excuses, of hopes and fears renders everything in us opaque, then only God can see clearly into the depths. But there He finds a name which he himself has written: Jesus Christ . . ."

"12th June 1939
"Deuteronomy 6:6: And these words which I command thee this day, shall be in thy heart.

"Acts 15:40: and Paul . . . departed, being recommended by the brethren to the Grace of God.

" 'Paul departed, being recommended by the brethren to the Grace of God'. Arrival in New York. To know during these first hours that brothers had recommended us to the Grace of God made all the difference. The Reverend Mr. Macy, from the Federal Council of Churches, greeted me on the quay. First night in Parkside Hotel. In the evening Dr. Sch. came to fetch me. The whole problem of the German emigration became apparent . . ."

"13th June 1939
"Breakfast with Leiper, who came to fetch me and greeted me most warmly. First conversation about the future. I made clear as a basis for everything, that I want to return in a year's time at latest. Surprise. But I am perfectly certain that I shall have to return . . . Four o'clock

meeting with President Coffin on Grand Central. I am to stay with him a few days in his house in the country . . .

"The country house in Lakeville, Connecticut, is in the hills, it is cool and the vegetation luscious. In the evening, thousands of fireflies in the garden, moving candleflames. I had never seen them. A quite fantastic sight. Very warm and 'informal' reception—In all this only Germany and the brothers are missing. The first lonely hours are hard. I cannot make out why I am here, whether it makes sense, whether the result will justify it. Last thing in the evening: the Bible readings and the thought of work at home. Nearly two weeks have passed now, without my hearing anything from over there. It is hardly to be borne. 'It is good that a man should both hope and quietly wait for the salvation of the Lord' (Lamentations 3:26)."

"14th June 1939
"Breakfast on the verandah at eight o'clock. It poured with rain in the night. Everything is fresh and cool. Then prayers. The short prayer—the whole family kneels—in which we remembered our German brothers, almost overwhelmed me . . ."

"15th June 1939
"Since yesterday evening I can hardly tear my thoughts away from Germany . . . I found a drive to visit a friend in the hills, in itself delightful, almost unendurable. We sat for an hour and chatted, not all that stupidly, but about matters to which I was entirely indifferent . . . and I thought how usefully I might have employed this hour in Germany. I should have liked best to board the next ship home. This being unoccupied, or occupied with indifferent matters, seems simply to be no longer bearable for us, when we think of the brothers and how precious time is. The whole weight of self-reproach for a wrong decision, rises up again and almost overpowers one . . . incidentally, a letter to Leiper; I must return in a year at the latest."

From Dietrich Bonhoeffer to Henry Smith Leiper
"15th June 1939
". . . these beautiful days in Dr. Coffin's country home are giving me some time to think about my future, and I am sure you will understand that I should like to put the situation before you as I see it, and ask your advice. Before I left Germany I had long talks with my Brethren from the Brethren Council and pledged myself to return to Germany after

about a year's time to take up the training work in the Confessing Church again, unless some unforeseen development would change the whole situation . . . The post which you are kindly intending to confer upon me attracts me from every point of view. I feel strongly the necessity of that spiritual help for our refugees . . . The only thing that makes me hesitate at the present moment of decision is the question of loyalty to my people at home. . . . I must not for the sake of loyalty to the Confessing Church accept a post which in principle would make my return to Germany impossible. Now my question is whether that would not be the case with any post that is officially concerned with refugee work? As a matter of fact I am afraid it would be so . . ."

"16th June 1939
"Only a fortnight since I left Berlin, and already so much longing for my work. Return to New York. Evening at last. I needed this badly. One is less lonely when one is alone . . . I am waiting for mail. It is hardly to be borne. I probably shall not stay long. God's word says today: 'Behold, I come quickly' (Revelations 3:11). There is no time to waste, and here I am wasting days and it may be weeks. At any rate, it looks like that at the moment. And then I think again: is it cowardice and weakness to run away from here now? But shall I ever be able to do really useful work here? Disturbing political news from Japan. If things become unsettled, I shall certainly return to Germany. I cannot stay alone outside the country. That is quite clear to me. I am living completely over there . . ."

"18th June 1939
". . . Through my intention and my interior necessity, continually to remember the brothers over there and their work, I have been almost abandoning my task over here. It would seem to me almost like disloyalty if my heart were not completely in Germany. I must find the right balance in this. Paul also writes that he is constantly present with his community in prayer, and yet he was able to devote himself entirely to the immediate task. That remains to be learnt. It will only be possible through prayer. May God give me in the next week a clear conviction about my future and maintain me in the fellowship of prayer with the brothers.

"The whole day without news from Germany. From post to post I have waited in vain. At the same time it is no use to get angry and write letters in that spirit. By the time the letter arrives, the news I am waiting for will have come long ago. I want to know how the work goes on over there, whether all is going well or whether they need me. I want some leading from over there for tomorrow's decisive conversation. Just as well perhaps that it has not arrived. Could one get home in time, if anything started?—All day in the library writing English lectures . . ."

"*20th June 1939*
"In the morning, a letter from the parents in South Germany. Nothing from Stettin. Visit to Leiper. I have refused. They were visibly disappointed and I think a little out of humour. For me it must certainly mean more than I can be aware of at this moment. Only God knows. It is strange, in any decision, I am never quite clear about my motives. Is that a sign of uncertainty, inner dishonesty, or is it a sign that God leads us over and beyond our own powers of discernment, or is it both? . . ."

"*21st June 1939*
". . . Of course I still go on wondering about my decision. One could have argued in quite another direction. I am here now (perhaps the misunderstanding itself was a leading?); they tell me that when my coming was announced it was like an answer to prayer; I was just the one they wanted, all future plans are upset; I have no news from home, whether all may not be going on just as well without me etc. Or one might ask, have I acted simply out of longing for Germany and the work there? And was my almost incomprehensible and hitherto unknown homesickness an accompanying sign from above which was to make the refusal easier? Or, is it not irresponsible in view of so many other people, simply to say no to my own future and to that of many others? Shall I regret it? I must not, that is certain. For me in spite of everything my promise stands in the first place, then the joy of the work at home and finally the other man whom I should be ousting. Again the Bible passage speaks hard words: 'he shall sit as a refiner and purifier of silver' (Malachi 3:3), I need it too. I no longer know where I am but He knows, and in the end all acting and doing will be clear and clean."

"*22nd June 1939*
". . . We cannot after all separate ourselves from our destiny, here less than ever . . ."

"*24th June 1939*
"Mail at last. It is a great release. But it is now quite clear to me again, that I must return to my work . . ."

". . . Today I read by chance in II Timothy 4, 'Do thy diligence to come before winter', Paul's petition to Timothy. Tomothy is to share the suffering of the apostle and not to be ashamed. 'Come before winter'—otherwise it might be too late. That has been in my mind all day. It is for us as it is for soldiers, who come home on leave from the front but who, in spite of all their expectations, long to be back at the front again. We cannot get away from it any more. Not because we are necessary, or because we are useful (to God?), but simply because that is where our life is, and because we leave our life behind, destroy it, if we cannot be in the midst of it again. It is nothing pious, more like some vital urge. But God acts not only by means of pious incentives, but also through such vital stimuli. 'Come before winter'—it is no misuse of scripture, if I accept that as having been said to me. If God gives me grace for it."

Paul Lehmann to Reinhold Niebuhr
"28th June 1939

"Immediately upon receipt of your letter May 11th, I got started. I wrote at once to Dr. Press and contacted Pauck and Paul Scherer. The enclosed letter[1] which I am sending out today to some thirty or forty places will speak for itself. I hope replies will not come in too slowly.

"Meanwhile a letter has come from Bonhoeffer who is already at Union. I don't quite know what to make of it, for he speaks already of going back. He says that he is not a refugee and must go back to Germany to take up his work over there, for Germany needs teachers . . ."[2]

Paul Lehmann to Dietrich Bonhoeffer
"June 28th 1939

"You cannot know with what joy and relief your letter was received. It came to me just when I had to be away for some days and to take part in a Conference here for some days, so that I have had to wait until now to reply. Evidently my letter of May 27th, sent to Berlin will not have reached you. Since that time Marion and I have been eagerly awaiting word of your arrival in Union. Now that you are there we can scarcely wait until you are here with us.

"Whether or not Dr. Niebuhr has been too optimistic I do not know.

[1] A circular letter offering Bonhoeffer as lecturer for the academic year 1939–40.
[2] *G.S.* II, pp. 353–4.

But I do know that it is unthinkable that you should return until America has had the fullest opportunity to be enriched by your contribution to its theological hour of destiny. At least, I like to think of it in this way. The tragic political occasion for these disturbed times may have one great and positive overtone in the widening of the American theological understanding by the present cross-fertilisation with the continental tradition. So that you must see this also as a responsibility, as well as the German need for teachers . . ."[1]

Postcard, Dietrich Bonhoeffer to Paul Lehmann
"June 28th 1939
"I wonder if you have received my letter last week. Things have changed for me entirely. I am going back to Germany on August 2nd or even July 25th. The political situation is so terrible. But of course I should like to have a word from you before I leave. I am enjoying a few weeks in freedom, but on the other hand I feel I must go back to the 'trenches' (I mean of course, the Church struggle)."[2]

Bonhoeffer's Journal
"June 28th 1939
". . . Newspaper reports grow more and more disturbing. They distract one's thoughts. I cannot believe it to be God's will that I should stay on here, in the event of war, without any particular assignment. I must return at the first possible opportunity."

Dietrich Bonhoeffer to Paul Lehmann
"June 30th 1939
"Thank you so much for your good letter, which is so full of friendship and hope for the future. I can hardly find it in my heart to tell you that in the meantime I have had to decide to return to Germany within the next weeks. My invitation to come over here was based on a misunderstanding to the effect that I intended to remain in America indefinitely. Therefore it was proposed to make me responsible for the care of Christian refugees here, a work which, necessary as it is, would have prevented any possibility of my returning to Germany. It must be done by a refugee. In the meantime everything has been decided and set in order with the Confessing Church; I return in July or August. I certainly regret it in some ways, but on the other hand I am glad that I

[1] *G.S.* II, p. 354-5.
[2] *G.S.* II, p. 356.

shall very soon be able to help again over there. I am drawn back into the struggles of the brothers. You will understand that! And now I have an urgent request: in your very kind letter to the Colleges you mentioned my work in Pomerania. If a page of information like this should fall into the hands of German authorities, this work, which is at present continuing, would be at an end. Will you understand me if I ask you, warmly and urgently, to write round again at once, saying that I have already returned home, so that the whole thing no longer arises, and perhaps also (which is important to me) that the suggestion was the result of a misunderstanding! I hope that the circles concerned are responsible enough not to allow the letter to go further. Now you have had a great deal of work, and I thank you for it most warmly. It is a bitter disappointment to me, that we shall not see each other . . ."[1]

Bonhoeffer's Journal
"July 1st 1939
". . . All day long I have been unable to forget the situation in Germany and in the Church. The Daily Readings are so good again! Job 41:11. God speaks: 'Who has prevented me that I should repay him? Whatsoever is under the whole heaven is mine,' and Romans 1:36: 'For of him and through him and to him are all things, to whom be glory for ever, amen.' The world, the nations, Germany and above all the Church, can never slip from his hand. It is terribly hard for me, in the face of the present situation to think and to pray 'thy will be done'. But it must be done. Tomorrow is Sunday. May God's word find hearers in all the world."

Paul Lehmann to Dietrich Bonhoeffer
"July 2nd 1939
"Your letter was awaiting me when I arrived here this morning. It was of great help in explaining your card which I received in Elmhurst on last Thursday. But I cannot tell you how deeply it troubles both Marion and me. I write now, believe me, with great heaviness of spirit.

"I shall, of course, comply immediately with your request. Please know that I do so with great reluctance and out of a full understanding of your situation. On such a basis you are not entitled to speak of effort expended and of kindnesses shown. The principal matter of concern is you, and the cause to which you are devoted.

"Now I have the following to propose: we must meet before you

[1] *G.S.* II, p. 357.

return. I simply could not think of your being here and going back without it. Therefore you must be good enough to let me know by return mail which time will be best for my coming to New York . . ."

Dietrich Bonhoeffer to Reinhold Niebuhr
"July 1939
"Sitting here in Dr. Coffin's garden I have had the time to think and to pray about my situation and that of my nation and to have God's will for me clarified. I have come to the conclusion that I have made a mistake in coming to America. I must live through this difficult period of our national history with the Christian people of Germany. I shall have no right to participate in the reconstruction of Christian life in Germany after the war if I do not share the trials of this time with my people. My brothers in the Confessional Synod wanted me to go. They may have been right in urging me to do so, but I was wrong in going. Such a decision each man must make for himself. Christians in Germany will face the terrible alternative of either willing the defeat of their nation in order that Christian civilisation may survive, or willing the victory of their nation and thereby destroying our civilisation. I know which of these alternatives I must choose, but I cannot make that choice in security . . ."

Bonhoeffer's Journal
"July 6th 1939
"I am writing on board ship. The last two days were so full, that I had no time to write. In the morning, down town to complete preparations for the journey. On the return, Stock Exchange. Shopping. At two-thirty I met Paul Lehmann in my room, who has travelled from Columbus, Ohio to see me. Great joy. From then on, all the remaining time spent with him. Prepared a lecture."

"July 7th 1939
"Last day. Paul tries to make me stay. No longer possible. Van Dusen lecture. Packing. Afternoon with Hans Wedell. Theological discussions with Paul. Farewell at the Seminar. Dinner with van Dusen. Drive to the ship with Paul. Eleven-thirty farewell, twelve-thirty departure. Manhattan by night. The moon riding above the skyscrapers. It is very hot. The journey is finished. I am glad to have been here and glad to be on the way home again. Perhaps I have learnt more in this month than in a whole year nine years ago; at least I have realised things

which will be important for future decisions. Probably this journey will have a prolonged effect upon me."

"*July 9th 1939*
". . . Since I have been on the ship, the interior conflict about my future has ceased. I can think about the abbreviated time in America without self-reproach. Passage for the day: 'It is good for me that I have been humbled; that I might learn thy statutes.' (Psalm 119:71). From my favourite psalm one of my favourite verses."[1]

---

[1] Where not otherwise stated, quotations are made from *G.S.* I, pp. 292–320.

CHAPTER XVI

BONHOEFFER knew very well into what sort of world he was returning; having been privy to the first plot against Hitler, and knowing through Dohnanyi's chronicle of scandals the increasingly criminal directions which National Socialism was taking, he was aware that the course of his own life might now be drastically affected. Up to the point of his departure for America he had been able to follow an obviously honourable course, fighting for the integrity of his Church out in the open and side by side with other Christians. When he returned he had chosen to put himself in a situation in which he might be drawn away into obscure and devious paths, where he would associate with any who were intriguing for the downfall of the regime, and where less than half of what he did or said could be what it seemed to be.

In the event, Bonhoeffer's involvement in the resistance did follow step by step upon his return. Bethge sees in this momentous decision a second vital landmark in his spiritual development. After his first return from America, facing the complete disillusionment of 1932 and driven to the abandonment of many personal hopes, the theologian had become a Christian; in this second return, the Christian became completely a man of his time. Still a theologian and more than ever a Christian, he became now also, little by little, but at last fully and unreservedly, a citizen of the world in which his fate had set him.

But deeply hidden below these observable changes, there lies another, invisible and seen only in its effects. For as Bonhoeffer became more and more deeply enmeshed in the evil necessities of his time, he was driven quietly to accept the loss of that particular personal treasure which he had many times struggled to abandon, but which yet had clung to him, wrapping its powerful tentacles round his inmost being: the sense of his own righteousness. His own righteousness. It had been the pursuing demon through all his past life. The maggot at the heart of the rose, the material of his most agonised confessions, the cause of his occasional black despondency, the subject of intense and seemingly unanswered prayer. For it was there. It was a fact. Its iron presence held him. His own righteousness. But now, as the last stages of his life unfolded, his prayers were answered in a manner which seemed almost paradoxically simple. For his righteousness was taken from him. Step by step he was to be involved in a conspiracy which would require the abandonment of much that Christian life demands, expert lying built up into layer upon layer of closely-woven deception, and ultimately the willingness to murder. Bonhoeffer never for a moment regarded these evils as anything but what they were—evil. He accepted them as necessary.

To sacrifice his life in open martyrdom for a clearcut Christian issue would not have been easy. Who would dare to say that martyrdom is ever easy? But for Bonhoeffer there is a real sense in which it would have been easier than this secret martyrdom, the death of his inmost claim to righteousness.

It seems no accident that it should have been in this year, when Bonhoeffer plunged back out of the safety and freedom of America into an extreme of moral and physical danger, that he began to write *The Ethics*. This book is no product of a professor's peaceful study. It comes to us red-hot out of a cauldron which boiled with agonising decisions, decisions which could mean life or death for the body and salvation or damnation for the soul.

"Today there are once more villains and saints, and they are not hidden from the public view. Instead of the uniform greyness of the rainy day we now have the black storm-cloud and the brilliant lightning flash. The outlines stand out with exaggerated sharpness. Reality lays itself bare. Shakespeare's characters walk in our midst. But the villain and the saint have little or nothing to do with systematic ethical studies. They emerge from primaeval depths and by their appearance they tear open the infernal or the divine abyss from which they come and enable us to see for a moment into mysteries of which we had never dreamed."[1]

With ruthless clarity Bonhoeffer demonstrates the impossibility of following a course which is reliably and satisfactorily good. Looking round him, he sees the solutions which men have attempted within the imprisoning evil of his time and rejects them, including his own:

"But if someone sets out to fight his battles in the world in his own absolute freedom, if he values the necessary deed more highly than the spotlessness of his own conscience and reputation, if he is prepared to sacrifice a fruitless principle to a fruitful compromise, or for that matter the fruitless wisdom of the *via media* to a fruitful radicalism, then let him beware lest precisely his supposed freedom may ultimately prove his undoing. He will easily consent to the bad, knowing full well that it is bad, in order to ward off what is worse, and in doing this he will no

[1] Dietrich Bonhoeffer, *Ethics*, p. 3.

longer be able to see that precisely the worse which he is trying to avoid may still be the better. This is one of the underlying themes of tragedy."[1]

Who then shall be saved? Bonhoeffer knows out of the depths of his own experience, that to such a question there is no direct answer. But drawing on these same depths he can tell us how to listen for the indirect answer in which truth must often be contained, and now were written those words which were the fruit of many years' experience in prayer and discipleship:

"Yet our business now is to replace our rusty swords with sharp ones. A man can hold his own here only if he can combine simplicity with wisdom. But what is simplicity? What is wisdom? And how are the two to be combined? To be simple is to fix one's eye solely on the simple truth of God at a time when all concepts are being confused, distorted and turned upside-down. It is to be single-hearted and not a man of two souls, an ἀνὴρ δίψυχος (Jas. 1:8). Because the simple man knows God, because God is his, he clings to the commandments, the judgements and the mercies which come from God's mouth every day afresh. Not fettered by principles, but bound by love for God, he has been set free from the problems and conflicts of ethical decision. They no longer oppress him. He belongs simply and solely to God and to the will of God. It is precisely because he looks only to God, without any sidelong glance at the world, that he is able to look at the reality of the world freely and without prejudice. And that is how simplicity becomes wisdom."[2]

The *Ethics* was begun in intervals of leisure in a life which was still active in the service of the Confessing Church. Upon returning to Germany, Bonhoeffer went back to Sigurdshof, the small and primitive hunting lodge buried in the Pomeranian forests to which the community at Gross Schlönwitz had very soon been removed. Here he continued quietly with his teaching, while the expected European war broke out, and the German armies opened it with their appalling onslaught upon Poland. It was not till after September 29th when Warsaw fell and the regiments began to return, that some civilians heard of the horrors of the campaign and of brutalities perpetrated by the S.S. on the direct orders of the party, and to the disgust of the regular soldiers.

Bonhoeffer travelled to Berlin as often as he could and was kept informed of the progress of the Resistance. Though not actively planning an immediate *coup d'état*, the organisation was taking form and substance. The able and busy group of conspirators, headed by

[1] *Ethics*, pp. 5–6.
[2] *Ethics*, p. 7.

General von Beck and centred round the *Abwehr*, formed the organising heart of the active movement. In addition to this group another was now in process of formation, which was later to be named the "Kreisau Circle" because its meetings would often be held in Kreisau, the country home of Helmuth von Moltke, who was among its leaders. These were less practical and more idealistic rebels, more concerned in discussing the future of Germany after the fall of Hitler than in bringing that fall about. A quiet and unobtrusive character formed the liaison between the two groups, the diplomat, Ullrich von Hassell, whose secret diary was published after the war. It gives not only insight into a sensitive and incorruptible mind under the strain of a tragic period, but also much veiled information about the activities of the movement.

By the end of the Polish campaign the aims of the main body of the movement were crystallising. Their intention was to bring about the fall of Hitler and his government and to bring the war to as speedy an end as possible. But before the next *coup d'état* could be attempted, certain foundations had to be laid. It was necessary to formulate intentions for a future government of Germany, and at the same time to secure if possible an assurance from Britain that she would be willing to discuss peace terms with a reconstituted democracy. If some reasonably favourable response could be elicited the movement hoped for the support of the leading generals, since the more military power Hitler arrogated to himself, the more restless they became. We find a note upon the state of mind in informed circles at the end of 1939 in the diary left by Ullrich von Hassell:

"The principal sentiments are: The conviction that the war cannot be won militarily, a realisation of the highly dangerous economic situation; the feeling of being led by criminal adventurers; and the disgrace that has sullied the German name through the conduct of the war in Poland, namely the brutal use of air power and the shocking bestialities of the S.S. especially towards the Jews."[1]

In view of the developing situation and in the hope of securing the generals' support, a first approach to the British government was made by a Catholic lawyer, Joseph Müller, who was attached to the *Abwehr* in Munich. He made an approach through the Vatican which was not unfavourably received in Britain, and the results of which were summarised by Hans von Dohnanyi in a document called the X Report, which in the last year of the war would be discovered and used in evidence against him.

[1] *The von Hassell Diaries*, p. 76.

It was at this time that Bonhoeffer first met Joseph Müller; and the two men, separated by a generation and by widely different backgrounds, took an instant liking to each other. Bonhoeffer admired Müller's stalwart integrity and the sheer momentum of his confident zeal, while Müller found in Bonhoeffer a man quick to appreciate the moral pressures towards resistance. They were to meet again.

Joseph Müller had performed a useful service in producing the material embodied in the report, and it should have been strong and circumstantial enough to rouse the generals, but they remained lethargic, and a few weeks later their attention was distracted by a curious pair of events.

Early in November, by means of some exceedingly able manoeuvres, two agents of the British Secret Service were taken prisoner by the Germans on the borders of Holland. One of these was Captain Payne Best, who was to meet Bonhoeffer in strange circumstances in the last weeks of his life. Now, almost simultaneous with the kidnapping, the extraordinary attempt on Hitler's life, for which the young ex-Communist Georg Elser was arrested, took place in the Bürgerbräukeller in Munich. The suspicion is strong that the "attempt" was engineered by the government in order to whip up popular enthusiasm for the war. It was quickly associated in all newspapers with the two captured Secret Service men, with the claim that the affair had been contrived by the British government. Popular emotions were not noticeably aroused, but it made the task of the resistance in approaching the British government more difficult.

While these curious dramas were being acted out, Bonhoeffer was living what would prove to be the last months at Sigurdshof. With an immense effort of the concentration of which he was master, he had put the restless intriguing world of Berlin out of his mind and was teaching the last group of students who would ever gather round him how to think with scholarly accuracy and live with Christian grace.

It was a hard winter that year. For months Sigurdshof was cut off from the outside world, and sunk in the silence of the snow-laden forest. But life in the little hunting lodge was still warm and vivid, still there was music and laughter, there were walks in the forest and games in the sunlit snow, singing and reading aloud in the evenings, all woven into a rich multifarious background for the learning and prayer that were the central purpose of every day. In his few hours of leisure Bonhoeffer wrote as before to the scattered brothers of Finkenwalde, many of whom were already at the front. Already there were deaths to announce, and Bonhoeffer wrote to the parents and wives of the fallen brothers. On March 15th this last group broke up. One by one the young men scattered. Two days after the last had gone, Sigurdshof was discovered and closed by order of the Gestapo.

Whilst Europe was enduring the shock of Germany's successful occupation of the Scandinavian countries, Bonhoeffer was beginning his last attempt to continue his work for the Confessing Church. Twice his work had been frustrated, but he was still technically free to pursue his calling. After some deliberation it was decided to send him as *visitator* to the churches in East Prussia. With the increasing problems of communication, *visitators* had acquired many functions. They kept the churches in touch with one another, discussed theological and practical problems and often acted as visiting preachers or helped out in a parish where a young pastor had been called up. While Bonhoeffer was preparing for this new post, all Europe waited for Germany's offensive in the west.

With consternation the members of the resistance listened to the underground news of Hitler's preparations for invading Belgium and Holland. Oster warned Holland through her Ambassador, but after their combined appeal for peace, Belgium and the Netherlands seemed paralysed. At last, on May 10th, the attack on Belgium and Holland began, and the blows fell with stunning rapidity. On May 15th the Dutch capitulated, on May 27th the Belgians. On the same day the evacuation from Dunkirk began, and the Germans were pressing into France. On June 14th Paris fell. On June 17th France capitulated.

On that day Bonhoeffer and Bethge were in Memel, engaged on the first visitation in East Prussia. They were sitting in the garden of a café outside the town, when the news came over the radio with a fanfare of trumpets. Immediately the little garden was in a joyful uproar; men and women jumped to their feet breaking into a jubilant shout of the Horst Wessel song. All raised their arms in the Nazi salute. Bethge remained rooted to his chair but he was surprised to see Bonhoeffer lustily joining in the song and salute. "Put your hand up, are you crazy?" his companion hissed in his ear. Later he whispered, "Now we shall have to take risks for other things, but not for a mere salute."

Bonhoeffer's reaction to this high point in Hitler's success was widely misinterpreted. Many misconstrued an address in which he frankly admitted that Hitler's claims were being justified by history, without guarding his statement by reference to the, for him, self-evident fact that historical and moral justification were not the same thing. A few months later he was to write those lines in the *Ethics* which expressed so clearly the depths of his own moral insight:

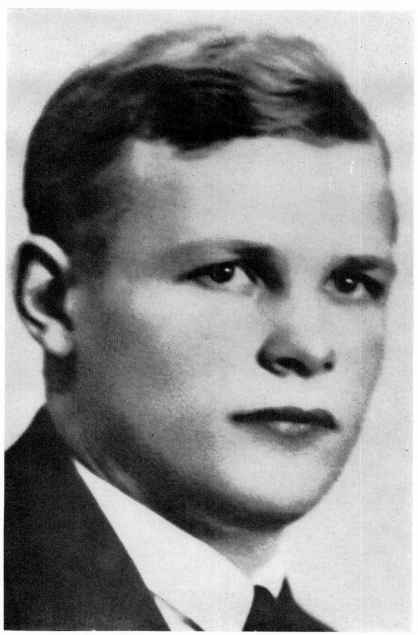

Dietrich Bonhoeffer at Union Theological Seminary, 1931

Dr. Eberhard Bethge, re
portrait

Hans von Dohnanyi, self-
portrait drawn in prison

"If evil appears in the form of light, beneficence, loyalty and renewal, if it conforms with historical necessity and social justice, then this if understood straightforwardly, is a clear additional proof of its abysmal wickedness."[1]

Meanwhile Bonhoeffer saw that the fall of France had radically changed the *de facto* situation. The hope of a quick end to Hitler's regime would have to be abandoned. The resistance was in for a long hard struggle. In this sense, and in this sense only, success had vindicated Hitler's actions. In the autumn, spending a quiet week at Klein Krössin, Bonhoeffer added to the *Ethics* a passage upon the place of worldly success:

"In a world where success is the measure and justification of all things, the figure of Him who was sentenced and crucified remains a stranger and is at best the object of pity. The world will allow itself to be subdued only by success. It is not ideas or opinions which decide, but deeds. Success alone justifies wrongs done . . . with a frankness and offhandedness which no other earthly power could permit itself, history appeals in its own cause to the dictum that the end justifies the means . . . The figure of the Crucified invalidates all thought which takes success as a standard."[2]

In 1940 it certainly appeared that Hitler was to secure the historical justification of unqualified and indeed uncanny success. After Germany had overrun Belgium and Holland, England stood alone. The whole continent of Europe was now either allied to Hitler or under his dominion. But it was in this year that the most important single event of the war took place. In the single country still opposing Hitler, Churchill took up the reins of government, and under his inspiration a few hundred young Englishmen in small fighter aircraft beat back the massed attacks of the Luftwaffe which were to be the prelude to invasion, and held the pass for western civilisation. It was a gallantry of the moment which could not look into the future, but in fact we can now see this as the year when the war was lost for Germany. Silently, secretly, far out on the invisible main where the future is made, the tide turned.

The resistance, depressed by Hitler's successes but not in despair, occupied the year in blue-printing constitutions for a future Germany. The Kreisau Circle planned a socialist Utopia replete with all the moderation, generosity and justice which every reasonable man desires and the most enlightened government fails to achieve. The circle

[1] *Ethics*, p. 4.
[2] *Ethics*, pp. 13–15.

around Beck considered the possibility of a return to the monarchy. Meanwhile they marked time. Bonhoeffer, away from Berlin, was encountering fresh difficulties in East Prussia.

On July 14th, in Blöstau near Königsberg, he had been preaching to a group of students who had gathered for a conference. He had come out of the church and was standing in conversation with some of the students, when a large posse of police arrived, led by an officer of the Gestapo. They ordered the conference to disperse in pursuance of an order made in the preceding month forbidding all such meetings. No one was arrested, and there was no interrogation, but Bonhoeffer was disturbed. He gave up an intended visit to Klein Krössin, and returned to Berlin to confer with Dohnanyi. Dohnanyi conferred with Canaris and Oster and concocted a plan. Before Bonhoeffer's next visit to East Prussia, the *Abwehr* would find some work for him. To have an assignment from them would both protect him from the attentions of the Secret Police and prevent his being called up. Since Hitler's intention of invading Russia was becoming common knowledge, it would be perfectly reasonable that the *Abwehr* should want a little spying done on the Eastern borders. "We use Jews and Communists, why not members of the Confessing Church?" was to be their disarming reply if any criticism was made. So on his third visitation, Bonhoeffer travelled with an assignment from the *Abwehr*. But it did not save him. Early in September came an urgent telephone call from Superintendent Block recalling him to Schlawe in Pomerania, which was still his official residence. Here he found an order awaiting him from the R.S.H.A.,[1] spying organisation for the Nazi Party and deadly enemy of the *Abwehr*, stating that because of "subversive activity" he was forbidden to speak in public, and would be required to report at regular intervals to the Gestapo at his official place of residence.

Now he was almost completely out of action for the Confessing Church. After some debate it was therefore decided to keep him still technically on the strength as a teacher, and in the meantime to allow him leave of absence for "theological study". This seemed a reasonable solution, and now he was taken officially on to the unpaid role of *Abwehr* assistants, with the position of what was called "V man", covering a multitude of *sub rosa* activities, and giving him a certain unofficial status. With the idea of removing him as far as possible from the eye of the authorities in Berlin, he was sent to Munich and attached to the local office of the *Abwehr*, to which his new friend Joseph Müller

[1] *Reichssicherheitshauptamt*, Principal Security Department of the Reich.

also belonged. He now changed his official residence from Schlawe to Munich, and the *Abwehr* was successful in getting him released from the necessity of reporting to the Gestapo.

Through Joseph Müller Bonhoeffer was quickly introduced to members of the resistance in Munich, and soon became acquainted with the community at the ancient Abbey of Ettal, who were secretly engaged in rescue operations and in passing on helpful information. The Abbot and Prior became personal friends of Bonhoeffer's, and through this friendship he was invited to be the guest of the Abbey for as long as he wished. In November he took up residence in Ettal sleeping at the hotel and having his meals in the Abbey. He was given a key to the enclosure, an exceptional honour, with free access to the library and all other parts of the building. Here he spent the winter months, working on the *Ethics* and waiting to receive his first serious assignment from the resistance centre located in the *Abwehr* headquarters. This was to be a journey to Switzerland where he was to meet members of the Oecumenical Movement. Ostensibly he was to collect information for counterespionage purposes, but in reality he was to discover whether any approaches might be made to the British Government through the Church.

Bonhoeffer spent in all five months in Munich and Ettal. It was his first separation from Bethge since their friendship had ripened, and the extent to which he had come to depend upon it appears vividly from the letters to Bethge which have been preserved; one gains the impression from the extant half of the correspondence that Bethge was less dependent upon constant close contact, than was Bonhoeffer. Bonhoeffer's power in human relationships was such as to render him almost invariably dominant, but in this exceptional friendship he both was, and was not, the stronger. Bethge combined an outstanding depth and range of response with a quiet integrity which would never be taken by storm. That Bonhoeffer valued this, a passage from one of the letters shows:

"You have endured the weight of this friendship, especially heavy because of my demanding nature (which I myself detest, and of which, happily you have again and again reminded me), with great patience and without becoming embittered . . ."[1]

Bonhoeffer might, and did, frequently besiege the citadel, but to his own intense relief the interior castle never fell. Such a siege began as soon as he was established at Kloster Ettal, when he set to work to get Bethge to come to him. The interior pressure to be reunited with his friend beats through his letters like an insistent *leitmotiv*:

[1] *G.S.* II, p. 397.

October 31st: "It is a beautiful winter here. I hope you will come!"

November 4th: "Now you will be preparing for the Bible week. A pity that we cannot again prepare for it together . . ."

November 16th: "How nice it would be, if we could do something together. Can you think of a solution to this ? . . . When are you coming ?"

November 18th, Ettal: ". . . I am here since yesterday, received in a most friendly manner . . . I only miss my writing table, and the opportunity to share my impressions which during the last six years has become a matter of course . . . I wanted also to tell you in addition to your invitation here that I have excellent personal contacts with the largest Catholic Missionary Society . . . I wonder whether that would not justify your journey ? . . ."

November 23rd, Ettal: "The inborn hospitality here, which is evidently something specifically Benedictine, the honour which is shown to the stranger for the love of Christ, makes one almost ashamed. You really ought to come here! It is an enrichment . . ."

Advent 1: ". . . So I suggest that you come here immediately after East Prussia . . ."

December 5th: ". . . In the meantime you will have read that from the 20th onwards, travelling is to be made more difficult. So we must soon make up our minds."

December 10th: ". . . of course, I will meet you in Munich."

December 11th: "Will you prefer to travel second class, a day journey ? If you take something pleasant to read . . . it might actually be quite restful . . ."[1]

A few days later, without haste, Bethge came. And the friendship, kept sound by his wisdom, stood up to the task of strengthening and refreshing them both.

"Because Christ stands between me and others, I dare not desire direct fellowship with them. As only Christ can speak to me in such a way that I may be saved, so others too can be saved only by Christ himself. This means that I must release the other person from every attempt of mine to regulate, coerce and dominate him with my love."[2]

The stronger a man's passions are, the harder it is to learn this lesson. Bonhoeffer learnt it in breadth—and taught it—at Finkenwalde; he learnt it in depth in the friendship with Bethge, and it may be that of the many human experiences that he underwent, this was ultimately the most searching of all.

---

[1] The foregoing quotations are taken from *G.S.* II, pp. 377 *et seq.*
[2] *Life Together*, pp. 25-6.

CHAPTER XVII

BONHOEFFER left Ettal bound for Geneva on February 24th. When
a few days later he was sitting with a small circle of friends in the home
of Visser 'tHooft, his host asked him: "What do you pray for in these
days?" and Bonhoeffer answered: "If you want to know the truth, I
pray for the defeat of my nation, for I believe that is the only way to pay
for all the suffering which my country has caused in the world."[1]
Bishop Bell recorded him as saying a year later, "If we claim to be
Christians there is no room for expediency. Hitler is Antichrist; therefore we must go on with our work and eliminate him, whether he be
successful or not."[2] Though Bonhoeffer did not see Hitler as Antichrist
in the eschatological sense, he saw him as the embodiment of all that was
evil, and the two answers give a clear impression of his attitude when
Hitler was still at the height of his success.

Bonhoeffer's assignment on this first visit to Switzerland was a
general one. He was to renew oecumenical contacts taking the opportunity to inform responsible people of the activities of the resistance
within Germany and to sound them as to what might be Britain's
attitude to the possibilities of a peaceful settlement. Bonhoeffer took the
opportunity of being in Switzerland to write a long letter to his beloved
sister Sabine, and to his old friend Bishop Bell, whose affection for him
had now been extended to the Leibholz family. He visited Erwin Sutz
and Karl Barth, but the visit to Barth may not have been altogether a
happy one. It seems that Barth could not immediately adjust to the arrival of this member of the Confessing Church, now provided with an
assignment by the German Counter-Espionage Department and at the
same time engaged in some oppositional activity which was, in its very
nature, hard to define. He struggled in vain to envisage a resistance
which could include members of the Gestapo, government officials and
men who were running the German Secret Service, and whose sub-
terranean activities wove tangling and criss-crossing in and out under the
rotten edifice of the Nazi government like rabbit runs under a hill. Barth
strove to open his mind to these possibilities, and Bonhoeffer strove to
explain them, but the two men tripped over one another as they had on

---

[1] Visser 'tHooft, *Zeugnis eines Boten*, p. 7.
[2] *G.S.* I, p. 397.

occasion done before, and parted without having fully met. They were never to meet again.

This impression of their last meeting is based on the personal recollection of Helmuth Traub, who was for many years a close friend of Barth's, and it might fit into the overall pattern of a friendship between Barth and Bonhoeffer which was seldom clear of small misunderstandings. Bonhoeffer's friends, on the other hand, carry no recollection of his having been disturbed by this interview, and certainly his affection and admiration for Barth remained undimmed to the end of his life, while the actual content of this last conversation must remain forever unknown.

The greater part of Bonhoeffer's time in Switzerland was spent in Geneva, where he had long conversations with Visser 'tHooft, which were the main purpose of his visit, and as a result of which Visser 'tHooft was able to send a report to Bishop Bell on the spirit of the resistance in Germany, which encouraged Christian leaders in England to give some thought to the problems of a new order for Europe after the possible downfall of the Nazi regime.

With his task accomplished, Bonhoeffer returned, and now moved his centre of operations back to Berlin. The command to report frequently to the Gestapo remained in suspension, so that he was not at the moment so closely watched; but he found that a new prohibition had been laid upon him, for he was now forbidden to publish. He continued, however, to work steadily at the *Ethics* in all his intervals of leisure. In fact the book was never to be completed, but all that was found after his death has been collected and edited by Eberhard Bethge, and the background against which it was written makes it permanently unique. Even since the days when he came under the influence of Barth, it had seemed manifest to Bonhoeffer that for the Christian, "ethics" could never mean the enunciation of a system of ethical principles by which he could be equipped to make correct moral decisions as required. As early as 1928, when he first attempted to formulate some thoughts on Christian ethics for his congregation at Barcelona, he had reminded them that a man has not always the good fortune to be able to choose simply between a right course and a wrong one, often he is faced with a decision in which every possible course has an element of evil in it. In 1938, at Zingst, he had reminded the Finkenwalde brothers, hard-pressed as they were by the temptations arising through the Church struggle, that: "the Christian cannot see his life as a series of principles, but only in its relation to the living God."[1]

[1] *C. and T.*, p. 98.

Now amid the horrifying demands of life within Hitler's Germany, the truth of these insights was becoming luridly manifest. And so, in the book which came into being in this morally tragic setting, Bonhoeffer moves with a certain sovereign freedom.

In an intense journey of the spirit which glows with life and burns with impassioned thought, he searches for the way by which, among a multitude of decisions few of which can be regarded objectively as right or good at all, he may yet find the way to give God his single-hearted obedience. It is a dark hard journey, and we shall not find the way lighted with useful maxims, but we find it illumined by Christ. The secret of man's ethical survival is his life in Christ, the man whom we meet in other men, as we learn to live for Christ encountered in them.

"The point of departure for Christian ethics is not the reality of one's own self or the reality of the world; nor is it the reality of standards and values. It is the reality of God as He reveals Himself in Jesus Christ."[1]

"To be conformed with the Incarnate—that is to be a real man."[2]

That the life in Christ must be lived in daily repentence and dying to self was a fact whose power was uniquely evident in these bitter days, when all were involved in their country's guilt. Bonhoeffer longed and prayed for a corporate repentance on the part of the Church, seeing it as the only way to a true resurrection. His hopes were not realised, and in these last years, through force of circumstance, he lived more and more entirely in a secular world. It is a world hard to penetrate in retrospect, tangled and obscure even to an accomplished historian, most clearly glimpsed even now through the words of those who suffered in it. Bonhoeffer's letters, the burning thoughts behind the *Ethics* and the sad, vivid diaries of Ullrich von Hassell, speak out of the past with a tragic immediacy which no recollections in tranquillity can equal.

"The situation," wrote Ullrich von Hassell, "of the majority of politically clear-headed and reasonably well-informed people today, while Germany is in the midst of a great war, is truly tragic. They love their country. They think patriotically as well as socially. They cannot wish for victory, still less for a severe defeat . . ."[3]

In September 1941, Bonhoeffer made a second journey to Switzerland. This time he went with more specific aims; chief among them was to find means of communicating with Britain regarding the possibilities

[1] *Ethics*, p. 56.
[2] *Ethics*, p. 18.
[3] *The von Hassell Diaries*, p. 77.

231

for peace and expectations for the future of Europe. Under the untiring leadership of Bishop Bell, a group of Churchmen and leading Christian laymen had been meeting to study peace-aims, and a fruit of these meetings had been Bishop Bell's book *Christianity and World Order*, in which he had frankly suggested that, "links should be strengthened between the Churches in warring countries on both sides in any way that is possible through the help of the Churches in neutral countries."[1] A companion to this book was William Paton's *The Church and the World Order*. Bonhoeffer found a way of communicating indirectly with the peace-aims study group by means of a commentary on Paton's book, which he made in conjunction with Visser' tHooft who was able to convey it to England.

It is in documents such as this, which are not concerned with theological discussion, but directed to a particular end, that one can sometimes find most clearly exposed the solid bones of Bonhoeffer's theological and ethical convictions. Basic assumptions which seem to Bonhoeffer to be too obvious to need expressing in a work of creative exploration like the *Ethics*, can often be discovered, put down *en passant*, in such occasional papers. This particular commentary, whose political interest would soon be superseded by more specific statements, contains two interesting formulations of this kind, which may usefully be read in conjunction with the *Ethics*, in which Bonhoeffer assumed them as basic.

"In the Ten Commandments God has revealed the limits which must not be exceeded, if Christ is to be Lord in the world. The decalogue is expressed negatively. Positive forms are brought out by living history, and are limited and judged by the decalogue."[2] Moreover, "Freedom in its Bibilical sense means: to be free for the service of God and our neighbour, to be free for obedience to God's commandments . . . Freedom does not mean, therefore, the dissolution of all authority; it means life within an authority and framework which is ordered by God's word."[3]

When Bonhoeffer speaks in the Ethics of "the man not fettered by principles" it is well to remember that the German word "*Prinzipien*" has a more lifeless and negative connotation than its English equivalent. "*Das Prinzip*" means for Bonhoeffer a precise and bloodless formula, and to be fettered by it is to try to apply it indiscriminately to the un-

---

[1] Bell, *Christianity and World Order*, p. 87.
[2] *G.S.* I, p. 358.
[3] *G.S.* I, p. 359.

predictable chances and changes of human life. *Prinzipien* are contrasted with God's commandments, which demand our obedience and which, alive and actual, bring us into his presence, not only guiding our actions, but at the same time bringing us face to face with the unattainability of a flawless righteousness, and so with the need for forgiveness which to sensitive Germans at that time was such an intensely immediate fact.

Bonhoeffer returned from the second Swiss journey to be involved in a new venture under the *Abwehr*, the enterprise which came to be known as "U7". By this time systematic deportation of the Jews had begun, while the German nation stood by helpless, when not actually indifferent. But a small group of distinguished Jews was now to be rescued and helped over the border into Switzerland. Bonhoeffer took a leading part in this protracted and complex operation. Eventually it was successful. After his arrest, his connection with it would be held in evidence against him.

Meanwhile the network of the resistance was extending, and its intentions hardening. When on December 19th 1941 the Commander-in-Chief of the Army was removed and Hitler took over his functions, the preparation for an attempt on Hitler's life went into a higher gear. At this time Bonhoeffer met again the young lawyer, Fabian von Schlabrendorff, whose acquaintance he had first made at Klein Krössin. Fabian von Schlabrendorff was now adjutant to Henning von Tresckow, the Commander-in-Chief of the Central Army Group at the Russian front. His headquarters were a hotbed of intrigue against Hitler. Now plans began forming to which Bonhoeffer was doubtless privy. It will have been in this winter that Bonhoeffer expressed himself as willing to take part in an attempt on Hitler's life if this were required of him. He only asked for sufficient warning to be able beforehand formally to sever his connection with the Confessing Church, as he knew it would be an act which they could not condone. Since Bonhoeffer was totally unversed in the arts of killing, these were in the most immediate sense academic points, but nevertheless this willingness to be totally involved represented a costly decision for Bonhoeffer, for he believed that after the fall of Hitler, when all was known, it might mean the end of his career as a pastor. For he knew that his Church, more concerned with *Prinzipien* than with the inexorable demands of reality, would be likely to repudiate him when the facts were known. It is a fact that his involvement with the active and uncompromising elements in the resistance has had an effect upon his reputation in some circles of Protestant Germany which dims the admiration with which he is regarded to this day. Bonhoeffer squarely faced the prospect of this loss of reputation, just as he faced the fact of increasing danger. For towards the end of the winter, Dohnanyi and Bonhoeffer received through a member of the *Abwehr* the first intimation that they were being watched. Dohnanyi's mail was being censored and his telephone tapped, but apart from increased vigilance and an avoidance of unreliable contacts, neither he nor Bonhoeffer made any change in their activities.

In April 1942 the *Abwehr* sent Bonhoeffer with Helmuth von Moltke to Norway, where on February 1st the Provost of Trondheim Cathedral had, by order of the Nazi puppet Government, been forbidden to exercise his ministry. This was to lead to a revolt of the whole Protestant Church in Norway, and a passing phase in the curious interplay of religion and politics, of military expediency and the designs of the resistance, is revealed in the story of these few weeks. Following his suspension on February 1st, the Provost was, on February 20th, summarily dismissed from his post, and this was the signal for all the Bishops of Norway to resign from all official functions connected with their office, remaining only as simple pastors to their flocks. A few weeks later, upon the announcement that a form of "Hitler Youth" was to be inaugurated in Norway, a thousand school-masters resigned, while on April 5th all parish priests abandoned their livings. On Maundy Thursday Bishop Berggrav, initiator and leader of the religious resistance, was placed under house-arrest, and on April 8th he was imprisoned.

Now the *Abwehr* went into action. They pointed out to their Government quite reasonably that by actions against the Church the Norwegian puppet government were exacerbating the resentment of the population and enhancing their determination to obstruct the German war effort. The *Abwehr* pressed for the release of Berggrav, which was secured on April 15th. Meanwhile, they sent their two emissaries, Bonhoeffer and Moltke, ostensibly to implement a general pacification, in fact to strengthen the resolve of the Church resistance.

To Bonhoeffer the religious revolt in Norway had a particular significance. In 1933 he had proposed a similar protest to the German Protestant Church: wholesale resignations and refusal to perform any function whatever required by the state. In Germany religious opinion was divided and the political motive was lacking, so that Bonhoeffer's proposal had fallen on deaf ears; in Norway where religious unity was combined with resentment against the occupying power, united action had been possible and had succeeded in its objective. A large measure of religious and educational freedom was secured, and Bonhoeffer, studying with interest this achievement of civil disobedience, was able at the same time to give its leaders practical advice based on his own experience in the German Church struggle.

The visit to Norway was short and concentrated. By April 16th the two men were already on their homeward journey. They returned by way of Stockholm and the two days that this required gave the two so different members of the resistance there an opportunity of exhaustive conversations. They discussed long and earnestly the many issues involved in political resistance. Upon the subject of Hitler's assassination, their views were irreconcilable. Moltke was not willing to take part in violence or in any of the more active aspects of the conspiracy. For Bonhoeffer, this reservation represented an unjustifiable moral luxury. Though the two men respected each other's opinions, the divergence of their views was too great for them ever to go further in collaborating.

On his return, Bonhoeffer snatched a week or two with Frau von Kleist-Retzow at Kieckow to continue with the *Ethics*, but in May he found himself once more in Switzerland. This third journey to Geneva proved abortive, since Visser 'tHooft and several other men whom he had hoped to see were absent. Among the noticeable absentees was Hans Schönfeld, who was still Director of the Research Department of the World Council of Churches, and so normally resident at Geneva. But Bonhoeffer picked up one item of news which affected him; he heard that his friend Bishop Bell was paying a "cultural" visit of some weeks to Sweden. Now, with an idea forming in his mind, he precipitately abandoned his visit to Geneva and hurried back to Berlin to confer with the *Abwehr*.

Meanwhile the Bishop was picking up oecumenical contacts in Sweden. His visit began as a comparatively conventional ecclesiastical tour, but a week or two after his arrival a curious double event took place which greatly added to the interest and importance of his journey. On May 24th, he was suddenly confronted with Hans Schönfeld. Schönfeld was nervy, intense, and loaded with detailed information about the German resistance. He described to Bell "the strong organised opposition movement inside Germany", which was "making plans for the destruction of the whole Hitler regime", and gave many facts in support of his claim. Having unloaded his information, Schönfeld enquired whether, in the event of a change of Government in Germany, Britain and her allies might be prepared to consider a negotiated peace. Bell could not show himself optimistic, for apart from what he knew of the stiffening of the allied attitude, he regarded Schönfeld as faintly compromised by his connection with the official Church Government. But then a totally unexpected factor was added to what was already a surprising situation. On May 31st, Dietrich Bonhoeffer arrived. His frame of mind was different from Schönfeld's. He was calm and steady, clothed as ever in that indefinable radiance which was his special quality. He had not come as a negotiator, trembling with political hopes and fears, desiring to do what he could to serve the interests of Germany. He had come first and foremost as a friend, acting on a free impulse, an impulse understood and supported by the generous-hearted men in the *Abwehr*, who had arranged courier's papers for him at a few days' notice, and sent him away with their blessing. Bonhoeffer, unexpectedly confronting Schönfeld, could confirm all that he had said, and even add to it the names of the resistance leaders, but then the divergence in their attitude appeared. Bonhoeffer's deep grief for the sins of Germany was evident to the Bishop. It was plain that he felt them as a stain on his own soul, and was deeply moved by his country's need for the forgiveness of God and men. When Bonhoeffer heard Schönfeld's attempts to negotiate comfortable terms for Germany, his Christian conscience was not easy. "There must be punishment by God," so runs the Bishop's report of his conversation, "we should not be worthy of such a solution. Our action must be such as the world will understand as an act of repentance. Christians do not wish to escape repentance, or chaos, if it is God's will to bring it upon us. We must take this judgement as Christians."[1]

After his conversation with Bonhoeffer, the Bishop was entirely convinced of the accuracy of the information about the German resistance. He returned to England determined to do all he could to gain from the government, if not an actual expression of support for the movement, at least some definite statement that their attitude to a reconstituted German government would be different from their attitude to one dominated by Hitler. Immediately on his return, Bell laid the information he had received before the Foreign Secretary, and pressed him as hard as he could to communicate in some way with the resistance. It was to no avail. The government no longer wished to hear of an underground opposition. For the present, the star of the European statesman, able to think in large terms and to look ahead towards the reconstruction of Europe, had set. The wind was setting fair for the demand of unconditional surrender, and that spirit by whose power wars are won, and which depends for its dynamic effect upon its very

[1] *G.S.* I, p. 405.

limitations, had taken hold of the leaders in Britain. Meanwhile to Bell a letter came from Bonhoeffer which transcended all the barriers thrown up by war:

"My Lord Bishop, *June 1st 1942*
"Let me express my deep and sincere gratitude for the hours you have spent with me. It still seems to me like a dream to have seen you, to have spoken to you, to have heard your voice. I think these days will remain in my memory as some of the greatest in my life. This spirit of fellowship and of Christian brotherliness will carry me through the darkest hour, and even if things go worse than we hope and expect, the light of these few days will never be extinguished in my heart. These impressions of these days were so overwhelming that I cannot express them in words. I feel ashamed when I think of all your goodness and at the same time I feel full of hope for the future.
"God be with you on your way home, in your work and always. I shall think of you on Wednesday. Please pray for us. We need it."
"Yours most gratefully,
"Dietrich"[1]

The Bishop returned home with his vital information to receive a cool rebuff from the British government. He could send no message of encouragement to the German opposition. But from now on, he was never to relax his efforts on behalf of the German people and the resistance movement. With complete disregard of his personal reputation, and against impassioned opposition, he insisted on speaking out. Keeping closely in touch with Dietrich's brother-in-law, Gerhard Leibholz, who was now in Oxford with his family, he prepared his material with the greatest care. On March 10th 1943, after enduring lengthy delays, he delivered a speech in the House of Lords in which he gave all the information which could safely be made public about the German Opposition, and elicited the last mildly sympathetic response that the Government was ever to make to his exhortations and warnings. To the Bishop's demand for a statement of intentions the Speaker replied: "I now say in plain terms, on behalf of His Majesty's Government, that we agree with Premier Stalin, first that the Hitlerite state should be destroyed, and secondly that the whole German people is not, as Dr. Goebbels has been trying to persuade them, thereby doomed to destruction." After this the Bishop never again met anything but a completely

[1] *G.S.* I, p. 382.

237

negative response, and it was not until many years later that the unremitting efforts during the war of this great statesman of the Church would be understood and valued; it remained for the military historian Liddell Hart to write their epitaph:

"For the wisdom and foresight of George Bell's wartime speeches in the House of Lords, although they met much disagreement at the time, have now come to be widely recognised—and especially by military historians of the war. Hardly anyone would now question the truth of his repeated warnings about the folly of the Allies' unconditional surrender policy . . . While the horizon of technical strategy is confined to immediate success in a campaign, grand strategy looks beyond the war to the subsequent state of peace—and thus tends to coincide with morality. In this way George Bell, standing for the principles of his creed, came to achieve a far clearer grasp of grand strategy than did the statesman. The present situation of the West would be better if more attention had been paid to his temporarily unpalatable warnings and guidance."[1]

Bell's particular combination of wide vision with penetrating understanding was doubtless the outcome of a native endowment developed to the full by the experience of a distinguished and fruitful life. But his unique appreciation first of the difficulties besetting the Confessing Church in Germany, and later of the extent and importance of the resistance as well as of the high calibre of its leaders, seem to have been to a considerable extent the result of his friendship with Dietrich Bonhoeffer, and of all that this friendship set in train.

[1] From an article in the *Daily Telegraph*, June 15th 1959.

CHAPTER XVIII

"IN the past few years I have written numerous letters to brothers on their marriage, and preached at numerous weddings. The main feature of the event rested always in the fact that a man was venturing, in the face of these 'last' times (which I do not mean altogether apocalyptically) to make this affirmative gesture to the world and the world's future. It was always quite evident to me that as a Christian one may only take this step as a powerful act of faith and in view of God's mercy. For by this act, in the midst of general destruction, a man desires to build; in the midst of a life lived from day to day and from hour to hour he demands a future, in the midst of our exile from the earth he demands some living space, in the midst of the general misery some happiness. And the overwhelming fact is, that to this improbable desire, God says Yes, that here God confirms our will with His, when one would expect the opposite. And so marriage becomes something quite new, majestic, glorious—for those of us in Germany who seek to be Christians."[1]

These words, written by Bonhoeffer to Erwin Sutz in 1941, might now have stood for a sign over the next months of his own life.

For on returning from Stockholm he went to spend a few weeks with Frau von Kleist-Retzow in Klein Krössin, and there he found her granddaughter, Maria von Wedemeyer. The charming child who seven years before had passed almost unnoticed among the crowd of others was now revealed: a young woman, beautiful, suddenly and startlingly unique.

Dietrich left Klein Krössin more deeply moved than he at first realised. What he had sought and failed to find some ten years earlier, had now, in this apparently inappropriate moment, blazed upon him. At first he was uncertain how far to pursue this new experience. When, in August, Maria's father was killed on the Russian front, he did not venture to write to her. But he wrote to her mother a letter of great warmth, which had all the more strength and comfort in it from the fact that it avoided even a word of direct sympathy; he knew how to express himself to a Junker's widow, and this letter evidently made Dietrich Bonhoeffer, hitherto only slightly known to the von Wede-

[1] *G.S.* I, p. 50.

meyers, a vivid reality to the bereaved family. Now he began to meet Maria quite frequently in Berlin and Klein Krössin, and soon there was no longer any doubt in his heart or mind; he loved her, and Maria's response to his love was joyful and immediate.

This turn of events in the lives of Dietrich and Maria surprised others as much as it surprised themselves. The widowed Frau von Wedemeyer felt some anxiety at discovering that her daughter had won the heart of a man who was not only seventeen years her senior, but who was also manifestly involved in secret and probably dangerous activities. The Bonhoeffers for their part would hardly have expected their able and intellectual son to have given his heart to a girl who was little more than a child, too young to have gained any distinction of character beyond what her birth conferred. But evidently this native distinction was already a striking quality in her. The courage and dignity, the inborn piety and leisurely culture which had endeared the Junker families to Bonhoeffer during his years in Pomerania, were all concentrated in this lovely girl, by whom they seemed personified. It was a life that Dietrich had fallen in love with, a life and Life itself. This moment, which seemed so tragically inappropriate for a love-affair, was yet the true moment for him. With the love for Maria, Dietrich affirmed his wholehearted faith in life, refusing to capitulate in any respect at all to the forces of evil and disintegration which were closing in upon him.

For now they were closing in on every side. Now it was a race for life between the resistance and their enemies who were feeling about for them everywhere. Which would come first, arrest of the leaders, or the death of Hitler? During the winter of 1942–3, plans for the assassination were moving towards a final stage. Meanwhile, though every department of the Reich was now mined with active resistance members, such perfect secrecy had been maintained that the government's suspicions remained entirely general.

The leading members of the *Abwehr*, by a curious irony, were in more danger from another quarter. Since the outset of the war their department had been feverishly hated by the rival intelligence agency, the R.S.H.A. who were the spying establishment of the Gestapo. Even here there were members of the resistance, though not in leading positions. Through these allies the *Abwehr* had been warned that the R.S.H.A. were on their track, not because of any suspicion that they were engaged in subversive activities, but hoping to discredit Dohnanyi and Oster by any available means, such as the exposure of their part in

Maria von Wedemeyer,
at the time of her
engagement

Dietrich Bonhoeffer
in Tegel prison

Steps leading down to the place of execution at Flossenbürg

the escape of the Jews through the U7 operation. The R.S.H.A. hoped to discover that members of the *Abwehr* had derived some pecuniary advantage from an enterprise which did not seem to them to be capable of any other explanation. Though less the target of their specific hatred than Oster and Dohnanyi, Bonhoeffer had also been involved in the U7 affair, and was vulnerable because of his repeated evasion of the call-up. So now, while plans for the death of Hitler and the total destruction of his regime were being perfected, the threatened members of the *Abwehr* did what they could to fabricate a web of protective evidence which should cover any suspect activities, however peripheral. Bonhoeffer wrote to Dohnanyi, on writing paper fortunately still surviving from the appropriate year, a letter in which he enumerated, as though with truly patriotic intentions, the uses which he could make of his oecumenical contacts for intelligence purposes if he were taken on to the strength of the *Abwehr*. Meanwhile Confessing pastors and other men who, for one reason or another, had been helped to avoid the call-up, were required to write innocent-looking notes of various kinds which could be discovered in the files. Hans von Dohnanyi made a journey to Switzerland in order to visit the escaped Jews and brief them in case they were interrogated. At the same time, whilst plans were laid for the immediate reorganisation of the country after the *coup d'état*, minute agreement was at the same time being reached as to what should be the cover story in case of arrest. It was against such a background that Dietrich's love-affair progressed.

As the months went by and the resistance trembled in balance between hope and fear, Dietrich's sense of urgency understandably increased. On November 24th, at her own request, he visited Frau von Wedemeyer, on her estate in Pätzig. Frau von Wedemeyer, still concerned for Maria, asked him to agree to a year's separation. Bonhoeffer was in a hard position. He wrote to Bethge that he believed he might have won her over by argument, but he hesitated to do so, for, as he wrote: "Frau von Wedemeyer has become, through the loss of her husband, that is to say precisely because of her weakness, stronger than if I had been able to deal with her husband; I have not the right now to make her feel defenceless; that would be dastardly, but it makes the situation more difficult."[1]

Dietrich endured the situation for a time, though with a rebellious heart, and after a few weeks Frau von Wedemeyer gave way to what were presumably her daughter's entreaties; for, on January 17th 1943,

[1] E.B., *D.B.*, p. 888.

Dietrich and Maria were engaged, though no announcement was made. Eberhard Bethge had become engaged a few months before to Dietrich's niece Renate, the daughter of his sister Ursula Schleicher, and now the two men went forward again abreast, to meet a new stage in their lives.

A month later Oster reported to General von Beck that the preparations for "Operation Flash" were completed. The "Flash" was to be Hitler's death, which would ignite the revolution throughout the Reich. Plans were prepared for the seizure of power by the military authorities in Berlin, Cologne, Munich and Vienna. The assassination was to take place on the Russian Front at the Headquarters of the Central Army Group in Smolensk. The master brains of the enterprise were to be Henning von Tresckow and his adjutant, Fabian von Schlabrendorff. A visit from Hitler was expected on March 13th. A short time before, Dohnanyi travelled out to Smolensk to confirm the final arrangements. Eberhard Bethge drove him to the night train in Karl Bonhoeffer's car; even he little suspecting that in Dohnanyi's briefcase reposed the material for a plastic bomb.

On the morning of March 13th, Major General von Tresckow and Field Marshal von Kluge drove to the airfield to welcome Hitler. While they were gone, von Schlabrendorff telephoned to Oster the code word to announce that Operation Flash was going into action. Hitler arrived. The visit went off without incident. During lunch von Tresckow asked one of the officers in Hitler's entourage, Heinz Brandt, whether he would take two bottles of brandy to his old friend General Helmuth Stieff for an anniversary. Colonel Brandt agreed. After lunch Hitler drove back to the airfield. Von Schlabrendorff followed in his own car, carrying a parcel. Hitler's plane stood on the runway. He boarded it; as Colonel Brandt prepared to follow him, von Schlabrendorff handed him the parcel, containing not brandy but the bomb. The time fuse was set to detonate this in half an hour. Hitler's plane took off and disappeared into the distance followed by its fighter escort.

Von Tresckow and von Schlabrendorff returned to headquarters, and waited in appalling suspense. If the bomb exploded punctually, they might receive a radio message from Minsk. To those waiting in Berlin the hours had already seemed endless. Half an hour went by. An hour. Two hours. Two hours and a half later a routine message came through. Hitler's plane had landed at Rastenburg without incident. The two conspirators went at once into action. Von Tresckow telephoned to Brandt asking him to hold the parcel. The next day von Schlabrendorff arrived in Rastenburg. He repossessed himself of the bomb, giving a parcel containing two real bottles of brandy in its place. On the night train back to Smolensk, in the privacy of a sleeping compartment, he dismantled the bomb. For some reason which will never be explained, the detonator had failed to ignite.

But the conspirators were not easily foiled. A week later the younger Bonhoeffers with their children and intimate friends were assembled in the Marienburgerallee. They were practising Walcha's cantata "*Lobe den Herrn,*" to be performed in ten days' time on Karl Bonhoeffer's seventy-fifth birthday. Dietrich, conducting, was pleasant and composed. Patiently he worked to bring the performance up to the high standard that was a *sine qua non* on all special occasions. As the young voices rose up, disciplined and trim, the page of music trembled in Christine's hand, but Hans von Dohnanyi's fine tenor voice never faltered, though his car stood at the door with the engine warmed up, and any minute could bring a telephone call which would mean an immediate dash to the *Abwehr* headquarters. To the rest of the family he appeared as usual, and no one looking at Dietrich's broad cheerful face would have guessed that he was listening for anything more dramatic than the balance of voices as they competently wove into a seamless whole the pattern of their several parts. The hours went by; the singers worked diligently. No sound came from the next room where the telephone stood. And when at last the family folded up their music and dispersed, three of them knew that another attempt on Hitler's life had failed.

This time the attempt was to have been made by Major von Gersdorff, another officer of the Army Group Centre which was such a hotbed of intrigue against Hitler. On March 21st, which was *Heldengedenktag*, the Sunday on which the dead from the first world war were commemorated, Hitler was to inspect an exhibition of material taken in the Russian campaign, by the Army Group Centre, and the young officer on duty at the exhibition took two plastic bombs in his pockets, and proposed to approach Hitler, set the fuses at an appropriate moment and explode the bombs, sacrificing his own life for the sake of ending the Führer's. Hitler, however suddenly altered his plans. He was to have stayed half an hour at the exhibition, but instead he left after eight minutes; von Gersdorff never got within twenty yards of him. The careful plan for the overthrow of the government in which Dohnanyi would have had a leading part had to be abandoned; and before another attempt could be made on Hitler's life Dohnanyi would be in prison.

Still the *Abwehr* remained unsuspected as a centre of the opposition,

243

and the net was closing round Hans and Dietrich on suspicion of comparatively minor offences: accepting bribes from the Jews who escaped through the U7 operation, and Dietrich's evasion of the call-up. But it was enough. When on March 31st the whole family assembled to celebrate Karl Bonhoeffer's seventy-fifth birthday, the two men had entered their last week of liberty.

After this four more days went by between hope and fear. On April 4th, Dohnanyi received the news from his ally, the Chief of the *Wehrmachtsabteilung* that no immediate danger was to be expected. But the next day, April 5th, at midday, when Dietrich tried to speak to Christine by telephone in her house at Sakrow, the telephone was answered by an unknown man's voice. Dietrich guessed the truth at once: that Hans and Christine had been arrested and that the secret police were ransacking the house. Without saying anything to his parents, he went next door to his sister Ursula Schleicher and asked her to prepare him a large meal. Then he went up to his attic bedroom in his parents' house, checked it once more for incriminating papers, and left about, not too conspicuously, one or two specially fabricated notes which he wished the Gestapo to find. Then he returned to the Schleichers' house and waited there with the Schleichers and Bethge. About four o'clock his father looked in: "Dietrich, two men want to see you in your room!" The two men were Roeder, Chief Investigator for the Air Force, and Sonderegger, a member of the Gestapo. They said little and without producing a search warrant or any formal notice of arrest, they ordered Bonhoeffer to accompany them to their car. Quietly, undramatically, the black Mercedes drove away. Soon Dietrich saw the gloomy façade of Tegel Military prison rising in front of them, a frowning cliff of masonry, pockmarked with barred windows. The car halted. They stood at the entrance. Roeder said a word to the warder who approached. Without ceremony, Bonhoeffer was bundled over the threshold. The iron gates crashed to behind him. He was in prison.

PART III

Suffering

A change has come indeed. Your hands, so strong and active,
are bound; in helplessness now you see your action
is ended; you sigh in relief, your cause committing
to stronger hands; so now you may rest contented.
Only for one blissful moment could you draw near to touch freedom;
then that it might be perfected in glory, you gave it to God.

Dietrich Bonhoeffer.

CHAPTER XIX

"THE formalities of admission were correctly completed. For the first night I was locked up in an admission cell. The blankets on the camp bed had such a foul smell that in spite of the cold it was impossible to use them. Next morning a piece of bread was thrown into my cell; I had to pick it up from the floor. A quarter of the coffee consisted of grounds. The sound of the prison staff's vile abuse of the prisoners who were held for investigation penetrated into my cell for the first time; since then I have heard it every day from morning till night. When I had to parade with the other new arrivals, we were addressed by one of the jailers as 'blackguards', etc. etc. We were all asked why we had been arrested, and when I said I did not know, the jailer answered with a scornful laugh, 'You'll find that out soon enough.' It was six months before I got a warrant for my arrest. As we went through the various offices, some N.C.O.s, who had heard what my profession was, wanted now and then to have a few words with me. They were told that no one was to talk to me. While I was having a bath an N.C.O. (I do not know who he was) suddenly appeared and asked me whether I knew Pastor N. When I said that I did, he exclaimed, 'He is a good friend of mine,' and disappeared again. I was taken to the most isolated cell on the top floor; a notice, prohibiting all access without special permission, was put outside it. I was told that all my correspondence would be stopped until further notice, and that, unlike all the other prisoners, I should not be allowed half an hour a day in the open air, although, according to the prison rules, I was entitled to it. I received neither newspapers nor anything to smoke. After forty-eight hours my Bible was returned to me; it had been searched to see whether I had smuggled inside it a saw, razor blades, or the like. For the next twelve days the cell door was opened only for bringing food in and putting the bucket out. No one said a word to me. I was told nothing about the reason for my detention, or how long it would last. I gathered from various remarks—and it was confirmed later—that I was lodged in the section for the most serious cases, where the condemned prisoners lay shackled.

"The first night in my cell I could not sleep much, because in the next cell a prisoner wept loudly for several hours on end; no one took any notice."

So runs Bonhoeffer's own description of his introduction to prison life. Of the twelve days of solitary confinement which immediately followed, very little impression can be gained from the cheerful and controlled letters written to his parents. The iron hardness and heartlessness of his surroundings not only emphasised the sudden break with his own life, but also seemed to symbolise the iron grip of disaster by which the past that he had loved was being destroyed. During the hours when Bonhoeffer sat silent in his cell, the horror of this destruction weighed him down to the point of death. Added to this was the fearful prospect of the interrogations, possibly of physical torture, under the stress of which he might reveal secrets which could constitute the death warrant for Hans von Dohnanyi and others to whom he was bound by ties of loyalty. Among notes scribbled on scraps of paper during the first days appears the sentence: "Suicide, not from a sense of guilt, but because basically I am already dead. Full stop. The end."[1] "Not from a sense of guilt". As he sat in prison he was once more involved in the interior struggle which was the background to his part in the resistance. "At first," he wrote, in his first letters to Bethge, "I wondered a great deal whether it was really for the cause of Christ that I was causing you all such grief."[2] And finally the awful oppression of the world of evil against which Bonhoeffer and so many others had been struggling, weighed upon him in his cell without relief. "We have been silent witnesses of evil deeds; we have been drenched by many storms; we have learnt the arts of equivocation and pretence; experience has made us suspicious of others and kept us from being truthful and open; intolerable conflicts have worn us down and even made us cynical. Are we still of any use? What we shall need is not geniuses, or cynics, or misanthropes, or clever tacticians, but plain, honest, straightforward men. Will our inward power of resistance be strong enough, and our honesty with ourselves remorseless enough for us to find our way back to simplicity and straightforwardness?"[3]

That Bonhoeffer's inward power of resistance was indeed strong enough, the letters written during the next two and a half years were abundantly to prove. It was a strength which can be seen as the gift of God through the prayer which had become the foundation of Bonhoeffer's life in the years of his success and freedom, and which did not fail him now. From the first days in the prison he continued the steady

[1] E.B., *D.B.*, p. 934.
[2] *Letters and Papers from Prison*, 1967 edition, p. 87.
[3] *L. and P.*, p. 40.

discipline of his Christian life: meditation, intercession and thanksgiving, the daily "praying" of the Psalms and Bible study. He wrote in November to Bethge that by that time he had already read the Old Testament through two and a half times. From this inexhaustible supply of spiritual strength, life once more began to well up. Bonhoeffer embarked upon an essay on "The Sense of Time", and as soon as it was permitted he was sending requests for the works of the great German novelists of the nineteenth century, Gotthelf, Stifter, Gottfield Keller and others, in whose work he might find the past reflected. Soon he was deep in their works, accompanying them with Kant's *Anthropology* and Heidegger's *Phenomenology of Time-Consciousness*, which spoke with a particular immediacy to his reviving sensibility. As his creative faculties came to life again, Bonhoeffer's irrepressible radiance began to shine out, and when his solitary confinement was lifted, he soon began to win friends among the warders, and among the prisoners too as opportunity offered.

Meanwhile there was another subject with which his mind had to be intensively occupied. His impression on April 5th that Hans von Dohnanyi had been arrested was only too well-founded. A few hours before his own arrest, Dohnanyi had been conveyed to the military prison for officers in the Lehrterstrasse to which Joseph Müller and his wife had already been delivered. Christine von Dohnanyi and Frau Müller were imprisoned at Charlottenburg, and were released after a few weeks, but the men were held, under conditions which were very much more stringent than those in the military prison of Tegel.

And now it was not only the lives of these two men which were at stake, but also the secret centre of the resistance in the *Abwehr*. It was of quite desperate importance that these two key figures and also Bonhoeffer should act their parts perfectly under interrogation and tell the same stories down to the minutest detail. Exact plans had been laid for them all in the event of their arrest. Hans, the brilliant and experienced lawyer, was to take full responsibility for all the questionable activities in which the three had been involved. Canaris, still at liberty and still, at present, Chief of the *Abwehr*, would corroborate all that Hans said and maintain that all had been done under his orders and solely in the interests of counter-espionage. Bonhoeffer was to act the part of the inexperienced patriotic pastor, drawn into the *Abwehr* solely through the anxiety to help his country. Notes prepared for his interrogator Manfred Roeder show that he acted the part of the simple unworldly pastor with considerable success. In an early note to Roeder he observes disarmingly: "I am the last who would deny that in an activity which is for me so complicated, so strange and unaccustomed as counter-espionage, I may have made mistakes."[1] And he adds in a later one that the opportunity to assist the *Abwehr* represented for him: "A great mental relief, when I found in this the welcome opportunity to rehabilitate myself in the eyes of the National Board, which I was very anxious to do, in view of the distressing, and in my view entirely unjustified accusation which had been made against me. The consciousness of being required by a military department was therefore of great importance to me . . ."[2] These notes were evidently written with great care, so as to complete the fabric of necessary lies which concealed the true nature of his activities with the *Abwehr*, and which at this stage stood up to all the tests of cross-examination.

While the interrogations proceeded, the resistance maintained an exact communication system with Bonhoeffer and Dohnanyi by means of codes employed in the food parcels and books which were handed in for them. Straightforward answers to questions might be conveyed by means of prearranged coloured wrappings, but whole sentences of information were often conveyed in the books; when there was a message the name of the book's owner was written in the flyleaf and underlined, then, beginning from the end of the book, appropriate letters were very faintly marked. It was not long before Dietrich began to discover many essentially goodhearted men among the warders, some of whom soon began to act as go-betweens for illicit letters and parcels, while others contrived to allow Dietrich occasional words with his family or friends in private, when the risk was not too great; then Dietrich would receive at great speed news of the progress of the conspiracy; and the code messages in books were supplemented with some direct information. The prisoner heard that attempts on Hitler's life were continuing, and an unsuspected little hunchback, Helmuth Stieff, had undertaken to make the attempt at the Führer's Headquarters in East Prussia. Explosives for a bomb had been successfully buried under a wooden tower inside the headquarters compound. But before the attempt could be made, the explosives unaccountably blew up. Soon after this a young officer succeeded in entering the Berghof with a revolver in his pocket, but could not get near enough to the Führer to shoot. In November, a young officer, Axel von dem Bussche, prepared himself to blow up Hitler while he acted as model to display a new type

[1] E.B., *D.B.*, p. 913.
[2] E.B., *D.B.*, p. 915.

of army overcoat. After many delays, the dress parade was ready, von dem Bussche was arrayed in the overcoat with a bomb in each pocket; just before the fateful moment however, the occasion was interrupted by an Allied air raid. Soon afterwards the entire consignment of overcoats was destroyed by enemy action. It was after the failure of this attempt that Dietrich began to hear for the first time in connection with the conspiracy the name of Claus von Stauffenberg.

Through all these months air raids continued with increasing intensity, and one of their effects in Tegel prison was further to strengthen Bonhoeffer's growing influence. It had become evident how strongly his perfect calm in the midst of the most violent attacks supported the morale of those in his neighbourhood. Very soon his skill in first aid was discovered, and after this he was always fetched down to the first aid post when the alarm sounded, and often remained there talking with the warders after the raid was over. By this time his spirit was affecting the atmosphere throughout the prison, and warders and prisoners alike would make use of all kinds of tricks and subterfuges for the comfort of exchanging a few words with him.

Meanwhile, within this framework of danger, conspiracy and prison regulations, his engagement to Maria continued its strange course. Her mother, with aristocratic *noblesse*, had chosen the occasion of Dietrich's arrest to make it public; and so Maria, known to be his fiancée, from time to time received permission to visit him. A letter written to Bethge in December of the first year, gives a vivid impression of the agonising constraint of these occasions: "Now we have been engaged for almost a year, and have not been for a single hour alone together! Is that not crazy? . . . We must write and talk about matters which are not really the important ones for us, we sit together once a month for an hour, like good children on the bench at school, and then are torn apart again; we know almost nothing of one another and have shared no experiences, for we are living through these months in separation. Maria regards me as a paragon of virtue, good behaviour and Christian perfection, and in order to set her mind at rest I have to write her letters like an early Christian martyr, and so her picture of me becomes more and more erroneous. Is not this an impossible situation for her? And yet she sustains it magnificently as a matter of course."[1] A poem written after one of these visits, and called with some prophetic instinct "The Past", expresses with a passion which he rarely allowed to appear, the anguish which could succeed them:

[1] E.B., *D.B.*, p. 938.

O happiness beloved, and pain beloved in heaviness,
you went from me.
What shall I call you? Anguish, life, blessedness,
part of myself, my heart—the past?
The heavy door falls to,
I hear your steps depart and slowly die away,
What now remains for me—torment, delight, desire?
This only do I know: that with you, all has gone.
But do you feel how I now grasp at you
and so clutch hold of you
that it must hurt you?
How I so rend you
that your blood gushes out,
simply to be sure that you are near me,
a life in earthly form, complete?
Do you divine my terrible desire
for my own suffering,
my eager wish to see my own blood flow,
only that all may not go under,
lost in the past?

after five more stanzas in this vein the poem concludes:

The past will come to you once more,
and be your life's enduring part,
through thanks and repentance.
Feel in the past God's forgiveness and goodness,
pray him to keep you today and tomorrow.[1]

The note of comfort, coming at the end of this prolonged cry of grief,
makes here an almost perfunctory impression. During this penultimate
year of his life, Bonhoeffer passed through an intensely painful stage in
his Christian formation, a final stage of purgation, in which at first he
was thrown with violence from one mood to another, and only maintained his equilibrium by means of his powerful self-discipline. The
letters and papers give us a succession of glimpses into what was going
on: "I often wonder who I really am—the man who goes on squirming
under these ghastly experiences in wretchedness that cries to heaven,
or the man who scourges himself and pretends to others (and even to

[1] *L. and P.*, pp. 225–6.

himself) that he is placid, cheerful, composed and in control of himself, and allows people to admire him for it."[1]

In the earlier letters the natural faults which are particularly his, and which limit his total effectiveness in the life with others, still show through from time to time. There is the vanity which "allows people to admire him", the fastidiousness which can still separate him from some of the more obnoxious of his fellow men, and the still surviving remains of a censorious self-satisfaction, which particularly governed his relations with a certain pitiable little government propagandist, who for some failure to toe the party line found himself in prison and was going to pieces in a welter of misery and self-pity. Bonhoeffer at first showed him some condescending kindness, but when the little man let fall some anti-Jewish sentiments, he turned against him, adopted a haughty attitude and appeared rather to admire himself for his behaviour. ". . .I have had to take a new line with the companion of my daily walks. Although he has done his best to ingratiate himself with me, he let fall a remark about the Jewish problem lately that has made me more offhanded and cool to him than I have ever been to anyone before; and I have also seen to it that he has been deprived of certain little comforts. Now he feels obliged to go round whimpering for a time, but it leaves me—I am surprised myself, but interested too—absolutely cold."[2]

These were the last remains of the "Old Adam", and as we make the journey with Bonhoeffer through these letters which give insight into these last years, we can watch the combined operation of suffering and love, as they burned them out of his soul. Bonhoeffer himself was aware of the operation to a certain extent; he wrote at the end of 1943: "There are two ways of dealing psychically with adversities. One way, the easier, is to try to ignore them; that is about as far as I have got. The other and more difficult way, is to face them deliberately and overcome them; I am not equal to that yet, but one must learn to do it . . ."[3]

"When we are forcibly separated for any considerable time from those whom we love, we simply *cannot* as most can, get some cheap substitute through other people—I don't mean because of moral considerations, but just because we are what we are. Substitutes repel us; we simply have to wait and wait; we have to suffer unspeakably from the separation, and feel the longing till it almost makes us ill. That is the only way, although it is a very painful one, in which we can preserve unimpaired

[1] *L. and P.*, p. 107.
[2] *L. and P.*, pp. 121–2.
[3] *L. and P.*, pp. 105–6.

our relationships with our loved ones . . . Above all, we must never give way to self-pity. And on the Christian aspect of the matter, there are some lines that say:

> *dass nicht vergessen werde*
> *Was man so gern vergisst,*
> *dass diese arme Erde*
> *nicht unsre Heimat ist*[1]

That is indeed something essential, but it must come last of all. I believe that we ought so to love and trust God in our *lives*, and in all the good things that he sends us, that when the time comes (but not before!) we may go to him with love, trust and joy."[2]

In the same letter Bonhoeffer comments that "through every event, however untoward, there is access to God". Perhaps it is no accident that only after an event so untoward that it would eventually cost him his life could Bonhoeffer write a sentence which rings like a gentle epitaph on his relations with the pitiful little prisoner: "It is weakness rather than wickedness that drags most people down, and it needs profound sympathy to put up with that."[3] But before this tragic event had scored the last deep line across his life, he was already growing towards that simple humility before his fellow men which for his fastidious, aristocratic nature was an exceptionally hard lesson to learn. In April 1943 he could already speak of: "a clearer and more sober estimate of our limitations and possibilities, which makes it possible for us genuinely to love our neighbour;"[4] and could describe the true nature of the life for others which he himself has been learning in depth at such great cost:

"There is a wholeness about the fully grown man which enables him to face an existing situation squarely. He may have his longings, but he keeps them out of sight, and somehow masters them; and the more he has to overcome in order to live fully in the present, the more he will have the respect and confidence of his fellows, especially the younger ones, who are still on the road that he has already travelled. Desires to which we cling closely can easily prevent us from being what we ought to be and can be; and on the other hand, desires repeatedly mastered for the sake of present duty make us richer. Lack of desire is poverty. Almost all the people that I find in my present surroundings cling to their own desires, and so have no interest in others; they no longer

---

[1] That we may remember what we so like to forget—that this poor earth is not our home.
[2] *L. and P.*, pp. 109–111.
[3] *L. and P.*, p. 212.
[4] *L. and P.*, p. 100.

listen, and they are incapable of loving their neighbour. I think that even in this place we ought to live as if we had no wishes and no future, and just be our true selves. It is remarkable then how others come to rely on us, confide in us, and let us talk to them."[1]

This is an element of the experience which he outlines in the notes for a book upon which he was then working:

"The experience that a transformation of all human life is given in the fact that 'Jesus is there for others'! His 'being there for others' is the experience of transcendence. It is only this 'being there for others' maintained till death, that is the ground of his omnipotence, omniscience and omnipresence. Faith is participation in this being of Jesus."[2]

While in the deepest areas of his being Bonhoeffer was enduring the later stages of this transformation, his day-to-day existence was complicated and enlivened by a hope which in the end would be deferred indefinitely. He was told that at last he was to be brought formally to trial, and that he might brief a lawyer to defend him. Letters on the subject of a suitable lawyer travelled to and fro between himself and his parents, and at last an honest and able man was found, who was neither too closely associated with the resistance nor on the other hand a sympathiser with the Nazi regime. But in the end it was to no avail. Joseph Müller stood his trial, conducted his own defence and was acquitted, though on release he was immediately arrested again, but Bonhoeffer's trial was too much dependent upon that of Hans von Dohnanyi to be undertaken apart from his and, in November, Dohnanyi was taken ill. The much harsher conditions of his imprisonment and his fearful battles with Roeder under interrogation had almost broken him, mentally and physically, and when on November 23rd, during an air raid, an incendiary bomb struck the cell where he was confined, he suffered a cerebral thrombosis and was partially paralysed. He was taken to the Charité hospital, where he remained until January, when Roeder finally succeeded in getting him removed and sent to the prison hospital at Buchenwald. Now he was declared to be sufficiently recovered to stand his trial, but in the meantime his arch-enemy Roeder had been transferred, and the authorities ceased to press for the trial. Now Carl Sack, the Judge Advocate General and unsuspected member of the resistance, who had been working for the prisoners behind the scenes, recommended a change of tactics. He suggested that they should no longer hope for a quick release through a trial and acquittal,

[1] *L. and P.*, p. 141.
[2] *L. and P.*, pp. 209–10.

255

but on the contrary try to escape notice by making no further sign, so that their case might fall into the background, *versanden*—"vanish into the sand"—as Sack expressed it. All members of the resistance believed that the defeat of Germany could not be much longer deferred, and meanwhile they pressed on with their last and boldest plan for the assassination of Hitler, the plan which so nearly succeeded on July 20th 1944. As soon as the government had fallen, the prisoners would be released in any case, so it was decided that they should endure just a few more months without further protest.

Both Hans and Dietrich saw the wisdom of this suggestion, and Dietrich now, by a supreme effort of the will, put all immediate thoughts of release out of his mind. And so it was that, forgetting his concern for physical freedom, he gained the mental freedom to embark upon the last great theological effort of his life, the effort to make creative use of the intense and painful, but also valuable and enriching experiences of his last years. It is through these experiences that the passionate and searching questions of the great theological letters gained their immediate character, but it was in the total and undivided experience of his whole life that their fundamental nature was rooted. Bonhoeffer was not destined to live on into the time when he might have explored these questions in depth and perhaps begun to approach here and there an answer; and in the years which have followed his death many have been appropriated and carried away, like stones from a half-built church, to be used as the foundation for theological superstructures for which he would have disclaimed any responsibility. But the first question, the central question, upon which all the others are simply an elaboration, has frequently been ignored: "Who is Christ for us today?" It had been the central question of Bonhoeffer's whole life: "Who art thou, Lord?" which is at the same time an answer to Christ's question to man, "Lovest thou me?" This is the same Bonhoeffer who told his young students in the far away days in Berlin University before the coming of Hitler: "The Church exists and God exists, and we are the ones who are being questioned. We are being asked whether we are ready to be used . . . to tell the right question from the wrong one was among the most vital problems in theology."[1] And a few years later, in his course of lectures on Christology, he was again concerned to dissociate the real from the unreal question. "Not 'How are you possible?'—that is the godless question, the serpent's question—but 'Who are you?' "[2]

[1] *Begegnungen*, p. 46.
[2] Dietrich Bonhoeffer, *Christology*, p. 30.

Bonhoeffer is now, in the last letters, as intensely convinced as he ever was before, that the right question can only be asked from within the faith. God is my centre at every moment. I may never return on to my own centre and make God the object of my enquiry; "How are you possible?" It is only from within the faith that a Christian has power to make the distinction, so vital to Dietrich Bonhoeffer, between ultimate and penultimate reality. Jesus Christ is the same yesterday and today and for ever, but my perception of Him may change with the changing world. It is from this understanding of Christ as the unchanging centre of man's existence that there follows the encounter with Christ as the beyond in our midst, ultimate in His unchanging totality, penultimate in the infinity of his changing manifestations. Around these certainties are grouped the intensely-worded, powerfully-felt contemporary questions, and in face of them the various distorted and incomplete answers are firmly rejected.

Bonhoeffer had now lived for a year in prison cut off from the Church and surrounded by sad, average, half-educated humanity, a cross-section of everyday modern man. Out of this experience had grown the conviction that man as a whole had ceased to be religious. And hence comes the question which runs through the whole of the great opening letter of April 30th; how can God be seen as the centre of a world which has ceased to be religious? "What kind of situation arises for us, for the Church? How can Christ become the Lord of the religionless as well?"[1] "We are moving towards a completely religionless time; people as they are now, simply cannot be religious any more."[2] These are the people around him in prison, but he could accept their condition the more easily, because of the negative connotations which the word "religion" bore for him. Since his student days, when his Barthian sympathies had led him to reject "religion" as being the "most grandiose and subtle" of man's self-centred efforts to gain possession of the infinite, the word had gathered many more specifically pejorative overtones. He had come to see in "religion" a particular department of culture, intent upon its own self-preservation, relying upon privilege, concerned to be rich and powerful, taking refuge now in "metaphysics" which for Bonhoeffer represented a flight from reality into convenient abstractions, and now in "conscience" and "inwardness" which he saw as an escapist world where religious man could take refuge from the harsh facts of reality in private experience. At best he saw it as an outgrown garment for the faith which must now

[1] *L. and P.*, 1967 edn., p. 153.
[2] *L. and P.*, p. 153.

be willingly put off, just as the demand for the symbolic act of circumcision had been abandoned by the early Church. Meanwhile, however, the religious were trying to clutch this threadbare garment round them, not daring to let it go, trying to preserve a foothold for God at the boundaries of existence, where human knowledge fails, or to make him a *deus ex machina*, to intervene in their extremity, calling upon him to do their will instead of abandoning their lives to his. Bonhoeffer indignantly repudiates these self-centred human solutions; we are to serve God, not press him to serve us, and perhaps now, far from relegating him to the boundaries of life, we have a better opportunity than ever before to see him, where he has always been, at the centre of the world. So we must accept the new situation, with all its revolutionary implications, and ask ourselves, "How do we speak (or perhaps we cannot now even 'speak' as we used to) in a secular way about God?"[1] This was how he expressed the challenge which he saw approaching the Christians of the twentieth century.

In the first two letters a single word appears, twice only and without explanation. No explanation was needed, for it carried a wealth of meaning for the two friends between whom the letters were passing; it is "*Arkandisziplin*", "secret discipline". This secret discipline meant for them a life of complete self-sacrifice lived together by dedicated Christians in all the churches in which "ultimate" truth, the revealed word of God, was remembered and shared, if necessary in secret until the new pattern of Christian life and language had, through their humble listening, and by the inspiration of the Holy Spirit, begun to form; and meanwhile the Christians within this discipline must be content to speak to the world through their lives. We may catch a glimpse of the hope that the two men held in common, from a passage in the *Thoughts on a Baptism* written some three or four weeks later for Bethge's infant son:

"We are once again being driven right back to the beginnings of our understanding. Reconciliation and redemption, regeneration and the Holy Ghost, love of our enemies, Cross and Resurrection, life in Christ and Christian discipleship—all these things are so difficult and so remote that we hardly venture any more to speak of them. In the traditional words and acts we suspect that there may be something quite new and revolutionary, though we cannot as yet grasp or express it. That is our fault. Our Church, which has been fighting in these years only for its self-preservation, as though that were an end in itself, is incapable of taking the word of reconciliation and redemption to man-

[1] *L. and P.*, p. 153.

kind and the world. Our earlier words are therefore bound to lose their force and cease, and our being Christians today will be limited to two things: prayer and righteous action among men. All Christian thinking, speaking, and organising must be born anew out of this prayer and action. By the time you have grown up, the Church's form will have changed greatly. We are not yet out of the melting-pot, and any attempt to help the Church prematurely to a new expansion of its organisation will merely delay its conversion and purification. It is not for us to prophesy the day (though the day will come) when men will once more be called so to utter the word of God that the world will be changed and renewed by it. It will be a new language, perhaps quite non-religious, but liberating and redeeming—as was Jesus' language; it will shock people and yet overcome them by its power; it will be the language of a new righteousness and truth, proclaiming God's peace with men and the coming of his kingdom. 'They shall fear and tremble because of all the good and all the prosperity I provide for it' (Jer. 33:9). Till then the Christian cause will be a silent and hidden affair, but there will be those who pray and do right and wait for God's own time."[1]

It seems to have been the reading of Weizsäcker's book, *das Weltbild der Physik*, "the World in the Language of Physics", that set light to those thoughts which led to the second stage in Bonhoeffer's questioning, and they are thoughts which seem to have come as the result of a real change in his attitude to the physical facts of the universe. Throughout the active years of his life a decision to ignore the discoveries of science, simply to avert his eyes from the scientific map of life, is from time to time negatively apparent. It is the retreat which may have begun during the youthful arguments with his elder brothers, and it was not until prison put an end to his normal activities that this aspect of reality seems to have caught up with him, so that the retreat was halted. In a letter to his parents written during the first months of his imprisonment, Bonhoeffer expressed his regret that he had never concerned himself with natural science. It was too late to do much to repair the omission, but the change in attitude which it represented is expressed in a letter of May 25th 1944: "We are to find God in what we know, not in what we do not know; God wants us to realise his presence, not in unsolved problems, but in those that are solved. That is true of the relationship between God and scientific knowledge . . ."[2]

[1] *L. and P.*, p. 172.
[2] *L. and P.*, pp. 174-5

". . . The autonomy of man (in which I should include the discovery of the laws by which the world lives and deals with itself in science, social and political matters, art, ethics and religion) has in our time reached an undoubted completion. Man has learnt to deal with himself in all questions of importance without recourse to the 'working hypothesis' called 'God'."[1]

And upon this followed his vivid definition: "a world come of age". It is a definition which has been taken up and bandied round the Christian world, and for Bonhoeffer it came to represent perhaps the most important of the "penultimate" realities which surround the "ultimate" reality of the Christian faith in the present age. It was particularly fruitful for his own thinking, since he himself stood before God in the conscious and loving relationship of a son to his father, and he understood this as a developing relationship, not only in the individual soul, but also in the history of the Christian Church. When a child is small, his father will give him the kind of protection that a small child needs; as he grows older and learns more, he will leave him more to his own devices; when the boy comes of age, he will expect him to accept still more adult responsibility for his own life. But he has not for this reason ceased to be a father; the relationship has only grown and developed, and by the time that the boy comes of age it is, though perhaps more demanding, at the same time potentially richer, deeper and more precious than it was in the boy's childhood. When an analogy is pressed too far, it recoils and imprisons the sense which it was intended to liberate, and this analogy of the coming of age must be handled with care. For Bonhoeffer it proved during the next weeks, simply a useful vessel in which to contain that area of the problem with which he was concerned.

Just as the "non-religious" world was represented for him by the inhabitants of Tegel, so in another sense those particularly associated in his mind with the "world come of age" were perhaps his own family and the many noble, gifted and heroic humanists who were sacrificing their lives to the resistance. It is for this reason, perhaps, that he is particularly vehement in his denunciation of what he sees as the principal method employed to counteract man's advance towards his majority. He sees existentialist philosophy and psychotherapy as "secularised offshoots of Christianity" intent on persuading "secure, contented and happy mankind that it is really unhappy and desperate," and as a companion to this he sees: "The 'clerical' sniffing around among people's sins in order to catch them out," as the result of a

[1] *L. and P.*, p. 178.

particular kind of isolation among the clergy which is parallel to the isolation of certain unhealthy gossip-mongers. In contrast to all this he declares characteristically, "that we should not run man down in his worldliness, but confront him with God at his strongest point, that we should give up all our clerical tricks, and not regard psychotherapy and existentialist philosophy as God's pioneers. The importunity of all these people is far too unaristocratic for the Word of God to ally itself with them. The Word of God is far removed from this revolt of mistrust, this revolt from below. On the contrary, it reigns."[1] And this leads back to the central question, always recurring in one form or another: "how to claim for Jesus Christ a world that has come of age?"

By this time Bonhoeffer had been occupied for rather over two months with these theological explorations. The mental detachment which he had achieved in order to concentrate upon them represented an exceptional feat of self-discipline, for news had been conveyed to him by means of the secret code and a few illicit conversations, that the resistance was crouching for the spring again. This time the young Count von Stauffenberg, handsome and gallant as a knight in a medieval romance, had been chosen to do the deed. Hopes rose among the conspirators, and on the upsurge of optimism, some of them began to act as though with a foretaste of freedom. Dietrich's uncle, General Paul von Hase, Commandant of Berlin, a member of the resistance but at that time still unsuspected, paid a surprise visit to the prison on June 30th, had his nephew brought down, and stayed drinking champagne and talking to him for five hours. Dietrich recorded a story that his uncle told. "At St. Privat a wounded ensign shouted loudly, 'I am wounded; long live the King.' Thereupon General von Löwenfeld, who was also wounded, said, 'Be quiet, ensign; we die here in silence.' "[2] They enjoyed this story as they drank their champagne, little guessing, accustomed though they were to danger, that before another six weeks had gone by, General von Hase himself would die in silence in the Gestapo prison.

Meanwhile, against this not wholly uneventful background, the theological letters continued and approached their climax. In the letter of July 16th, after a veiled reference to the intensive preparations in the resistance movement, Bonhoeffer returns once more to the subject of the world come of age, attempting to resolve the paradox inherent in his own analogy, that though he is come of age, man must remain for

[1] *L. and P.*, pp. 192–3.
[2] *L. and P.*, p. 189.

ever, in "ultimate" reality, a child before God. " 'Except ye be converted and become as little children, ye shall in no wise enter into the Kingdom of heaven." Our true state as children of God can only be rediscovered through repentence, through *ultimate* honesty." And then follows the passage which describes an experience deeply lived and understood by Bonhoeffer through his own prayer and suffering, that passage which leads us to the foot of the Cross:

"Before God and with God we live without God. God lets himself be pushed out of the world on to the cross. He is weak and powerless in the world, and that is precisely the way, the only way, in which he is with us and helps us."[1]

Two days later he continues:

"Man is summoned to share in God's sufferings at the hands of a godless world. He must therefore really live in the godless world without attempting to gloss over or explain its ungodliness in some religious way or other ... That is metanoia: not in the first place thinking about one's own needs, problems, sins and fears, but allowing oneself to be caught up into the way of Jesus Christ, into the messianic event . . ."[2] He had reached this point, at which for him all else was blotted out by Christ's sacrifice on Calvary, and at which he saw man's whole duty as the duty to suffer with him, when the news of the failure of the July plot flared across Europe. In the days that followed, details of the catastrophe filtered into the prison: plans had been laid for the *coup d'état* throughout the whole of Germany and occupied Europe, Hitler had escaped by a miracle, Claus von Stauffenberg was dead and a wave of arrests and executions was sweeping the country.

Bonhoeffer knew himself involved in the calamity, now in mortal danger, and with small hope of escape. The search for incriminating evidence against himself and hundreds of others would now become intensive. It was at this moment, with his perceptions heightened to their most sensitive pitch by the suddenly much nearer approach of death, that Bonhoeffer wrote the great letter of July 21st, which crowns the series of his theological letters.

"I am still discovering," he wrote, "right up to this moment, that it is only by living completely in this world that one learns to have faith. One must completely abandon any attempt to make something of oneself, whether it be a saint, or a converted sinner, or a churchman (a so-called priestly type!), a righteous man or an unrighteous one, a sick

[1] *L. and P.*, p. 196.
[2] *L. and P.*, pp. 198–9.

man or a healthy one. By this worldliness I mean living unreservedly in life's duties, problems, successes and failures, experiences and perplexities. In so doing we throw ourselves completely into the arms of God taking seriously, not our own sufferings, but those of God in the world— watching with Christ in Gethsemane. That, I think, is faith, that is metanoia; and that is how one becomes a man and a Christian."[1] Now the letters to Bethge begin to take a new direction; they give glimpses of a life lived simply in quiet faith, with speculations and reflections left behind, and they give flashes of insight into that resurrection of the spirit which is the counterpart to the Cross, and which, though he lived to know it, Bonhoeffer did not live to describe. The few letters to his friends which were still able to filter out of Tegel are instinct with a great peace which is the fruit of this quiet resurrection; and there are many passages whose power is the greater for having been written in face of the now almost certain approach of death. Less than a week after the failure of the plot he wrote: "How great a power there is in a hope that is based on certainty, and how invincible a life with such a hope is! 'Christ our hope'— this Pauline formula is the strength of our lives."[2]

On August 21st came a few words which were the last recorded fruit of his morning meditation, the meditation which he had taught to his students in Finkenwalde, and which remained his strength and stay to the last day of his life:

"Once again I have taken up the *Losungen*[3] and meditated on them. The key to everything is the 'in him'. All that we may rightly expect from God, and ask him for, is to be found in Jesus Christ. The God of Jesus Christ has nothing to do with what God, as we imagine him, could do and ought to do. If we are to learn what God promises, and what he fulfils, we must persevere in quiet meditation on the life, sayings, deeds, sufferings, and death of Jesus. It is certain that we may always live close to God and in the light of his presence, and that such living is an entirely new life for us; that nothing is then impossible for us, because all things are possible with God; that no earthly power can touch us without his will, and that danger and distress can only drive us closer to him."[4]

The last published letter to Bethge from the Tegel prison opens with

---

[1] *L. and P.*, pp. 201-2.
[2] *L. and P.*, p. 204.
[3] The Bible passages for the day—Num. 11; 23; II Cor. 1: 20.
[4] *L. and P.*, pp. 213-14.

the words: ". . . Please don't ever get anxious or worried about me, but don't forget to pray for me—I'm sure you don't! I am so sure of God's guiding hand that I hope I shall always be kept in that certainty. You must never doubt that I am travelling with gratitude and cheerfulness along the road where I am being led."[1]

After this no more illicit letters came out of Tegel. The watch on political suspects of all kinds was continually intensified, and a few weeks later, on September 20th or 22nd, the Gestapo made a find which was to constitute the final disaster for the members of the Resistance who had been in the *Abwehr*. In a secret file in Zossen, a centre outside Berlin to which part of the *Abwehr* material had been evacuated, Sonderegger, who with Roeder had been originally responsible for the arrest of Dohnanyi and Bonhoeffer, discovered material which incriminated Dohnanyi deeply and beyond dispute, and with him the other members of the *Abwehr* who had been active or passive members of the conspiracy. The news quickly spread along the secret channels of the conspiracy's network; Bonhoeffer heard it, and now prepared, as a last attempt to survive, to put into operation a plan hatched some time before and held in reserve, to escape with one of the guards, a trusted friend, and go "underground" until the fall of Hitler. It was a desperate measure, for to remain hidden from the diabolical vigilance of the Secret Police was almost impossible. But it was a last hope. On September 24th, Ursula and Rüdiger Schleicher with their daughter Renate, now the wife of Bethge, met the prison guard in the outskirts of Berlin, and gave him food, clothes and ration cards to be hidden in a shed on an allotment garden for the use of himself and Bonhoeffer after their escape. But the escape was never to be made. On October 1st, after a night of near despair, when it was perhaps only the splendid courage of his sister Ursula that saved him from suicide, Klaus Bonhoeffer was arrested. Next day the guard from Tegel prison came to the house in the Marienburgerallee with a message. Dietrich had given up the plan to escape, for fear of reprisals against the family and Klaus.

Meanwhile on October 4th, Rüdiger Schleicher was arrested, and on the next day Dietrich's faithful friend Friedrich Justus Perels. Later in the month, Eberhard Bethge was brought home from war service in Italy and imprisoned with them in the Lehrterstrasse. On October 8th, Bonhoeffer himself was transferred from Tegel to the Gestapo prison in the Prinz Albrecht Strasse. Round their intended victims, the Secret Police were closing the net.

[1] *L. and P.*, p. 215.

PART IV

DEATH

Come now thou greatest of feasts on the journey to freedom eternal;
death, cast aside all the burdensome chains, and demolish
the walls of our temporal body, the walls of our souls that are
blinded,
so that at last we may see that which here remains hidden.
Freedom how long we have sought thee in discipline, action and
suffering;
dying we now may behold thee revealed in the Lord.

Dietrich Bonhoeffer.

CHAPTER XX

THE months spent in the cellar of the Gestapo prison in the Prinz Albrecht Strasse were a strange phantasmagoria of hunger, darkness, squalor and fear, shot through with rays of hope. Bonhoeffer was now almost completely cut off from his family. Klaus, Rüdiger Schleicher and Bethge were all imprisoned in the Lehrterstrasse, and he was never to see them again. Hans von Dohnanyi was in the concentration camp in Sachsenhausen. Bonhoeffer's parents and sisters and Maria von Wedemeyer never again had permission to see him. Food parcels and books he might still receive, and two short, closely-censored letters which he was allowed to write to his parents have survived, but of his family, only Hans von Dohnanyi, who was transferred for a few weeks in February to the Prinz Albrecht Strasse, ever saw him again.

Since the finding of the Zossen documents, interrogations were taking a much more serious turn. Communication could no longer be maintained between those who had been privy to the conspiracy; Klaus Bonhoeffer, Perels and others were being examined under torture, all were on trial for their lives. But at the same time there were curious elements in the interrogations which kept hope alive for the prisoners. Their captors were plainly ill at ease. They could not remain unaware of the crumbling fortunes of the Nazi party. Suddenly, disconcertingly, prisoners would find themselves asked for their opinion of Germany's political prospects, warders would try, through motives of anxiety, to gain their friendship, even the governor of the prison in the Lehrterstrasse, was as Dohnanyi put it, "fishing for an anchor in the future". Meanwhile Hitler, though he thirsted for the conspirators' blood, gave orders that their trials were to be prolonged in order that they might be forced to reveal as much as possible about the nationwide network of whose existence he was now convinced. To Fabian von Schlabrendorff, whom he found already installed in the Gestapo prison, Bonhoeffer confided during conversations in the washroom under cover of the running shower that he was still hopeful of the outcome of the interrogations and that, "if the investigations were to carry on at the present pace, years might pass till they reached their conclusion".[1]

Meanwhile the decline in his fortunes had not dimmed Bonhoeffer's

[1] *Begegnungen*, p. 188.

radiance or disturbed his peace. "He was always good tempered," von Schlabrendorff writes, "always of the same kindliness and politeness towards everybody, so that to my surprise, within a short time, he had won over his warders, who were not always kindly disposed. It was significant for our relationship that he was rather the hopeful one, while I now and then suffered from depressions. He always cheered me up and comforted me; he never tired of repeating that the only fight which we lose is that which we give up."[1] It is the Tegel pattern repeating itself in the much more rigorous conditions of the Prinz Albrecht Strasse cellars. As Bonhoeffer by the magic of his personality won himself more freedom of movement, he contrived fleeting meetings with old friends; Joseph Müller, Canaris and Oster, the two latter arrested after the July plot, were his neighbours in nearby cells. And in hours of solitude he seems to have been working at his book. All through the autumn and winter the improbable existence continued, but no news leaked out to those who waited for it. Bishop Bell wrote to Gerhard Leibholz in Oxford, "I can't tell you how deeply I share your and your wife's anxieties for Dietrich. May God spare him for the survival of the Church in Germany and the world . . ."[2] Visser 'tHooft wrote to Bell from Geneva that he believed Bonhoeffer to be safe, but the family in Berlin knew that his life hung by a thread. On February 2nd 1945, his brother Klaus and his brother-in-law Rüdiger Schleicher were condemned to death by the People's Court.[3]

But all was not yet lost. The British and Americans from the West and the Russians from the East were converging on Berlin. On the same day a letter came from Maria von Wedemeyer's mother in Pätzig in Pomerania: "Dear Frau Bonhoeffer! I have had to deal very hardly with you, please forgive me. I have sent Maria with my three children, with Fräulein Rath who is ill of fever and Frau Dienel who is very delicate, through twelve degrees of frost and an icy north wind to travel west in the wagonette, in the direction of Celle, where relations of Herr Dopkes live in a nearby village.

"I needed her desperately. It is a task which is really far beyond her strength. She has a Pole for coachman and the three best workhorses. Pray with me that she may prove fit to cope with this hard assignment . . . when Maria has installed the children in the village, she will try to thrash her way back to you . . ."[4]

[1] *Begegnungen*, p. 188.
[2] E.B., *D.B.*, p. 1004.
[3] They were shot on April 22nd 1945.
[4] E.B., *D.B.*, p. 1019

Two days later artillery fire laid Pätzig level with the ground.

In this same fateful month, Hans von Dohnanyi was transferred from Sachsenhausen to the Prinz Albrecht Strasse. He was still ill, and made himself appear much iller than he was, in order to avoid further interrogations. He wrote to his wife a tiny round letter in minute handwriting, smuggling it out in the lid of a food container. "I am using my illness," he wrote, "as a weapon. I succeed in making people think me iller than I am . . . actually I feel all right, and through you I am really well fed. At night I am secretly learning to walk again. I am getting on quite well; I must become independent. By day I am the helpless invalid . . .

"Playing for time is the only solution . . ."[1]

And then he unfolds, in his tiny writing, a desperate plan. He is recovering too quickly, he cannot keep up the fiction of incapacitating illness much longer. So he must really become ill again. Christine is to procure a diphtheria culture, conceal it in a specially-marked food container, and send it in to him. Two weeks later Dohnanyi was back in the hospital. This time he would not leave it again until he went to his death.[2]

But by this time Dietrich had vanished. A packet and letters from his father intended for his birthday, and delivered one day late owing to the complete paralysis of the city by the appalling daylight raid of February 3rd, was the last word from home that he received. The last moving note from his parents was never delivered.

"We have had no news of you," this letter ran, "since your departure from Berlin, and you will have had no news of us . . . We should like you to go on receiving the clean linen and the other such things which till now we have been able to send, but at present we have found no means of achieving this. I hope that Christel may discover something today at the Prinz Albrecht Strasse . . . to such old people as we now are, permission to write should be more frequent. Affectionately your father."

"My thoughts are with you day and night in anxiety as to how you are. I hope you can work and read a little and are not too much dejected! God help you and us through this hard time. We shall remain in Berlin, come what may. Your old mother."[3]

Christel returned from the Prinz Albrecht Strasse with nothing dis-

---

[1] E.B., *D.B.*, p. 1020.
[2] Dohnanyi was executed in Sachsenhausen.
[3] E.B., *D.B.*, p. 1030.

covered and the note still in her hand, and when Maria battled her way back to Berlin at last, there was nothing to tell her. But Maria, who had courage and endurance in her blood, had grown in stature to meet the hour. She took a suitcase of Dietrich's warm clothes and set out alone in the chaotic conditions of that last nightmare winter, to follow him into the south down the line of the Nazi retreat. She found her way out to Dachau, hidden in the Bavarian woods, but receiving no news of him there, and led by some agonised instinct of love, she pressed on on foot carrying the suitcase, to the extermination camp at Flossenbürg. But she was turned back; and that, for Maria, was the end of a life to which nothing which came after could seem more than a postscript.

Meanwhile Bonhoeffer's life had continued, quiet, intense and vivid. Berlin was at breaking point, laid waste by the constant bombardments from the air, and awaiting the imminent arrival of the Russians and Americans. On February 7th, twenty of the most distinguished prisoners in the Prinz Albrecht Strasse were ordered to assemble in the prison yard. Two lorries stood ready for departure. Bonhoeffer was ordered to enter one, with, among others, Dr. Joseph Müller and Dr. Hermann Pünder, who was to enjoy a stimulating friendship with Bonhoeffer during the last weeks of his life, and Captain Ludwig Gehre, who was to play a brief part in the drama of the last days. Assembled beside the other truck stood another group of outstanding men, including Canaris and Oster, Carl Sack, the former Judge Advocate General and friend to Bonhoeffer during his earlier interrogations, Dr. Hjalmar Schecht and von Schuschnigg, the one-time Chancellor of the Republic of Austria. The men waited. Gradually some information materialised out of the air and was passed round among the prisoners. The trucks were to head south, down the narrowing strip of country which had not yet been overrun from East or West. One was bound for the concentration camp of Buchenwald, in the forests of Thuringia, the other for the dreaded Flossenbürg. The twenty prisoners, accustomed to live daily in an intensity of hope and fear, waited impassively, their thoughts locked within them. At last the trucks started. Bonhoeffer's carried its freight to Buchenwald.

And now happened one of those curious coincidences which the tangled skein of the war sometimes provided. Captain Payne Best, one of the two British officers taken prisoner on the borders of Holland in 1940 by means of a German hoax, who had been a prisoner in Sachsenhausen during the last year, was transferred to Buchenwald two weeks after Bonhoeffer's arrival and shared in his adventures during the last weeks of his life. Payne Best has published a book, *The Venlo Incident*, to which we may turn for detailed information about these last days, and for a few glimpses of Bonhoeffer that for depth and clarity of insight surpass those of his friends. This detached and ironical spectator, highly trained in the arts of critical observation, and without any knowledge of Bonhoeffer's previous history, appreciated without reserve the spiritual stature to which he had now attained. "Bonhoeffer," he wrote, "was different; just quite calm and normal, seemingly perfectly at his ease . . . his soul really shone in the dark desperation of our prison."[1]

Bonhoeffer was passing the last landmarks in his spiritual journey. The struggles of the Tegel days had ended in victory, and he seems to have attained that peace which is the gift of God and not as the world giveth. The struggle to abandon to God his rich and treasured past, the struggle with the last vestiges of his pride, the struggle to suffer, in full measure and yet in gratitude, his human longings and to remain open to others in the midst of his own pain; all this had led him to that experience of the Cross, in which at last, through a grasp of reality so intense that it fused all the elements of his being into a single shining whole, he learnt what life can be when "we throw ourselves completely into the arms of God, taking seriously not our own sufferings, but the sufferings of God in the world." Out of this death to the last vestiges of self Bonhoeffer seems to have been raised up quietly, unspectacularly, into the last stage of his life, in which he was made whole, made single, finally integrated in Christ. In a way more complete than any that had gone before, the Christian had become "the man for others", the disciple "as his Lord".

As we look back, struggling with such help as we have to pierce the obscurity that surrounds him in these last months, this seems to be the truth. To claim it is to claim a definite event, a concrete happening, not sudden in the sense of being discontinuous with what had gone before, but actual in the sense that it represents an intensive experience of spiritual reality, a condition of being united to God to an extent unknown until it is known from within, and which saints throughout all the Christian centuries have struggled in vain to describe. Apart from the change discernible in his letters after July 21st, 1944, Bonhoeffer himself has left no record of it, and it seems unlikely that he himself was conscious of it as of the consummating stage in his spiritual development, although in his Tegel days he had once written: "If I were to

[1] Letter from Payne Best to Sabine Leibholz March 2nd 1951.

end my life here, in these conditions, that would have a meaning that I think I could understand."[1]

Those looking back to that life and striving to discover, here and there, traces of that meaning which unfolds at a deeper level than the exterior event, have no right to do more than touch it lightly, and with the reserve that Bonhoeffer, in a like situation, would have imposed upon himself. The most it would be fair to say is that there are one or two indications of a profound and subtle change, and that the man who could, for instance, write in 1944: "I have had to take a new line with the companion of my daily walks . . . a remark he let fall . . . has made me more offhanded and cool to him than I have ever been to anyone before . . . I have even seen to it that he has been deprived of certain little comforts . . ."[2] was hardly the man of whom Payne Best could write: "Bonhoeffer was all humility and sweetness." It is the "all" which seems the operative word here, and the passage continues: "He always seemed to diffuse an atmosphere of happiness, of joy in every smallest event in life, and of deep gratitude for the mere fact that he was alive," and at the end of this sober, factual passage, Best quietly exposes the roots of the matter, "He was one of the very few men I have ever met to whom his God was real, and ever close to him."[3]

And meanwhile though hopes and fears still alternated for Bonhoeffer, as for others, amid the continual uncertainties of these last phantasmagoric days, fear in the deeper areas of his being was gone. "He had always been afraid," Best wrote later to Sabine Leibholz, "that he would not be strong enough to stand such a test, but now he knew that there was nothing in life of which one need ever be afraid."

These are only few and simple words, slight indications, not to be pressed too far, yet it may be that they afford glimpses into a victorious world of the spirit which few enter and which even a host of words could do little to describe. But whatever may be the truth about God's working in the unknown depths of Bonhoeffer's life, the exterior fact is evident that his capacity to cheer and inspire his fellow prisoners went on increasing; and that the majority were in a state of controlled desperation is apparent from Payne Best's record. Happily, however, Bonhoeffer and the other "Special Prisoners" who arrived at Buchenwald in the night of February 7th, were not to be exposed to the most extreme of the "tests" to which in those black days they might have

[1] *L. and P.*, p. 206.
[2] *L. and P.*, pp. 121-2.
[3] Payne Best, *The Venlo Incident*, p. 180.

been subjected. They were not accommodated amid the horrors of the main compound, but were delivered into the cellar of a high yellow-painted house which stood on the edge of the woods among others that had been built to house the staff of the concentration camp.

Their cells were ranged along the two sides of a wide corridor which was divided into three lengthways by two long concrete partitions. After the arrival of Payne Best with some other prisoners, Bonhoeffer shared a cell with the soldier-theologian General von Rabenau, to their great mutual enjoyment; opposite to them across the corridor was Payne Best and next to them Dr. Pünder and Franz Liedig, a one-time member of the *Abwehr*; further down the corridor Joseph Müller shared a cell with Ludwig Gehre.

There was no possibility of walks in the open, since the house was outside the walls of the compound. Food was increasingly hard to provide, for refugees from East and West, fleeing before the advancing armies, were pouring into the district in a state of complete destitution. But somehow a bowl of soup was provided at midday and some slices of bread with jam in the evening. For exercise the prisoners walked up and down the corridor, making one another's acquaintance and enjoying in the increasingly chaotic conditions a freedom from individual super-vision. Meanwhile in the dark cell, General von Rabenau wrote his memoirs and Bonhoeffer in all probability continued with his book; at other times Dr. Pünder in the next cell listened through cracks in the wall to animated theological conversations. In this way seven weeks went by.

On Easter Sunday, April 1st, American guns were heard firing across the Werra. The hearts of the prisoners leapt up with that curious amalgam of hope and fear which was the product of the time. For them the coming of the Americans would mean life and liberty, if it did not first mean death. Surely there could be no more question of trials and the death sentence with the British and Americans pressing on faster and faster to meet the Russians across this ever-narrowing strip of unoccupied country? They could hardly have guessed that the single element in the Nazi machine which was still functioning efficiently was the horrible apparatus of vengeance. But though they will not have suspected this, they were not without more immediate fears. As Easter Sunday ran its course, orders went round that the prisoners were to be prepared for immediate evacuation. At first, rumour had it that they were to leave on foot. This might have a sinister meaning. The general order to concentration camps required that at the approach of the enemy important prisoners should be marched into the woods and shot. By means of the invisible lines of communication upon which such news carried, the fact of this order was well known to all on the Special Prisoners' corridor.

But such was not to be their fate. It seemed that with regard to them particular orders had been received from Berlin. On April 3rd, a curious vehicle drew up in the yard. It was a prison van, propelled by means of power generated with the help of a wood fire, to such a pass had civil transport been reduced. The prisoners were commanded to enter it. They shared the passenger accommodation area with the piles of wood which provided fuel; at little over twenty miles an hour, the conveyance chugged away. Every quarter of an hour it halted, so that the cylinders might be cleaned and the fire brought back to the required heat. The men sat crushed together in the airless interior of the van, without food or water. Bonhoeffer sat next to Payne Best, who records that he insisted upon sharing with other smokers the last treasured remnants of his tobacco; "he was a good and saintly man".

By slow and painful stages, this load of living freight went rumbling down the roads in a south easterly direction. With sinking hearts the men began to suspect that they were on the way to the dreaded camp at Flossenbürg. Breakfast after a day and night in the van was their first meal. They were nearing Flossenbürg. Towards noon they reached the little town at the foot of the valley up which the Flossenbürg camp lay hidden. The van stopped at the police station. Driver and guards climbed out. The men locked into the dark interior strained their ears to hear the conversation. They seemed to gather the words, "Keep on; they can't take you; too full!" As men again reprieved from death, the passengers relaxed a little as the van once more set out, still heading south. But a few kilometres further on the driver was flagged down by motorised police. Joseph Müller and Franz Liedig were called out, so still, at this eleventh hour, individuals were being pursued! Then a third man jumped down, Ludwig Gehre, to whom love and loyalty to Müller, the fruit of those weeks in which they had shared a cell, mattered more than his life. He would not be parted from his friend now, when he was evidently going to his death.[1] As the door was opened for the three men to depart, Bonhoeffer drew back into the darkness behind it. He was not observed, and the truck drove on.

Now the guards themselves seemed to relax. On one of the numerous

[1] This act of friendship did in fact cost Gehre his life, for he was executed at Flossenbürg, while Müller and Liedig unaccountably survived.

halts, they allowed the prisoners to get out and wash themselves at the pump in a farmyard. The farmer's wife, pitying their condition, brought out a jug of milk and a long loaf of rye bread. In the evening, with some modest hope rising in every breast, the party drove into Regensburg. There seemed to be no accommodation. The city was crammed with refugees of every description. At last, with an ill grace, the men were received into the prison reserved to the Law Courts. "More aristocrats?" growled the warder who admitted them. "Push them up with the others on the second floor." They were locked up five together in single cells. Sleeping in the corridors outside lay the relations of many distinguished men already executed for their part, or supposed part, in the July plot. Among others, the families of Goerdeler, von Stauffenberg, von Halder, von Hammerstein and von Hassell lay on mattresses on the floor outside the cells.

On Thursday morning, when the prisoners were let out of their cells to wash, there followed a cheerful flurry of reunions and introductions. The corridors rang with animated conversation not without laughter. The warders, mastered by the pressures of their extraordinary situation, were totally unable to persuade the newcomers back into their cells. Only when breakfast came up to the first floor did the hungry men make a gradual voluntary return. With relief the warders turned the keys in their locks, but conversation continued through the small grilles intended for observation of prisoners. In the afternoon a severe air raid drove prisoners and guards down to the cellars, and when they returned the social scene of the morning was repeated. But the men were not to remain in Regensburg another night. In the evening they were once more called together and ordered back to the now familiar van. Cheered and increasingly hopeful now, they climbed in, and rattled away along the banks of the Danube. But the journey was soon interrupted. The van skidded to a halt. The fact was soon established that the steering gear was broken. The driver sent word back to Regensburg that fresh transport was needed. To everyone's surprise, at dawn on April 6th, another vehicle appeared. Plainly this group of prisoners possessed some unaccountable priority, for it was petrol-driven, and petrol in Germany in 1945 barely existed for civil transport. But here it was, a comfortable bus with unbroken windows. In rising spirits, the prisoners climbed on board. The guards from Buchenwald were left behind with the crippled van, and a group of armed secret police took over the transport. But nothing could now repress the prisoners' optimism as the bus set out in the spring sunshine of Friday morning along the Danube valley and then climbed up into the rolling hills of the Bavarian Forest. The driver, infected by the atmosphere of restrained hilarity, picked up some village girls who asked for a lift. Asked who his passengers were, he replied resourcefully that they were members of a film company, on their way to make a propaganda film. Dirty and unshaven as they were, the supposed film stars did what they could to act the part.

Early in the afternoon, the bus-load reached their goal, the little village of Schönberg, twenty-five miles north of Passau. Disembarking at the school, the men found the prisoners whom they had met at Regensburg already established there. They were on the ground floor, while the men were led up to a large room on the floor above. It was bright and warm, with windows looking out on three sides up and down the wooded valley. After two whole years Bonhoeffer saw windows with curtains and a row of clean beds with bright covers. For many hours he sat by the open window in the sun, talking to Pünder and a young Russian, Kokorin, and enjoying the dear sounds and colours of that normal life to which so soon now he might be returning.

Around him, all was animation. Men were laughing and chatting and writing their names up over their beds. The prospects of food were discussed with animation. But enquiry from the guards brought the information that the village was alive with refugees and provisions stretched to the limit. There was nothing to be requisitioned. At last, however, where the orders of the guards had failed the humble requests of the prisoners succeeded, and kind-hearted villagers sent in a huge bowl of steaming potatoes.

Saturday was a bright spring day. The prisoners, their first elation spent, were quieter now, daring to relax and at last to entertain the hope that the end of their troubles was in sight. Surely no one would have opportunity now to continue proceedings against them? With all the experience that they had of danger, still none would have guessed that against one of their number, in Berlin and in the hateful camp at Flossenbürg, the machinery of vengeance still worked on.

Tragically, in the very last weeks of the war, the diary of Admiral Canaris had been found, full of damning material. Upon this Saturday which Bonhoeffer was passing at Schönberg surrounded by his hopeful companions, Huppenkothen, his one-time interrogator in Berlin, arrived at Flossenbürg with orders for the immediate summary trial and execution of Canaris, Sack, Oster, two others of whom one was Müller's friend Gehre, and finally Dietrich Bonhoeffer. During the night of Saturday, search was made for Bonhoeffer through the cells in the camp. Von Schlabrendorff, who was one of the inmates, was twice woken and accused of being the wanted prisoner. At last the search was given up. Bonhoeffer must have travelled on southwards with the transport from Buchenwald. Well, mistakes could still be rectified. Petrol and a prison van were provided. In the morning of April 8th, the transport set out for Schönberg.

Meanwhile, in the schoolhouse at Schönberg, Low Sunday had dawned. It occurred to Pünder to ask Bonhoeffer to hold a small service. Bonhoeffer hesitated; most of his companions were Roman Catholic, and there was Kokorin from Communist Russia. But Kokorin himself begged for it, and under general pressure Bonhoeffer yielded. He gave an exposition of the Scripture passages for the day: "Through his stripes we are healed" (Isaiah 53:5) and "Blessed be the God and Father of our Lord Jesus Christ, which according to his abundant mercy hath begotten us again into a lively hope by the resurrection of Jesus Christ from the dead" (1 Peter 1:3). "He reached the hearts of all," Payne Best remembers, "finding just the right words to express the spirit of our imprisonment, and the thoughts and resolutions which it had brought."[1] Together with Bonhoeffer, all looked forward thankfully and hopefully into the future. The little service ended. Then, during the moment of stillness that succeeded it, the door was flung open and two men stood in the doorway. "Prisoner Bonhoeffer, take your things and come with us."

Bonhoeffer gathered his few belongings. In a copy of Plutarch that he had received for his birthday he wrote his name in large letters and left it on the table. His last words to Payne Best, were a message to his trusted English friend Bishop Bell. "Tell him," he said, "that for me this is the end, but also the beginning. With him I believe in the principle of our universal Christian brotherhood which rises above all national interests, and that our victory is certain—Tell him too that I have never forgotten his words at our last meeting."[2]

It must have been evening before Bonhoeffer reached Flossenbürg. The "trial" went on throughout the night. The prisoners were interrogated once more and confronted with one another. All were condemned.

The last picture that we have of Bonhoeffer comes from the prison doctor, who wrote many years later:

[1] Payne Best, *The Venlo Incident*, p. 200.
[2] *G.S.* I, p. 412.

277

"On the morning of the day, some time between five and six o'clock, the prisoners, among them Admiral Canaris, General Oster and Sack the Judge Advocate General, were led out of their cells and the verdicts read to them. Through the half-open door of a room in one of the huts I saw Pastor Bonhoeffer, still in his prison clothes, kneeling in fervent prayer to the Lord his God. The devotion and evident conviction of being heard that I saw in the prayer of this intensely captivating man moved me to the depths."[1]

So the morning came. Now the prisoners were ordered to strip. They were led down a little flight of steps under the trees to the secluded place of execution. There was a pause. For the men about to die, time hung a moment suspended. Naked under the scaffold in the sweet spring woods, Bonhoeffer knelt for the last time to pray. Five minutes later, his life was ended.

[1] *Begegnungen*, p. 192.

POSTSCRIPT

"THE isolated use and handing down of the famous term 'religionless Christianity' has made Bonhoeffer the champion of an undialectical shallow modernism which obscures all that he wanted to tell us about the living God."[1] These are Eberhard Bethge's own words.

The task before the Church today, clearly foreseen by Bonhoeffer, is that of becoming fully identified with the modern world without losing her Christian identity. Bonhoeffer is quoted continually as the prophet of identification; that he was equally concerned with the Christian's identity is commonly forgotten.

For him, as for Bethge, the means by which identity was to be maintained was defined by the phrase "secret discipline", while the demands of identification were summed up in the term "religionless Christianity", or, more often, "non-religious interpretation of the Gospel". Secret discipline meant for him all that had power to deepen and sustain Christian life: prayer, meditation, common worship, the sacraments, and experiments in life together such as Finkenwalde had been, all in fact that helped to fit the Christian for a life of love lived with God and for his fellow men. It meant besides a recognition of the fact that the truths of the gospel can and must be shared with fellow Christians in a way different from that by which they may be communicated to others, while religionless Christianity meant the christian's complete openness to those others, it meant his complete and joyful openness to the whole multifarious world around him, it meant his being without any reserve the man for others.

The *Letters and Papers from Prison*, which are the most widely read and quoted of all Bonhoeffer's works, explore extensively the problems of identification which face the Christian in the present century, while saying little about that secret discipline by which his identity as a Christian is maintained. But what the writer did not say he was living, daily and hourly, and the eloquence of his life counterbalances the reticence of the letters.

His life had in fact represented a continuous effort to hold the two in balance, an attempt complicated by powerful inward and outward

[1] From a lecture entitled "The Living God Revealed in this Church", delivered in Coventry Cathedral on October 30th 1967.

pressures, so that at certain stages the scale tipped more heavily to the one side and at certain stages to the other. It would probably be true to say that his exploration of the subject of Christian identity reached its high point during the years at Finkenwalde and its most effective expression in the two books in which that period culminates: *The Cost of Discipleship* and *Life Together*. During the period which followed his return from the U.S.A. in 1939, and which only ended with his death, he was intensely preoccupied with the practical and theological problems of identification, and the *Letters and Papers* show us the direction in which his thoughts on the subject were moving, without however attempting any definite pronouncement. It is a hindrance to the full understanding of what Bonhoeffer was and is that sections of the *Letters and Papers* have so frequently been quoted as though they represented the end of a theological journey instead of its quite tentative beginning.

No one can do more than attempt to conjecture how the journey would have continued, but one thing may be taken as certain: the exploration of the means of identification with the world would never have been pursued by Bonhoeffer at the price of his Christian identity. He would doubtless have continued to explore and extend the means by which the Christian might be identified with the world, but at the same time, and for this very reason, he would have continued the exploration of how Christian life in this age may be deepened and intensified, and of how its content may be evermore widely communicated. Through the peculiar magic of his passion and genius he has continued in a real sense to live and communicate to the present day. His thought is more and more widely known; to understand it in the context of his life can give it the dimension which hitherto it has lacked.

In Eberhard Bethge's phrase, "Secret discipline without worldliness becomes pure ghetto; worldliness without the secret discipline pure boulevard." Bonhoeffer's life was lived far from the boulevard and progressively further from the ghetto; it was lived with God and for God, with men and for men, ever more fearlessly exposed by the multifarious world, and it is by his life as much as by his words that he spoke and can speak today.

INDEX

Abwehr (Counter Espionage Department), 198, 200, 204, 222; B's connexion with, 226–7, 229, 233, 234, 235, 236, 240–1, 243, 249–50, 264, 273
Act and Being, 79–81
Ammundsen, Valdemar, Bishop of Haderslev, 99
Andersen, Hans (1805–75), 32
Anglican Church, 56, 156
Anglo-Saxon theology, B's early distrust of, 100–1, 104
Aryan Paragraph, 119, 121, 128, 138
Augsburg, Synod at (1935), 164–5

Bach, Johann Sebastian (1685–1750), 32
Bailie, Professor John, 84
Barcelona, B's ministry at (1928–29), 66–77
Barmen, Synod of (1934,) 139–40, 141–2, 146, 165, 176
Barth, Professor Karl (1884–   ), his relations with Liberal theologians in Berlin, 58–60; B's view of, 79–80; visited by B, 96–8; visits Berlin University, 101–2; influence on B, 112–13, 116; intervenes in German Church struggle, 124–6, 128; receives letter from B, 129–30; critical of B's going to England, 131; suspicious of B's Finkenwalde curriculum, 159; transfers to Basle University, 162; last meeting with B., 229–30
Basle University, 162
Beck, Colonel-General Ludwig (1880–1944), leads resistance to Hitler, 200–1, 203, 222, 226, 242
Beethoven, Ludwig van (1770–1827), 32
Belgium, 40, 47, 224, 225
Bell, Dr. George Kennedy, Bishop of Chichester (1883–1958), learns of B's death, 16; his first meeting with B, 105; growing friendship with B, 134–5, 138; letters exchanged with B, 139–41, 142; keen interest in German Church struggle, 183; visited by B (1938), 206; hears from B (1941), 229; receives report of B's visit to Switzerland, 230; visits Sweden and confers with B (1942), 235–7; writes to Leibholz about B's fate, 268; receives final message from B, 277
Berchtesgaden, Chamberlain at (1938), 204
Berggrav, Eivind, Bishop of Oslo (1884–   ), 234
Berlin, Bonhoeffer family reside at Bellevue, 25; then Wangenheimstrasse, 26 *et seq.*, 34 *et seq.*, 62, 172, 198; finally at Marienburgerallee, 172, 185, 198 *et seq.*, 204, 243, 264

Berlin University, B educated at, 55, 57–60, 61, 62; on staff of, 79 *et seq.*, 81, 96, 101–2; B quits (1933), 123; his right to lecture there withdrawn, 174; his subsequent attitude towards, 174, 255
Best, Captain S. Payne, 223; with B at Buchenwald, 270–71, 272, 273, 274; and at Schönberg, 276–77 *see also Venloo Incident, The*
Bethel Community, 120, 126–7, *see also Confession of Bethel*
Bethge, Eberhard, 57; *quoted*, 103; reconstructs B's notes on Christology, 123; at Finkenwalde as Leader of House of Brothers, 155, 156, 157; defends practice of meditation there, 157–9; close relationship with B, 177; accompanies B to Switzerland, 179; at Klein Krössin, 184; witnesses Niemöller's arrest, 185; holiday with B., 186; becomes Director of Studies at Gross Schlönwitz, 193; with B at Zingst, 194; growing intimacy with B, 197–8; helps Leibholzes escape, 201–3; records conversation between B and Dohnanyi, 205; in charge whilst B in U.S.A., 207, 208; accompanies B on East Prussia visitation, 224; nature of his friendship with B, 227, 228; receives letter from B about the Wedemeyers, 241; becomes engaged to B's niece, 242; present at B's arrest, 244; receives letters from B in prison, 248, 249, 251, 258, 263; himself arrested and imprisoned, 264, 267; final comments on B, 279, 280
Biesenthal, community at, 106
Bismark, Otto, Prince von (1815–98), 22, 25
Block, Superintendent, 193, 226
Blöstau (East Prussia), 226
Bodelschwingh, Friedrich von (1830–1910) 120, 126; Bishop Fritz von, 120–1, 126
Bonhoeffer, Caspar von (ancestor), 17; Christine (sister) *see* Dohnani, Christine von; Dietrich (1906–45);
   I *His Life* (a) *Pre-Hitler Years* (1906–33), birth and ancestry, 16–23; childhood, 24–30; education at Friedrichswerder Gymnasium, 31 et seq., 40 *et seq.*; at Tübingen University, 49–50; visits Italy and North Africa, 51–4; at Berlin University, 55–65 (where does pastoral work among children, 61–2 and presents first thesis, *Sanctorum Communio*, 62–5); acts as curate to German community in Barcelona, 66–77; returns to Berlin, becomes assistant lecturer and produces second thesis (*Act and Being*)

Bredow (Pomerania), meeting of pastors at, 166
Breslau, 11, 24, 55
bull-fighting, B's view of, 75
Bruderhaus (Finkenwalde), 156, 157, 168–170
Bruderrat (National), 146, 150, 162, 165–6, 167, 169, 170; (Pomeranian), 151, 166, 173; (Prussian), 147, 156, 166, 173, 178, 179, 185, 192; (Saxon), 157, 168
Buchenwald Concentration Camp, 185, 255, 275, 277; B at, 270–274
Buchman, Dr. Frank N. D., 132
Buddha (Buddhism), 73, 76
Bürgerbräu Keller Putsch (1923), 51; anniversary bomb plot (1939), 223
Bussche, Baron Axel von dem, 250–1

Calvin, John (Calvinism), 56, 159, 162, 163
Cambridge, B attends World Alliance Conference at, 99–101
Canaris, Admiral Wilhelm (1885–1945)—Head of *Abwehr*, 15, 198, 199, 200, 226, 268, 270, 276, 278
Canterbury, Archbishop of (Cosmo Gordon Lang), 138
Catholicism, B's contact with in Italy, 52–4; Spain, 68; and Mexico, 90; his attitude towards, 71, 159–60, 228, 277 *see also* Concordat
Cauer (family of Countess Stanislaus Kalckreuth), 32
Cernohorske Kupele, B attends conference at, 105
Chamberlain, Neville (1869–1940), 204
Chamby, B attends Life and Work Conference at (1935), 178–9
Charité Hospital (Berlin), 24 *et seq.*, 39, 204, 255
Charlemagne, 17
Charlottenburg Prison, 249
Christianity and World Order, 232
Christology, 123–4, 175
Church and the World Order, The, 232
Churchill, Winston, L.S. (1874–1965), 225
Coffin, Dr. Henry Sloan, 211, 217
Columbia University, 207
Columbus (Ohio), 217
Communism (Marxism), 38, 44, 79, 89, 117, 143, 223, 226
Concordat (1933), 122–3
Confessing Church, its birth, 127 *et seq.*; holds Synod at Barmen, 141; receives support from Fano Conference, 143, 144–5; holds second synod at Dahlem and establishes its own independent government (Reichsbruderrat), 146–7; commissions B to train its pastors in Pomerania, 150 *et seq.*; divisions amongst, 161–2; holds third synod at Augsburg, 165–7; further tribulations of, 168 *et seq.*; persecuted by Government in Fifth Emergency Measure, 173 *et seq.*; its seminaries (including Finkenwalde) closed,

182 *et seq.*; Neimöller arrested, 185; invention of the *Sammelvikariate* to conduct secret seminaries, 192; B assists in this at Kösslin and Gross Schönwitz, 192 *et seq.*; and then at Sigurdshof, 221, till its suppression, 223–4; assistance given to by *Abwehr*, 226, 227, 229
Confession of Bethel, 127, 130
Confirmation candidates, B's work for, 103–4, 106
Cordoba, 68
Cornelius, Peter (1824–74), 32
Cost of Discipleship, The, 56–7, 187–91, 279
Craske, F. W. Tom (Bishop of Gibraltar), 99
Creation and Temptation, 112–16
Czechoslovakia, 99; crisis of 1938–39, 200–1, 203–6
Czeppan, Dr., 48

Dachau Concentration Camp, 270
Dahlem, Synod and Declaration of (1934), 146–7, 162, 165, 175
Dawes, Plan, 48, 96
Delbrück, Hans (1848–1929), 26, 46
Denmark, B's visits to, 144–6, 174
Deutsches Hilfsverein (at Barcelona), 67
Dewey, James, 85
Diestel, Superintendent, 83, 98
Dohnanyi, Christine (Bonhoeffer), von, 24, 30, 48, 66, 172, 198, 243, 244, 249, 269–70; Hans Adam von (died 1945), 46, 47; marries Christine Bonhoeffer, 48; lives in Berlin, 172; becomes agent for *Abwehr*, 198–9; involved in Fritsch crisis, 200; compiles dossier on Hitler, 204, 219; influence on B, 205; compiles X Report, 222; helps B evade Gestapo surveillance, 226; suspected by R.S.H.A., 234, 241, 242; visits Switzerland, 241; involved in Operation Flash, 242–3; arrested, 244; imprisoned, 248, 249, 250, 255, 256, 264, 267; executed, 269
Dolfuss, Dr. Engelbert (1892–1934), 144
Dudzus, Otto, 144, 146

Eisenach, 121
El Greco (Domenico Theotocopuli), 68
Elser, Georg, 223
Emergency League of Pastors (*Pfarrernotbund*), 127–8, 135, 136, 137, 140
Epsom, B attends World Alliance meeting at, 104
Ethics, 227, 230–1, 235
Ettal Abbey, 227–8, 229
Evangelische Theologie, B's article in, 176

Fano, Life and Work Meeting at (1934), 139, 144–6, 163
Fiesco in Genoa, 31
Fifth Emergency Measure (1935), 173, 182, 184

285